The Financial Times
Guide to Options

The Financial Times Guide to Options

The plain and simple guide to successful strategies

Lenny Jordan

Second Edition

 Pearson

Harlow, England • London • New York • Boston • San Francisco • Toronto • Sydney • Dubai • Singapore • Hong Kong
Tokyo • Seoul • Taipei • New Delhi • Cape Town • São Paulo • Mexico City • Madrid • Amsterdam • Munich • Paris • Milan

PEARSON EDUCATION LIMITED

Edinburgh Gate
Harlow CM20 2JE
Tel: +44 (0)1279 623623
Fax: +44 (0)1279 431059
Website: www.pearsoned.co.uk

First published as *Options: Plain and Simple* in Great Britain in 2000
Second edition published in Great Britain in 2011

© Pearson Education Limited 2011

The right of Lenny Jordan to be identified as author of this work has been asserted
by him in accordance with the Copyright, Designs and Patents Act 1988.

Pearson Education is not responsible for the content of third party internet sites.

ISBN: 978-0-273-73686-8

British Library Cataloguing-in-Publication Data
A catalogue record for this book is available from the British Library

Library of Congress Cataloging-in-Publication Data
Jordan, Lenny,
    The Finacial Times guide to options : the plain and simple guide to successful
        strategies/Lenny Jordan. – 2nd ed.
        p. cm.
    Rev. ed. of: Options plain & simple. 2000.
    Includes index.
    ISBN 978-0-273-73686-8 (pbk.)
    1. Options (Finance)   I. Jordan, Lenny. Options Plain & simple. II. Title.
    HG6024.A3J664 2011
    332.64'53–dc22

                                                                    2010045453

10 9 8 7 6 5 4 3 2 1
14 13 12 11 10

Typeset in 9pt Stone Serif by 30
Printed and bound in Great Britain by Ashford Colour Press, Gosport

This book is dedicated to
the memory of my parents

Contents

Preface

What an option is

The difference between a commodity, a futures contract and an options contract is illustrated in the following three paragraphs, which will take you a minute and a half to read.

Suppose you're in the market for an oriental rug. You find the rug of your choice at a local shop, you pay the shopkeeper $500, and he transfers the rug to you. You have just traded a **commodity**.

Suppose instead you wish to own the rug, but you prefer to purchase it in one week's time. You may be on your way to the airport, or maybe you need the short-term use of your money. You and the shopkeeper agree, verbally or in writing, to exchange the same rug for $500 one week from now. You have just traded a **futures contract**.

Alternatively, you may like the rug on offer, but you may want to shop around before making a final decision. You ask the shopkeeper if he will hold the rug in reserve for you for one week. He replies that your proposal will deny him the opportunity of selling the rug, and as compensation, he asks that you pay him $10. You and the shopkeeper agree, verbally or in writing, that for a fee of $10 he will hold the rug for you for one week, and that at any time during the week you may purchase the same rug for a cost of $500, excluding the $10 cost of your agreement. You, on the other hand, are under no obligation to buy the rug. You have just traded an options contract.

About this book

The Financial Times Guide to Options is a straightforward and practical guide to the fundamentals of options. It includes only what is essential to basic understanding. It presents options theory in conventional terms, with a minimum of jargon. It is thorough; not simplistic.

The purpose of this book is to give you a basis from which to trade most of the options listed on most of the major exchanges. Its precursor, *Options Plain and Simple*, is used by traders, market-makers and broker-dealers. It is used by investment clubs. It is used as a textbook in universities. And it has been read by those who serve the industry: administrative staff, accountants and others.

When you have finished this book, you will be prepared for advanced derivatives subjects, including quantitative finance.

This book will not make you rich in 20 minutes. It will, however, give you tools to make *prudent* investment decisions.

Like all investment strategies, options offer potential return while incurring potential risk. The advantage of options trading is that risk can be managed to a greater degree than with outright buying or selling. This book continually discusses the link between risk and return. It will help you choose justifiable and manageable strategies. Reading it will develop an awareness of the risks involved.

This book is the product of my training courses for new traders, brokers and support staff. My method has been tested and revised over the years. It has proved successful for those whose livelihoods depend on thorough understanding and flawless execution under circumstances that allow no error. Because I am an options trader, the strategies presented here are the very same that I have traded time and again, day by day, year after year.

In fact, you and I have the same goals: to make money and to manage risk.

Many theoretical concepts are included, but the focus of this book is on practice, not theory. I teach how to swing the golf club; not how to design it.

While it is impossible to coach an investor at a distance, it is possible to recount many of the situations that often arise in the marketplace, and to discuss ways of approaching them. In this new edition I have added many examples of practical applications, or as it were, scenarios or anecdotes.

The mathematics in this book involve only addition, subtraction, multiplication and division. These four functions plus a pricing model are all that we professionals use in order to trade most of the options products on the major exchanges.

The focus of this book is options: it is not a comprehensive guide to trading. As professional traders know, trading technique is only gained through experience. For this, you should engage a professional adviser to help you to decide the best strategies to use. Or better yet, contact me at lenny@lennyjordan.com.

About the author

Lenny Jordan has trained countless traders in the options markets of Chicago and London. He was a market-maker at the Chicago Board of Trade (CBOT) and at the London International Financial Futures and Options Exchange (LIFFE). He now lectures for London-based exchanges and international banks. He can be contacted at lenny@lennyjordan.com.

Acknowledgements

The author would like to thank the following for their assistance:

- The Chicago Board of Trade and the Chicago Mercantile Exchange (CBOT and CME)
- The Chicago Board Options Exchange (CBOE)
- The London International Financial Futures and Options Exchange (LIFFE)
- Eurex and Deutsche Borse
- PM Publishing website (pmpublishing.com).
- Marty O'Connell, one of the great trainers

Introduction

Why options are useful

A word I often hear when people are discussing options is 'risky'. The other evening at dinner, a guest made the same comment. An hour later, I was sorry to hear him say that he had recently lost 84 per cent of an investment in stocks in emerging markets.

It is an unfortunate and costly reality that few investors know how to protect their investments from downside risk. Their sole investment strategy is to select a stock to buy, or a fund to buy into. Over the long term, and if value is found at the time of purchase, this strategy makes sense. Unfortunately, it hasn't made sense with many stocks from 1999 through 2009.

Of course, a competent financial adviser can outperform the indexes. But for those who take a more active role in their investments, options offer the two advantages of flexibility and limited risk.

Call and put purchases are excellent ways of developing market awareness and building confidence. This is because with these strategies traders can take either a bullish or bearish position while limiting their maximum loss at the outset. Because the cost of options is paid for up front on most exchanges, the options buyer is forced to be more disciplined than a trader who must simply post margin. And he won't be stopped out.

Because options have lives of their own, they are indicators of market sentiment. Implied volatility, which we will discuss, often anticipates changes in price activity in the underlying contracts. Simply knowing about options can improve market awareness.

Options strategies are only 'risky' when, like other investments, their potential return does not justify the risks taken, or when the parties involved do not know the fundamentals. This book presents a sensible approach to profit opportunities with a manageable degree of risk.

How to use this book

This book is designed for readers whose time is limited, and for those seeking different levels of expertise. A basic understanding of calls and puts, for those who do not wish to trade, can be obtained by reading Part 1. For investors willing to enter the market, Parts 1 and 2 provide enough information to take positions under most market conditions. Part 3 presents more sophisticated ways of approaching options. Part 4 covers basics that are not essential for most private investors, but which may be useful. It is recommended that those willing to commit capital read the whole book.

Each chapter presents explanatory material followed by a section with questions/examples. Use the latter as additional material from which to learn; don't expect to know all the answers the first time you go through the book.

An understanding of stocks, bonds or commodities is advisable before you start. You should also understand the simple mechanics of buying and selling through a broker or an exchange. You should also understand what a short position is, and this is explained in Part 4. Because stocks, bonds and commodities are often traded as futures contracts, a basic explanation of a futures contract is given in Part 4.

The substance of this book is accessible to all who have a basic understanding of one of the principal markets mentioned above. Occasionally subjects are presented that are at a slightly more advanced level than the immediate context in which they appear. These subjects are not difficult; they may merely require rereading after later portions of the book have been assimilated.

The examples in this book are drawn from exchange listed products. These products serve the needs of most investors, and their prices are reported in most daily business journals, on the internet and through many data vendors. Once the principles of this book are understood, you will be prepared for foreign currency and OTC (over the counter) options, as well as for more advanced topics such as exotic options.

Because this book is designed to help US and European investors, the examples chosen are from these markets. I have traded many products in the US and Europe; all the options strategies discussed in this book are identical, and only the nomenclature or jargon varies.

Options fundamentals

Introduction

Puts

We encounter options frequently in our daily lives, but we probably aren't aware of them. They occur in situations of uncertainty, and they are helpful in managing risk.

For example, most of us insure our home, our car and our health. We protect these, our assets, by taking out policies from insurance companies who agree to bear the cost of loss or damage to them. We periodically pay these companies a fee, or premium, which is based in part on the value of our assets and the duration of coverage. In essence, we establish contracts that transfer our risk to the companies.

If by accident our assets suffer damage and a consequent loss in value, our contract gives us the right to file a claim for compensation. Most often we exercise this right, but occasionally we may not: for example, if the damage to our car is small, it has been incurred by our teenage son, and filing a claim would produce an undesirable rise in our future premium level. Should we file a claim, however, our insurer has the obligation, under the terms of the contract, to pay us the amount of our loss.

Upon receipt of our payment we might say that the cost of our accident has been 'put to' the insurer by us. In effect, our insurance company had sold us a **put option** which we owned, and which we have exercised.

In the financial markets 'puts', as they are called, operate similarly. Pension funds, banks, corporations and private investors have assets in the form of stocks and bonds that they periodically protect against a decline in value. They do this by purchasing put options based on, or derived from, their stocks and bonds. These options give them the right to put the amount of an asset's decline onto the seller of the options. They transfer risk.

Subsequent chapters explain how this process of risk transfer works, but for now let's turn to another everyday use of options.

Calls

Suppose we need to purchase a washing machine. In our local newspaper we see an advertisement for the machine that we want. It is 'on sale' at a 20 per cent discount from a local retailer until the end of the week. We know this retailer to be reputable and that no tricks or gimmicks are involved.

From our standpoint we have the right to buy this machine at the specified price for the specified time period. We may not exercise this right if we find the machine cheaper elsewhere. The retailer, however, has the obligation to sell the machine under the terms specified in the advertisement. In effect, he has entered into a contract with the general public.

If we decide to exercise our right, we simply visit the retailer and purchase our washing machine. We might say that we have 'called away' this machine from the retailer. He had given us a **call option** which we accepted and which we have exercised. In this case our option is commonly known as a 'call'. It was given to us as part of the general public, free of charge. The retailer bore the cost of the call because he had a supply of washing machines that he wanted to sell.

Because, under the terms of the contract, the retailer is obligated to sell, he has also incurred a risk. Suppose we visit his shop within the week and find that all washing machines have been sold. The retailer underestimated the demand that the advertisement generated, and he is now short of supply. He and his sales staff are anxious to meet the demand, and he has his good reputation to uphold.

Our retailer will now try to rush delivery from a distributor, even at additional cost to him. If no machines are available through the distribution network, he may give us a voucher for the purchase of our machine when more arrive.

This voucher is, again, a call option. It contains the right to buy at the sale price, but its duration has been extended. If in the meantime the factory or wholesale price of our machine rises, the retailer will still be obligated to sell it to us at the sale price. His profit margin will be cut, and he may even take a loss. The call option that he gave us may prove costly to him.

Suppose that we become enterprising with our voucher, or call option. Early the next week we are talking to our neighbour who expresses disappointment at having missed the sale on washing machines. The new supply has arrived, and the new price is above the old, pre-sale price. By missing the sale, he will need to pay considerably more than he would have paid. We, after careful negotiations with our wife, decide that we can live with our old machine. We offer to sell him a new machine for an amount less than the new retail price but more than the old sale price. He accepts our offer. We then return to the retailer, exercise our option, purchase the machine, and resell it to our neighbour. He has a saving and we, including our wife, have a profit. We are now options traders.

Calls are a significant feature of commodity markets, where supply shortages often occur. Adverse weather, strikes or distribution problems can result in unforeseen rises in the costs of basic goods. Petroleum distributors, importers and food manufacturers regularly purchase calls in order to ensure that they have the commodities necessary to meet output deadlines.

Options in the markets

Part 1 tells you why options are useful, and it tells you how an option can give you an alternative to making an outright purchase or sale. Part 1 also lays down the fundamentals: what options do, how they are priced, the Greeks, volatility and substitution trades. If you're going to be in the business, then you'd better learn the fundamentals, otherwise, sooner or later, you or one of your clients will lose a lot of money. I've seen it happen many times.

It's possible to skip over this part, but only if you limit your trading to contract neutral spreads such as 1 × 1 call and put spreads, and butterflies and condors. These are described in Part 2. However, it's better to read Part 1 – you don't want to become one of the market casualties.

1

The basics of calls

In the previous chapter we saw that options are used in association with a variety of basic, everyday items. They derive their worth from these items. For example, our home insurance premium is derived, naturally, from the value of our house. In the options business, each of these basic items is known as an underlying asset, or simply an 'underlying'. It may be a stock or share, a bond or a commodity. Here, in order to get started, we will discuss an underlying with which we are all familiar, namely stock, bond or commodity XYZ.

Owning a call

XYZ is currently trading at a price of 100. It may be 100 dollars, euros, or pounds sterling. Suppose you are given, free of charge, the right to buy XYZ at the current price of 100 for the next two months. If XYZ stays where it is or if it declines in price, you have no use for your right to buy; you can simply ignore it. But if XYZ rises to 105, you can exercise your right: you can buy XYZ for 100. As the new owner of XYZ, you can then sell it at 105 or hold it as an asset worth 105. In either case, you make a profit of 5.

What you do by exercising your right is to 'call XYZ away' from the previous owner. Your original right to buy is known as a **call option**, or simply a 'call'.

It is important, right from the start, to visualise profit and loss potential in graphic terms. Figure 1.1 is a profit/loss graph of your call, or call position, before you exercise your right.

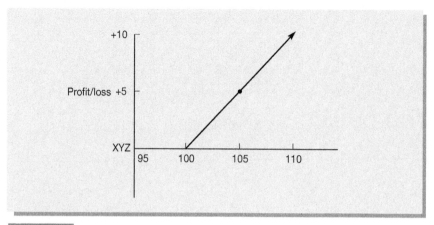

Figure 1.1   Owning a call

If you choose, you can wait for XYZ to rise further before exercising your call. Your profit is potentially unlimited. If XYZ remains at 100 or declines in price, you have no loss because you have no obligation to buy.

Offering a call

Now let's consider the position of the investor who gave you the call. By giving you the right to buy, this person has assumed the obligation to sell. Consequently, this investor's profit/loss position is exactly the opposite of yours.

The risk for this investor is that XYZ will rise in price and that it will be 'called away' from him. He will relinquish all profit above 100. In this case, Figure 1.2 represents the amount that is given up.

On the other hand, this investor may not already own an XYZ to be called away. (Remember our retailer in the introduction to this part who was short of washing machines.) He may need to purchase XYZ from a third party in order to meet the obligation of the call contract. In this case, Figure 1.2 represents the amount this investor may need to pay for XYZ in order to transfer it to you. Your potential gain is his potential loss.

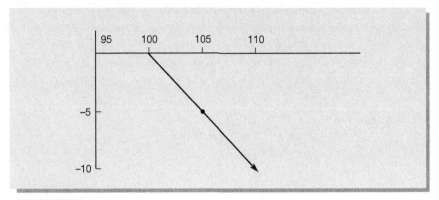

Figure 1.2   Offering a call

Buying a call

Obviously, then, the investor who offers a call also demands a fee, or premium. The buyer and the seller must agree on a price for their call contract. Suppose in this case the price agreed upon is 4. A correct profit/loss position for the buyer, when the call contract expires, would be graphed as in Figure 1.3.

By paying 4 for the call option, the buyer defers his profit until XYZ reaches 104. At 104 the call is paid for by the right to buy pay 100 for XYZ. Above 104 the profit from the call equals the amount gained by XYZ. Between 100 and 104 a partial loss results, equal to the difference between 4 and any gains in XYZ. Below 100 a total loss of 4 is realised. A corresponding table of this profit/loss position at expiration is shown in Table 1.1.

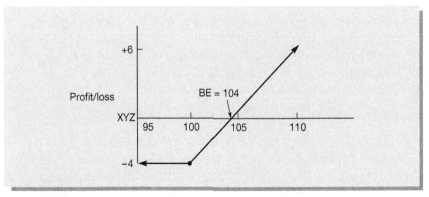

Figure 1.3   Buying a call

The first advantage of this position is that profit above 104 is potentially unlimited. The second advantage is that by buying the call instead of XYZ, the call buyer is not exposed to downside movement in XYZ. He has a potential savings. The disadvantage of this position is that the call buyer may lose the amount paid, 4.

Table 1.1 Buying a call

XYZ	95	96	97	98	99	100	101	102	103	104	105	106	107	108	109	110
Cost of call	−4	−4	−4	−4	−4	−4	−4	−4	−4	−4	−4	−4	−4	−4	−4	−4
Value of call at expiration	0	0	0	0	0	0	1	2	3	4	5	6	7	8	9	10
Profit/loss	−4	−4	−4	−4	−4	−4	−3	−2	−1	0	1	2	3	4	5	6

All options contracts, like their underlying contracts, have contract multipliers. Both contracts usually have the same multiplier. If the multiplier for the above contracts is $100, then the actual cost of the call would be $400. The value of XYZ at 100 would actually be $1,000. In the options markets, prices quoted are without contract multipliers.

When trading options, it is important to know the **risk/return** potential at the outset. In this case, the potential **risk** of the call buyer is the amount paid for the option, 4 or $400. The call buyer's potential **return** is the unlimited profit as XYZ rises above 104. For a discussion of an actual risk/return scenario, see Question 2 (concerning Unilever) at the end of the book.

Calls can be traded at many different strike prices. For example, if XYZ were at 100, calls could probably be purchased at 105, 110 and 115. They would cost progressively less as their distance from the current price of XYZ increased. Many investors purchase these 'out-of-the-money' calls, as they are known, because of their lower cost, and because they believe that there is significant upside potential for the underlying.

Our 100 call, with XYZ at 100, is said to be 'at the money'.

In addition, if XYZ were at 100, calls could also be purchased at 95, 90 and 85. These 'in-the-money' calls, as they are known, cost progressively *more* as their distance from the underlying increases. Where the underlying is a stock, many investors purchase these calls because they approximate price movement of the stock, yet they are less expensive than a stock purchase.

For both stocks and futures, the limited loss feature of these calls also acts as a built-in stop-loss order.

Out-of-the-money, in-the-money and at-the-money calls will be discussed in later chapters, but for now let's return to the basics.

An example of a call purchase

Suppose GE is trading at 18.03, and the April 18.00 calls are priced at 0.58 If you purchased one of these calls, the break-even level would be the strike price plus the price of the call, or 18.58. If GE is above this level at expiration, you would profit one-to-one with the stock. Below 18.00, your call expires worthless. Between 18.00 and 18.58 you take a partial loss, equal to the stock price minus the strike price minus the cost of the call.

Table 1.2 GE April 18.00 call profit/loss

GE	17.00	17.50	18.00	18.50	18.58	19.00	19.50	20.00	20.50	21.00
Cost of call	–0.58	--------	--------	--------	--------	--------	--------	--------	--------	--------
Value of call at expiration	0	0	0	0.50	0.58	1.00	1.50	2.00	2.50	3.00
Profit/loss	–0.58	–0.58	–0.58	–0.08	0.00	+0.42	+0.92	1.42	1.92	2.42

In graphic form, the expiration profit/loss is summarised in Figure 1.4.

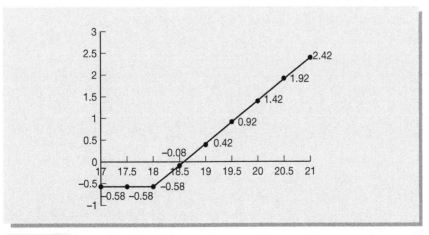

Figure 1.4   GE 18.00 profit/loss

The contract multiplier for GE, and most stock options at the Chicago Board Options Exchange (CBOE), is $100. Therefore, the cost of the April 18.00 call, and your maximum risk, would be 0.58 × $100 = $58.00. In other words, for $58 you have the right to purchase 100 shares of GE at a price of $18 per share. These shares have a total value of $1,800.

Selling a call

Now let's consider the profit/loss position of the investor who sold you the XYZ call for 4. Like the previous example, his position, when the contract expires, is exactly the opposite of yours (see Figure 1.5).

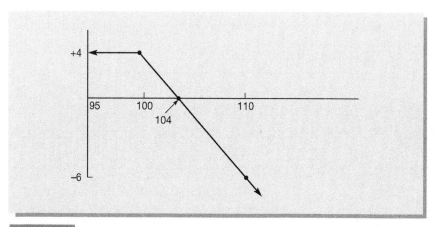

| Figure 1.5 | Selling a call

In tabular form this position would be as shown in Table 1.3.

Table 2.3 Selling a call

XYZ	95	96	97	98	99	100	101	102	103	104	105	106	107	108	109	110
Income from call	4	4	4	4	4	4	4	4	4	4	4	4	4	4	4	4
Value of call at expiration	0	0	0	0	0	0	−1	−2	−3	−4	−5	−6	−7	−8	−9	−10
Profit/loss	4	4	4	4	4	4	3	2	1	0	−1	−2	−3	−4	−5	−6

Consider also that the risk/return potential is opposite. The seller's potential return is the premium collected, 4. His potential risk is the profit given up, or the unlimited loss, if XYZ rises above 104.

The advantage for the call seller who owns XYZ is that by selling the call instead of XYZ, he retains ownership while earning income from the call sale. The disadvantage is that he may give up upside profit if his XYZ is called away. For the call seller who does not own XYZ, i.e. one who sells a call 'naked', the disadvantage is that he may need to purchase XYZ at increasingly higher levels in order to transfer it to you. His potential loss is unlimited. For this reason, *it is not advisable to sell a call without an additional covering contract, either a purchased call at another strike or a long underlying.*

Clearly, then, the greater risk lies with the seller. Through selling the right to buy, this investor incurs the potential obligation to sell XYZ at a loss-taking level. His loss is potentially unlimited. In order to assume this risk, he must receive a justifiable fee. The call seller must expect XYZ to be stable or slightly lower while the call position is outstanding or 'open'.

An example of a call sale

Again, suppose that GE is trading at 18.03, and the April 18.00 calls are trading at 0.58. If you sold one of these calls, then at April expiration the break-even level would be the strike price plus the price of the call, or 18.58. Above 18.58 you would lose one-to-one with the stock. Below 18.00 you would collect 0.58. Between 18.00 and 18.58 you would have a profit equal to the strike price minus the stock price plus the call income. An expiration profit/loss table would be as in Table 1.4.

Table 1.4 Sold GE April 18.00 call

GE	17.00	17.50	18.00	18.50	18.58	19.00	19.50	20.00	20.50	21.00
Income from call	0.58	----	----	----	----	----	----	----	----	----
Value of call at expiration	0	0	0	0.50	0.58	1.00	1.50	2.00	2.50	3.00
Profit/loss	+0.58	+0.58	+0.58	+0.08	0.00	−0.42	−0.92	−1.42	−1.92	−2.42

An expiration graph of your profit/loss would be as in Figure 1.6.

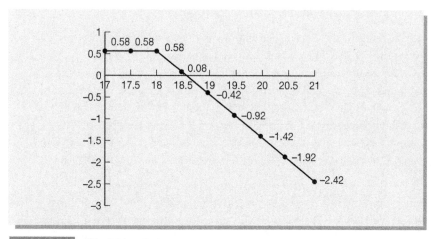

GE 18.00 call site

Again, the contract multiplier is $100, and therefore the maximum profit on the sold call would be 0.58 or × $100 = $58.

Summary of the terms of the call contract

A call option is the right to buy the underlying asset at a specified price for a specified time period

A call option is the right to buy the underlying asset at a specified price for a specified time period. The call buyer has the right, but not the obligation, to buy the underlying. The call seller has the obligation to sell the underlying at the call buyer's discretion. These are the terms of the call contract.

Summary of the introduction to the call contract

A call is used primarily as a hedge for upside market movement. It is also used to hedge downside movement because it's an alternative to buying the underlying. By buying the call instead of the underlying stock or commodity, etc. you have upside potential but have less money at risk.

The buyer and the seller of a call contract have opposite views about the market's potential to move higher. The call buyer has the right to buy the underlying asset, while the call seller has the obligation to sell the underlying asset. Because the call seller incurs the potential for unlimited loss, he must demand a fee that justifies this risk. The call buyer can profit substantially from a sudden, unforeseen rise in the underlying. When exercised, the buyer's right becomes the seller's obligation.

By learning the basics of call options, you have also learned several characteristics of options in general. This will help you to understand the subject of the next chapter, puts.

2

The basics of puts

Put options operate in essentially the same manner as call options. The major difference is that they are designed to hedge downside market movement. Some common characteristics of puts and calls are as follows:

- The buyer purchases a right from the seller, who in turn incurs a potential obligation.
- A fee or premium is exchanged.
- A price for the underlying is established.
- The contract is for a limited time.
- The buyer and the seller have opposite profit/loss positions.
- The buyer and the seller have opposite risk-return potentials.

A put option hedges a decline in the value of an underlying asset by giving the put owner the right to sell the underlying at a specified price for a specified time period. The put owner has the right to 'put the underlying to' the opposing party. The other party, the put seller, consequently incurs the potential obligation to purchase the underlying.

> A put option hedges a decline in the value of an underlying asset

Buying puts

Suppose you own XYZ, and it is currently trading at a price of 100. You are concerned that XYZ may decline in value, and you want to receive a selling price of 100. In other words, you want to insure your XYZ for a value of 100. You do this by purchasing an XYZ 100 put for a cost of 4. If XYZ declines in price, you now have the right to sell it at 100.

First, let's consider the profit/loss position of the put itself. At expiration, this position would be graphed as shown in Figure 2.1.

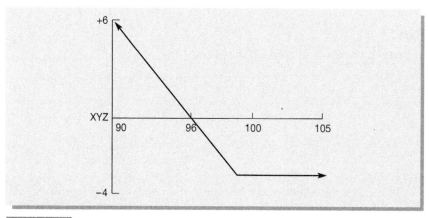

Figure 2.1   Buying a put

This graph should appear similar to the graph for a call purchase, Figure 1.3. In fact, it is the identical profit/loss but with a reverse in market direction. Both graphs show the potential for a large profit at the expense of a small loss. Here, profit is made as the market moves downward rather than upward. In tabular form, this profit/loss position would be as shown in Table 2.1.

Table 2.1 Buying a put

XYZ	90	91	92	93	94	95	96	97	98	99	100	101	102	103	104	105
Cost of put	–4	–4	–4	–4	–4	–4	–4	–4	–4	–4	–4	–4	–4	–4	–4	–4
Value of put at expiration	10	9	8	7	6	5	4	3	2	1	0	0	0	0	0	0
Profit/loss	6	5	4	3	2	1	0	–1	–2	–3	–4	–4	–4	–4	–4	–4

The break-even level of this position is 96. There, the cost of the put equals the profit gained by the right to sell XYZ at 100. Between 100 and 96 the cost of the put is partially offset by the decline in XYZ. Above 100, the premium paid is taken as a loss. Below 96 the profit on the put equals the decline in XYZ.

As the owner of XYZ, your loss is stopped at 96 by your put position. The cost of the put has effectively lowered your selling price to 96. But if XYZ falls sharply, you have a substantial saving because you are fully protected. In other words, you are insured. In the meantime, you still have the advantage of potential profit if XYZ gains in price.

The purchase of a put option can be profitable in itself. Suppose that you do not actually own XYZ, but you follow it regularly, and you believe that it is due for a decline. Just as you may have purchased a call to capture an upside move, you now may purchase a put to capture a downside move. (Your advantage, as an alternative to taking a short position in the underlying, is that you are not exposed to unlimited loss if XYZ moves upward.) The most you can lose is the premium paid. Figure 2.1 and the accompanying table (Table 2.1) illustrate the possible return from your put purchase.

Again, note the risk/return potential. With a put purchase the potential risk is the premium paid, 4. The potential return is the full amount that XYZ may decline below 96.

An example of a put purchase

Suppose GE is trading at 18.03, and the April 18.00 puts are trading at 0.52. If you purchased one of these puts, the break-even level would be the strike price minus the price of the put, or 17.48. If GE is below this level at expiration, you would profit one to one with the decline of the stock. Above 18.00, your put would expire worthless. Between 18.00 and 17.48, you would take a partial loss, equal to the strike price minus the stock price minus the cost of the put. A table of your expiration profit/loss would be as Table 2.2.

Table 2.2 Purchased GE April 18.00 put

GE	15.50	16.00	16.50	17.00	17.48	18.00	18.50	19.00
Cost of put	−0.52							
Value of put at expiration	2.50	2.00	1.50	1.00	0.52	0	0	0
Profit/loss	1.98	1.48	0.98	0.48	0	−0.52	−0.52	−0.52

In graphic form, your expiration profit/loss would be as in Figure 2.2.

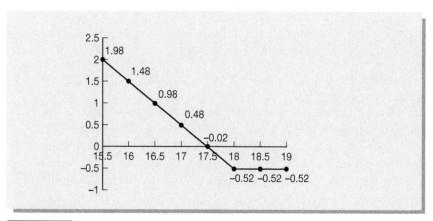

Figure 2.2   Expiration profit/loss relating to Table 2.2

The multiplier for stock options at the Chicago Board Options Exchange (CBOE) is $100, therefore the cost of the put, and your maximum risk, would be 0.52 × $100 = $52.

Selling puts

Now let's consider the profit/loss position of the investor who sells the XYZ put. After all, you may decide that the put sale is the best strategy to pursue. Because the put buyer has the right to sell the underlying, the put seller, as a consequence, has the potential obligation to buy the underlying.

At expiration, the sale of the XYZ 100 put for 4 would be graphed as in Figure 2.3.

This position should appear similar to that of the call sale, Figure 1.5. In fact, the profit/loss potential is exactly the same, but the market direction is opposite, or downward.

In tabular form, this profit/loss position would be as shown in Table 2.3.

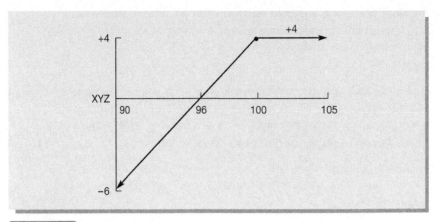

Figure 2.3 Selling a put

Table 2.3 Selling a put

XYZ	90	91	92	93	94	95	96	97	98	99	100	105
Income from put	4	4	4	4	4	4	4	4	4	4	4	4
Value of put at expiration	−10	−9	−8	−7	−6	−5	−4	−3	−2	−1	0	0
Profit/loss	−6	−5	−4	−3	−2	−1	0	1	2	3	4	4

The put seller's potential return is a maximum of 4 if XYZ remains at or above 100 when the contract expires. Between 100 and 96, a partial return is gained. The break-even level is 96. Below 96, the put seller incurs a loss equal to the amount that XYZ may decline.

Again, the risk/return potential for the put seller is exactly opposite to the put buyer. The potential **return** of the put sale is the premium collected, 4. The potential **risk** is the full amount that XYZ may decline below 96.

An investor may wish to purchase XYZ at a lower level than the current market price. As an alternative to an outright purchase, he may sell a put and thereby incur the potential obligation to purchase XYZ at the break-even level. The advantage is that he receives an income while awaiting a decline. The disadvantage is that XYZ may increase in price, and he will miss a

> The risk/return potential for the put seller is exactly opposite to the put buyer

buying opportunity, although he retains the income from the put sale. The other disadvantage is the same for all buyers of an underlying: XYZ may decline significantly below the purchase price, resulting in an effective loss.

For the investor who has a short position in XYZ, the sale of a put gives him the advantage of an income while he maintains his short position. The disadvantage is that he may give up downside profit if he must close his short position through an obligation to buy XYZ.

Practically speaking, there are few investors who adopt the latter strategy, although many market-makers do, simply because they supply the demand for puts.

Clearly then, as with calls, the greater risk of trading puts lies with the seller. He may be obligated to buy XYZ in a declining market. The put seller must therefore expect XYZ to remain stable or go slightly higher. He must demand a fee that justifies the downside risk.

An example and a strategy

Suppose that GE is, as before, trading at 18.03, and the April 18.00 puts are trading at 0.52. If you are decidedly bullish, you could sell one April 18.00 put. At expiration your break-even level would be the strike price minus the price of the put, or 17.48. Above 18.00, you would collect the premium. Below 18.00, you would be obligated to buy the stock, and your profit/loss is the closing price of the stock minus the strike price plus the premium income. A table of the expiration profit/loss would be as Table 2.4.

Table 2.4 Expiration profit/loss for sold GE April 18.00 put

GE	15.50	16.00	16.50	17.00	17.48	18.00	18.50	19.00
Income from put	0.52							
Value of put at expiration	2.50	2.00	1.50	1.00	0.52	0	0	0
Profit/loss	−1.98	−1.48	−0.98	−0.48	0	0.52	0.52	0.52

In graphic form, the expiration profit/loss would be as shown in Figure 2.4.

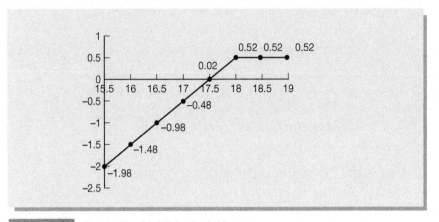

Figure 2.4 Graph of sold GE April 18.00 put

Remember that if GE declines significantly, you are still obligated to purchase it at an effective price of 17.48. Be mindful that all markets can drop suddenly, leaving the investor virtually no opportunity to take corrective action. For this reason, *selling naked puts*, as this strategy is called, contains a high degree of risk. A preferred strategy is the *short put spread*, which is discussed in Part 2.

On the other hand, suppose you think that stock in GE would be a good investment. If the stock is currently trading at 18.03, you may, quite reasonably, think that an effective purchase price of 17.48 represents good value. After all, this would represent a decline of approximately 3 per cent, and bear in mind that you receive an additional 3 per cent from the sale of the put. You may decide to sell the April 18.00 put as an alternative to buying the stock. If the stock remains above 18.00, then you are content to collect the 0.52 premium. You may even decide on a combined strategy of an outright stock purchase with put sales, i.e. you might purchase a number of shares at 18.03 and sell a number of April 18.00 puts, therefore averaging down the purchase price.

In order to apply the above strategy you must be convinced that the stock is good value at the level of the effective purchase price. In fact, it is not advisable to sell naked puts if you do not wish to own the stock or other underlying. Should you, as a result of employing this strategy, eventually purchase the stock, and should the stock, as it often does, decline below the purchase price, you must be secure in the knowledge that buying stock at the lowest point of a move is a matter only of luck. Few investors in 1932 bought the stocks in the DJIA when it was at 41.22.

Summary of the terms of the put contract

A put option is the right to sell the underlying asset at a specified price for a specified time period. The put buyer has the right, but not the obligation, to sell the underlying. The put seller has the obligation to buy the underlying at the put buyer's discretion. These are the terms of the put contract.

A comparison of calls and puts

Now that you've learned how calls and puts operate, it will be constructive to compare them.

- The **call buyer** has the right to **buy** the underlying, consequently the **call seller** may have the obligation to **sell** the underlying.
- The **put buyer** has the right to **sell** the underlying, consequently the **put seller** may have the obligation to **buy** the underlying.

If the underlying is a futures contract, the above terms are modified.

- The **call buyer** has the right to take a **long position** in the underlying, consequently the **call seller** may have the obligation to take a **short position** in the underlying.
- The **put buyer** has the right to take a **short position** in the underlying, consequently the **put seller** may have the obligation to take a **long position** in the underlying.

If these statements seem confusing, bear in mind that they are related to each other by simple logic: if one is true, then the others must be true. It may be helpful to review the graphs and tables presented. As you work through the examples in the next few chapters, familiarity will help comprehension.

In conclusion, markets can be bullish, bearish, or range-bound, and different options strategies are suitable to each. Any particular strategy cannot be said to be better than any other. These strategies, and those that follow, vary in terms of their risk/return potential. They accommodate the degree of risk that each investor thinks is appropriate. It is this flexible and limiting approach to risk that makes options trading appropriate to many different kinds of investors.

3

Pricing and behaviour

Now that you understand the nature of calls and puts, you need to know how they are priced and how they behave. In this chapter you will learn that options are both dependent on, and independent of, their underlying asset. They have lives of their own because they are traded separately as hedges. They indicate market sentiment, or the outlook for price changes in the underlying.

Options are both dependent on, and independent of, their underlying asset

Price levels

We will begin with a straightforward options contract. Its underlying is the short-term cost of money in the US. Table 3.1 is the Eurodollar futures contract, traded at the Chicago Mercantile Exchange, the CME.[1]

Table 3.1 December Eurodollar options

Strike price	93.50	93.75	94.00	94.25	94.50	94.75	95.00
Call value	0.805	0.56	0.32	0.12	0.04	0.02	0.01
Put value	—	0.01	0.02	0.065	0.23	0.46	0.70

On this day the December futures contract settled at 94.305, or an equivalent interest rate of 5.695 per cent. As the interest rate falls, the futures

---

[1] Because current short-term interest rates are at unsustainably low levels, this example is left at a more historical level. It still serves the need of this discussion.

contract increases; as the interest rate rises, the price of the futures contract decreases. An investor wishing to hedge a rise in the interest rate to 6 per cent could pay 0.02 for the 94.00 put. An investor wishing to hedge a fall in the interest rate to 5.5 per cent could pay 0.04 for the 94.50 call. The contract multiplier is $25, which means that the 94.50 call has a value of 4 × $25, or $100. There are 132 days until the options contracts expire on 14 December.

The number of different options contracts listed is designed to accommodate investors with different levels of interest rate exposure. Each listed price level is known as a **strike price**, e.g. 94.00, 94.25, 94.50, etc.

When an option is closest to the underlying, it is termed **at-the-money** (ATM). Here, both the 94.25 call and the 94.25 put are at-the-money. When a call is above the underlying, it is termed **out-of-the-money** (OTM), e.g. all the calls at 94.50, 94.75 and 95.00. When a put is below the underlying, it is also out-of-the-money, e.g. the puts at 93.75 and 94.00.

When a call is below the underlying, it is termed **in-the-money** (ITM), e.g. the calls at 93.75 and 94.00. When a put is above the underlying, it is also in-the-money, e.g. all the puts at 94.50, 94.75 and 95.00.

The options most traded are those at-the-money or out-of-the-money   Generally speaking, the options most traded are those at-the-money or out-of-the-money. If an upside hedge is needed, then at-the-money or out-of-the money calls will work, and they are less costly than in-the-money calls. For a downside hedge, the same reasoning applies to puts.

Aspects of premium

The premium of an option corresponds to its probability of expiring in the money. The 94.75 call and the 94.00 put are each worth only 0.02 because most likely the underlying will not reach these levels before expiration. More specifically, the 0.02 value of each of these is termed the **time premium**.

The premium of an in-the-money option consists of two components. The first of these is the amount equal to the difference between the strike price and the price of the underlying, and it is termed the **intrinsic value**. The second component is the **time premium**. The 94.00 call, with the underlying at 94.305, is worth 0.32; it has an intrinsic value of 0.305 and contains a time premium of 0.015.

When an option is deeply in the money, it will trade as a proxy for the underlying, and its premium will consist of intrinsic value only. This kind of option is said to be **at parity** with the underlying. The 93.50 call, with a value of 0.805, is at parity with the underlying at 94.305.

An at-the-money option will contain the most time premium because there the two advantages to owning an option are equal and greatest. A call that is exactly at-the-money, whose strike price equals the price of the underlying, can profit fully from upside market movement, less the cost of the call. As an alternative to purchasing the underlying, it can also save the call buyer the full amount that the underlying may decline, less the cost of the call. With an at-the-money call, the potential profit theoretically equals the potential savings. An at-the-money put has the same **profit/ savings potential**.

Duration and time decay

Another aspect that determines the amount of an option's premium is, quite reasonably, the time until expiration. A long-term hedge will cost more than a short-term hedge. Time decay, however, is not linear. Figure 3.1 illustrates that an option loses its value at an accelerating rate as it approaches expiration.

Another way of stating this is that the proportion of an option's daily time decay to its value increases toward expiration. Using two options based on Corn futures, Table 3.2 illustrates this in percentage terms.

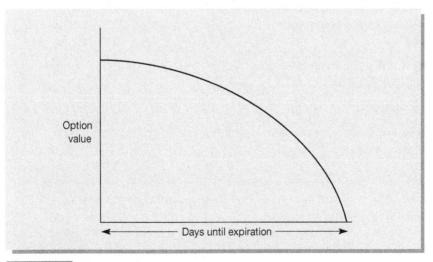

Option value

Days until expiration

Figure 3.1 **Value of option with respect to time**

Note that the out-of the-money option enters its accelerated time decay period much earlier than the at-the-money option. This is true for in-the-money options as well.

To the trader this means that the risk/return potential also accelerates with time. Because near-term options cost less, they have the potential to profit more from an unexpected, large move in the underlying. However, their time decay can be severe. The risk of time decay is great, but the return of substantial savings or large profit is also great.

Options with accelerated time decay are best utilised by professionals who are certain of their outlook for the underlying at expiration. The risks can be reduced by spreading, but for most investors a straight long call or put position with 2 per cent time decay should either be closed or be 'rolled' to a later contract month. Trading time decay is discussed further in Part 3.

Table 3.2 December Corn calls[2]

December Corn at $2.20 Implied volatility at 20 per cent				
Days until expiration (DTE)	120 DTE	90 DTE	60 DTE	30 DTE
Price of December 220 call with multiplier included	493.75	431.25	350.00	250.00
Cost of time decay per day	1.97	2.31	2.88	4.13
Daily time decay as percentage of option's value or theta/price ratio	0.40%	0.54%	0.82%	1.65%
Price of December 250 call with multiplier included	87.50	56.25	25.00	0
Cost of time decay per day	1.16	1.10	0.90	—
Daily time decay as percentage of option's value or theta/price ratio	1.33%	1.96%	3.60%	—

Based on data from FutureSource – Bridge; the percentage calculations are the author's.

---

[2] Corn is currently trading much higher, but this example can still be applied to it and other options products.

Interest rates, dividends and margin versus cash payment

It is best to check with the exchange where you wish to trade as to whether margin or cash payment applies. The following are general guidelines for interest rate and dividend pricing characteristics. Except under special circumstances, interest rate and dividend pricing components are outweighed by the volatility component of options.

Check with the exchange where you wish to trade as to whether margin or cash payment applies

Futures options

On most exchanges a purchased option on a futures contract must be paid for in full at the outset. Accordingly, its price will be discounted by the cost of carry on the option until expiration. Given the current low rates of interest, this discount is minor when compared to other pricing components. This discount becomes greater, however, with deep in-the-money options.

The LIFFE, however, charges margin for purchased options on futures contracts, and therefore the interest on the cash or bonds held by the clearing firm is retained by the options buyer.

All sold or short options on most exchanges have margin requirements because their potential risks are greater than bought or long options.

Stock options

The situation is different for options on stocks. Because a call is an alternative to buying stock, the call holder has the use of the cash that he would otherwise use to purchase the stock. The cost of a call is therefore increased by the cost of carry on the stock via the strike price of the option, until the option's expiration.

Because the holder of a call on stocks does not receive dividends, the cost of the call is discounted by the amount of dividends for the duration of the call contract.

For example, suppose DuPont pays a dividend of $0.35 on 14 December. The current short-term interest rate is 5 per cent as determined by the December Eurodollar futures contract at 95.00. There are 60 days until the DuPont options expire on the third Friday of January. The interest rate and dividend components of the DuPont January 55 call can be estimated as follows. A more accurate calculation is obtained with an options model.

(a) $55 × $^{60}/_{360}$ × 0.05 = $0.46 interest added to call price

(b) $0.35 dividend subtracted from call price

(c) $0.46 − 0.35 = $0.11, total added to call price

Note that the price of the stock is not a factor in this calculation. In fact, DuPont was trading at 57 at the time of this example. There is a difference of opinion, however. Some traders think that the current price of the stock is a more accurate basis from which to calculate the interest rate component of the option. Practically speaking, the difference between these two methods is not significant unless the options are far out-of-the-money with many days until expiration. Again, an options model accounts for this. More important would be a change in the dividend or the interest rate until expiration. Also note that unless special circumstances occur with respect to dividends and interest rates, these pricing components are far less significant than the volatility component.

Puts on stocks have the opposite pricing characteristics to calls with respect to cost of carry and dividends. Purchased calls and puts on stocks are paid for in cash up-front on most exchanges. Sold or short options, however, are margined because short calls incur potentially unlimited risk, and short puts incur extreme risk.

Options on stock indexes

A stock index is a proxy for all the stocks that comprise it. Calls and puts on a stock index are priced according to the cost of carry of the index, and the amount of dividends contained in the index. The costs of carry and dividends are added and discounted in the same manner as options on individual stocks. These options are also paid for in cash.

Long and short options positions

In practice, once a call or put is bought, it is considered to be a **long options position**. 'I'm long 10, June 550 puts,' you might say. Conversely, a call or put sold is considered to be a **short options position**. 'I'm too short for my own good,' means that you have sold too many calls or puts, or both, for your peace of mind.

It may be helpful to think that when the terms 'long' and 'short' are applied to options, they designate **ownership**. The same terms applied to a position in the underlying designate exposure to **market direction**. To be short puts is to be long the market, i.e. you want the market to move upward. The following chapter on deltas clarifies this.

Exercise and assignment

In practice, most options are not held through expiration. They are closed beforehand because the holders of options do not want to take delivery of the underlyings. The exceptions are options

In practice, most options are not held through expiration

on stock indexes and options on short-term interest rate contracts such as Eurodollars. In these contracts, no delivery of an underlying is involved.

Long and short options positions that are in the money at expiration will be converted into underlying positions through **exercise** and **assignment**, respectively. The clearing firms manage this procedure. The resulting positions are similar to those stated at the end of Chapter 2 under *a comparison of calls and puts* (page 24). There are slight differences for each type of contract.

Stocks

Through exercise, the holder of a long call will buy, at the strike price, the number of shares in the underlying contract. Through assignment, the holder of a short call will sell the shares. If the short call holder does not own stock to sell, he will be assigned a short stock position.

Through exercise, the holder of a long put will sell, at the strike price, the number of shares in the underlying contract. If the long put holder does not own shares to sell, he will be assigned a short stock position. Through assignment, the holder of a short put will buy the shares.

Futures

Through exercise, the holder of a long call will acquire, at the strike price, a long futures position in the underlying. Through assignment, the holder of a short call will acquire a short futures position at the strike price. On many futures exchanges, an options contract expires one month before its underlying futures contract.

For example, expiration for options on November soybeans at the Chicago Board of Trade (CBOT) normally occurs on the third Friday in October. If on the day of expiration the November futures contract settles at 552, then the holder of a long November 550 call will exercise to a long November futures position at the price of 550. The holder of a short November 550 call will be assigned a short November futures position at a price of 550. In this case the former long call holder obviously has a credit of 2, but he may have originally paid more or less than that for his November 550 call.

Through exercise, the holder of a long put will acquire, at the strike price, a short futures position in the underlying. Through assignment, the holder of a short put will acquire a long futures position at the strike price.

For example, if on the day of expiration the November soybeans futures contract settles at 552, then the holder of a long November 575 put exercises to a short November futures position at a price of 575. The holder of a short November 575 put is assigned a long November futures position at 575. The 23 credit for the former long put holder is no indication of the price at which he originally traded the option.

Cash settled contracts: stock indexes and short-term interest rate contracts

Through exercise, the holder of a long call will receive the cash differential between the price of the index or underlying and the strike price of the call. Through assignment, the holder of a short call will pay the cash differential.

For example, if at expiration the OEX settles at 527.00, the holder of an expiring long 525 call position receives 2.00, while the holder of an expiring short 525 call position pays 2.00. The contract multiplier for the OEX is $100, so in this case $200 changes hands.

Through exercise, the holder of a long put will receive the cash differential between the strike price of the put and the price of the index or underlying. Through assignment, the holder of a short put will pay the cash differential.

For example, if at expiration the OEX settles at 527.00, the holder of an expiring long 530 put position receives 3.00, while the holder of an expiring short 530 put position pays 3.00.

The same procedures apply to short-term interest rate contracts such as Eurodollars and Short Sterling. For example, in either of these contracts if an option settles one tick in the money, then the long is credited with one tick times the contract multiplier, and the short is debited one tick times the contract multiplier. The multiplier for Eurodollars is $25, and the multiplier for Short Sterling is £12.50.

Pin risk

Pin risk is rare, but it is important to know about it. Occasionally, options expire exactly at-the-money, i.e. the underlying equals the strike price at the time of expiration. We say that these options, both the call and the put, are **pinned**. This causes a problem for options on stocks and options on futures contracts, but not for options on stock indexes and short-term interest rate futures contracts.

While there is no immediate profit to be made from exercising these options, those who hold them may have a short-term directional outlook for the underlying that warrants exercising them.

For example, if the expiration price of XYZ is 100, the owner of a 100 call may exercise because he thinks that XYZ will increase in price during the next trading session, or he may simply want to own it while risking a short-term decline. The owner of a 100 put may exercise for the opposite reasons.

The problem lies with the holder of a short position in either of these options. He may or may not be assigned a position in XYZ. The assignment process is carried out on a random basis by the clearing firms. If the short option holder is assigned, he will be notified by the opening of the next trading session. If as usual he does not want to keep a position in XYZ, he will need to make an offsetting buy/sell transaction at the opening. If the market opens against him, he will cover his position at a loss.

There is no pin risk with cash settled index options such as the OEX and the FTSE-100 because with these contracts there is no underlying futures contract or quantity of shares to be assigned, or to exercise to. The same is true of most short-term interest rate contracts such as Eurodollars and Short Sterling.

How to manage pin risk

If you are short an option that is close to the underlying with a week until expiration, it is advisable to buy it back rather than ring the last amount of time decay from it and risk an unwanted position in the underlying. If you wait until the morning of expiration, you may find that you are joined by others with the same position, and you may be forced to pay up to get out.

European versus American style

An option is **European style** if it cannot be exercised before expiration. The only way to close this style of option before expiration is to make the opposing buy/sell transaction. One example is the SPX options on the Standard and Poor's 500 Index (S&P 500) traded at the CBOE. Another example is the ESX options (at the 25 and 75 strikes) on the Financial Times 100 Index (FTSE-100) traded at the London International Financial Futures and Options Exchange (LIFFE).

Also available is the **American-style** option, which can be exercised at any time before expiration. If such an option becomes so deeply in-the-money that it trades at parity with the underlying, then it has served its purpose and represents cash tied up. As a result, it can be sold, or it can be exercised to a position in the underlying stock or futures contract. In the case of a stock index, such as the OEX, it can be exercised for the cash differential. Most stock options and futures options are American style.

Black–Scholes and other models

The Black–Scholes options pricing model was the first to succeed. By itself it practically created an industry. It assumes that the option is held until expiration. This model is therefore appropriate for European-style options, but it is less appropriate for American-style options. For index options subject to early exercise, it must be, and has been, modified significantly.

Most options models assume that volatility is constant through expiration, which it seldom is. This brings challenges to both options buyers and options sellers. These challenges are discussed later in this chapter.

For more on models and their assumptions please refer to the reading list given at the end of the book.

Early exercise premium

Because American-style options can be exercised before expiration, those in-the-money will often contain an additional early exercise premium. This is not a significant amount for most options on futures contracts. It is more significant for puts on individual stocks because they can be exercised to sell stock and as a result, interest is earned on the cash.

Early exercise premium is a highly significant amount for in-the-money index options such as the OEX options on the S&P 100 traded at the CBOE. The reason is that at the end of each trading session, this contract closes at a different time from its index. Their in-the-money options, especially their puts, can be driven to parity with the cash index, and can then become an exercise. To be assigned in this manner often results in a loss. It is advisable not to sell, or have a short position in, the in-the-money options of this and similar contracts.

Conversely, because of the potential for early exercise, long out-of-the-money or at-the-money positions in the above two contracts can profit significantly. As these options become in-the-money, their early exercise premium increases drastically. Holders of these options then profit twofold.

A trader's story

This brings to mind a story concerning risk and early exercise premium.

I have a personal rule with American styled index options, and that is always to cover a short position when it becomes 0.50 delta. I made this rule after one or two incidents when I was short the former FTSE-100 American styled options[3] and they went deep in-the-money on me. Their early exercise premium mounted, and I became reluctant to pay up in order to buy them back. I lost more sleep than usual, and then eventually, a few days or weeks later, they became an exercise at the close. As a result, I lost my hedge, i.e. I was no longer delta neutral, which is what all market-makers strive to be. The next morning at the opening, the market moved against me and I took a loss.

One or two incidents such as this are not serious, but I could see the potential for serious damage in a highly volatile market. It was then that I decided on my rule. Subsequently, I paid up whenever I had a short position that went to 0.50 deltas. This wasn't often, but it seemed as if it was because it always cost me. Anyway, that was the price of a good night's sleep, or just a better night's sleep.

A year or so later, during mid-1997, the emerging market crisis started to develop. At first, the US seemed to ignore it, and that held London up. Still, I thought it was time to buy a little extra premium in case the US changed its mind. The extra premium cost me in time decay, especially

---

[3] These options are no longer listed.

because the FTSE implied was around 20 per cent. In the back of my mind was, and always is, 19 October 1987.

In October 1997 the UK market started to weaken because of its exposure to Hong Kong, and one day towards the close, I found myself short a number of 4800 puts which were at-the-money, or 0.50 deltas. A rule is a rule, I said, which was some consolation for the amount I paid up to buy them back. I was now longer premium than I generally like to be, and because we were at the close, I knew I was going to bear the cost of the time decay.

That night the US cracked. The next morning, the BBC news was calling for serious losses in London, and I knew there were going to be casualties at the opening. I arrived early at the office, and I had my clerks do an extensive risk analysis, though I knew, as all market-makers do, that at a time like this, options theory takes a back seat. I went to the floor and wedged my way into the crowd, and I waited, knowing that I was covered.

The bell sounded and the shouting began, and after a few brief stops the FTSE landed at 4400. The traders who were short options were screaming to buy them back, paying any price from those willing to sell. The implied volatility leaped to 70 per cent before settling down to a cool 50 per cent after the opening. I made few trades that day, but they were the ones I wanted to make. I had my best day ever.

Make a plan to cover your risk and stick to it   One lesson from this is obvious. Make a plan to cover your risk and stick to it. Your goal here is not to make money but to avoid taking a serious loss. Had I not covered my short options over the course of a year or more, I would have been one of the casualties. My profit on that day more than offset all my days of paying up.

Another lesson is that by covering risk, you leave your mind clear to deal with the circumstance at hand. You can make rational trading decisions. This is equally true for an extraordinary event or for a more routine trading day.

4

Volatility and pricing models

The most sophisticated and the most significant aspect of options pricing is that of volatility. After all, the primary purpose of options is to hedge exposure to market volatility. Increased market volatility leads to increased options premiums, while decreased market volatility has the opposite effect. Although a thorough review of volatility involves a study of statistics, a layman's explanation is practical and sufficient for the purpose of trading options.

> The most sophisticated and the most significant aspect of options pricing is that of volatility

Volatility is generally described in terms of normal price distribution. On most days, an underlying settles at a price that is not very different from the previous day's settlement. Occasionally, there occurs a large price change from one day to the next. One can safely say that the greater the price change, the less frequent its occurrence will be.

A typical set of price changes for an underlying can be graphed with a bell curve (see Figure 4.1).

The bell curve places each day's closing price at the centre, and plots the next closing day's price to the right or left, depending on whether the next day's price is upward or downward, respectively. The x-axis denotes the magnitude of the price changes, and the y-axis denotes their frequency.

Some underlying contracts routinely have greater daily price changes than others. They are said to be more volatile. In these cases their bell curves indicate greater price distribution by exibiting a lower, flatter curve. A particular contract may also undergo periods of higher volatility. In both cases the bell curve becomes more like the example shown in Figure 4.2.

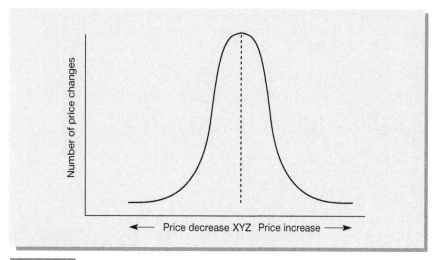

Figure 4.1   Low volatility

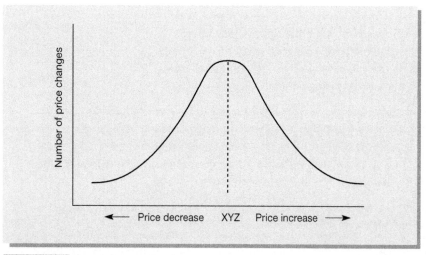

Figure 4.2   High volatility

The bell curve is a helpful way of visualising the concept of volatility. It illustrates the need for higher options prices due to higher volatility.

Normal price distribution is similar to waiting for public transport. In normal circumstances, the bus appears shortly before or after you arrive at the bus stop. Occasionally, the previous bus has already departed some time ago, and the next bus arrives at the stop just as you do. At other times, you just miss the bus, and you need to wait longer than usual.

Unfortunately, normal circumstances, like normal markets, are themselves unusual. Arrivals and departures are subject to a variety of traffic, weather and professional complications, making it difficult to anticipate bus movements. Sometimes, the street is bumper to bumper with buses. At other times, you may wait for 20 or more minutes in the rain, and then find yourself passed by a bus with a sign that says 'Out of Service'. At these times you are at the ends of the bell curve.

There are two types of volatility used in the options markets: the **historical volatility** of the underlying, and the **implied volatility** of the options on the underlying.

Historical volatility

The historical volatility describes the range of price movement of the underlying over a given time period. If, for a certain time period, an underlying's daily settlement prices are three to five points above or below its previous daily settlement prices, then it will have a greater historical volatility than if its settlement prices are one to two points above or below. Historical volatility is concerned with price movement, not with price direction.

> The historical volatility describes the range of price movement of the underlying over a given time period

Properly speaking, volatility itself is calculated as a one-day, one standard deviation move, annualised. The annualised figure is used in computing historical volatility. For example, a stock, bond or commodity with a volatility of 20 per cent has a 68 per cent probability of being within a 20 per cent range of its present price one year from now; and it has a 95 per cent probability of being within a 40 per cent range of its present price one year from now. If XYZ is currently at 100 and the current historical volatility is 20 per cent, then we can be 68 per cent certain that it will be between 80 and 120 one year from now. We can be 95 per cent certain that XYZ will be between 60 and 140 one year from now.

Most trading firms have mathematical models to calculate volatility, but for most underlyings there is a simplified way to calculate an annualised volatility based on a day's price movement.

An annualised volatility for an underlying can be computed by multiplying the day's percentage price change by 16.[1] For example, if XYZ settles

---

[1] 16 is the approximate square root of 250, the approximate number of trading days in a year.

at 100, and the next day it settles at 102: $^2/_{100}$ = 2%. 2% × 16 = 32% annualised volatility. Note that if on the following day XYZ retraces to 100: $^2/_{102}$ = 1.96%. 1.96% × 16 = 31.36% annualised volatility.

This way of calculating volatility is, as mentioned before, simplified, but it will provide insight into how price changes and the value of the underlying affect the volatility calculation. The above formula is insufficient for short-term interest rate contracts such as Eurodollars, where the volatility calculation should be based on the change in the yield or interest rate, and not on the change in the underlying futures contract.

Volatility fluctuates from day to day, but over a time period it often trends up or down, or remains in a range. In order to put daily volatility fluctuations in perspective, they are averaged into time intervals of 10, 20, 30 days or more. This process of averaging creates a useful historical volatility. It is similar to the more familiar moving average of daily settlement prices.

Because markets frequently change their volatility levels, and because options are short-term investments, many traders use a 20-day average

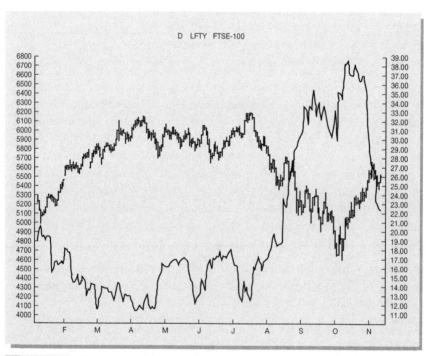

Figure 4.3 Chart of historical volatility of FTSE-100 index compared to daily price changes, January–November 1998

Source: FutureSource – Bridge.

in order to compute their historical volatility. For longer-term options it is beneficial to examine the 20-day historical volatility over longer time periods, perhaps a year or more. In markets that are undergoing a sudden change of volatility, a five-day average or less may be used for near-term contracts. It is particularly useful to know what a contract's historical volatility can be under extraordinary circumstances, both active and quiet. See Figure 4.3 for an example.

Pricing models

Once the historical volatility is known, it becomes an input for an options pricing model. The primary model used in the options industry is the Black–Scholes model; almost all other models used are variations of it. This model has been revised

> Once the historical volatility is known, it becomes an input for an options pricing model

over the past 35 years or so in order to price options on different underlyings, but it remains the foundation of the business.[2]

The other pricing inputs are those already discussed:

- strike price of the option
- price of the underlying
- time until expiration
- short-term interest rate
- dividends
- volatility, historical or implied.

With these inputs the model yields an option price which can become a basis from which to trade. If we compare this option price to its current market price, however, we will probably find a discrepancy. The reason for this is simply a difference between theory and practice.

Implied volatility

Although a theoretical value for an option can be determined by the historical volatility, an option's market price is determined by supply and

---

[2] There are many books that discuss the differences between options models. Needless to say this topic requires an extensive maths background. See the bibliography for recommended readings.

demand. An options market accounts for past price movement, but it also tries to anticipate future price movement. The market price of an option, then, implies a range of expected price movements for the underlying through expiration.

If we insert the market price of the option into the pricing model, and if we delete the former historical volatility, the model substitutes another volatility number, the implied volatility of the option.

This implied volatility can then be used as *the* implied volatility to calculate market prices of options at other strike prices within the same contract month. As a result, market prices of options spreads can also be calculated.

For example, if the December Corn futures contract is at 220,[3] and the December 220 calls, with 60 days until expiration, are priced at 7 ($350), an options model can calculate that these calls have an implied volatility of 20 per cent. If the demand for these options bids up their price to 10.5 ($525), while at the same time the price of the underlying and the days until expiration remain constant, the model will calculate that they have an implied volatility of 30 per cent.

If demand has bid up the 220 calls, then the 240 calls are also worth more because they are a hedge for underlying price movement as well. The last traded price of the 240 calls may have been 1.375 but that was before the 220 calls became bid up. Suppose we want to estimate the new theoretical value for the 240 calls.

If we know that the 220 calls have increased their implied to 30 per cent, we can assume that the implied for all the options, including the 240 calls, has increased to 30 per cent.[4] We can assume this because the market is implying a new volatility for the underlying through expiration, and all the options will be priced to account for it.

We then insert the 30 per cent implied into the options model, and it yields a price of 3.375 ($193.75) for the December 240 calls.

You can experiment with the effect of implied volatility changes on options prices by using an options calculator. Several options' websites, including cboe.com, offer one of these. In fact, anyone who seriously wants to learn about the effects of all the options variables on options prices should spend a minimum of several hours with this device.

---

[3] Corn is now priced much higher, but this example still holds true.

[4] This assumption becomes modified with respect to volatility skews, which are discussed in Part 3.

Comparing historical and implied volatility

Historical and implied volatility move in tandem; they seldom coincide. Figure 4.4 compares the historical and implied volatilities for January Crude Oil, traded at the New York Mercantile Exchange (NYMEX).[5] Here, the dotted line is the historical volatility and the solid line is the implied volatility.

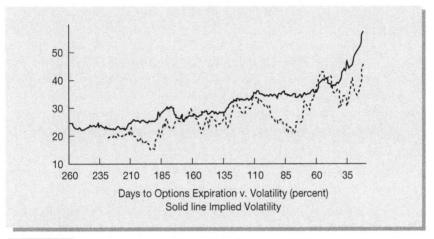

Figure 4.4   **Historical and implied volatilities, January Crude Oil 1998**

Source: Based on data from pmpublishing.com.

This chart can be interpreted in at least two ways. Because it is an indicator of expected price movement for the underlying, the implied volatility can be seen as the leader of historical volatility. Conversely, the historical volatility can be seen as the trend volatility of the underlying, to which movements in the implied volatility eventually return. Again, this kind of analysis is similar to that associated with moving averages and trendlines. The study of volatility is a form of technical analysis.

The study of volatility is a form of technical analysis

---

[5] A great chart from the start of the bull market in commodities. It shows perfectly how the implied volatility can anticipate an increase in the historical volatility.

Conventional usage

Although it is confusing, in the options markets the term 'volatility' can refer to the daily, historical, or implied volatility. But when an options trader says 'Exxon's at 20 per cent,' he is referring to the implied volatility of the front-month, at-the-money call and put. This is the basis of the Vix contract at the CBOE.

Risk/return

By now, it should be apparent that volatility can be traded in its own right, independently of market direction. There are many approaches to this, and several are discussed in later chapters. For now, bear in mind that if the volatility of an underlying contract increases or decreases, the volatility component of an option will likely increase or decrease respectively.

Because volatility can trend, there is a **risk/return** potential associated with volatility direction. Like more conventional kinds of directional trading, an options trader can take a position that follows the volatility trend, or not. The options buyer is actually a volatility buyer, while the options seller is the opposite.

For the volatility buyer, the potential return is the increased volatility component, or time premium, of the option as the underlying becomes more active. He can profit significantly if the underlying makes an unexpected, large move. The volatility buyer's major risk is that the underlying may suddenly come to a halt, and that options premiums collapse.

For the volatility seller, the potential return is the decreased volatility component of the option as the underlying becomes less active. He can profit significantly if the underlying quickly settles into a range. The volatility seller's major risk (and nightmare) is that an unexpected event will cause the underlying to move sharply while options premiums explode.

The main problem for options traders is to anticipate changes in volatility. It is comparable to the problem of price direction for stock or commodity traders.

Traders and the bell curve

The bell curve can be a useful reference when evaluating your performance. Please refer to Figures 4.1 and 4.2 earlier. Imagine that profitable days fall to the right of the vertical dotted line (the mean) while loss days fall to the left.

Now let's assume that you've survived your first year or so, and that you've established a trading *style*. Some traders have P/L swings like the curve in Figure 4.1: they are nip and tuck traders. They try to make small profits and take small losses while earning a good living. Their results are not spectacular, but they don't take a lot of risk either.

Other traders have P/L swings like the curve in Figure 4.2. They take more risk. On the profit days they are handsomely rewarded. On loss days, they have their risk managers emailing their résumés.

All traders have occasional large P/L swings, i.e. further from the mean. Just because a trader makes a large profit doesn't necessarily mean that he's a hero, and conversely, if he takes a big loss, it doesn't mean that he's a bum. Traders are like underlying contracts: they have profit swings that resemble standard deviation moves.

Many people in the industry, including, it seems, senior management of some very large banks, insurance firms and hedge funds, don't have a practical understanding of the bell curve. Keep the bell curve in mind.

A final note

The volatility calculation is based on statistical analysis of asset price movement. It has the benefit of a great deal of data, but like any other form of analysis, it cannot predict the future. Ultimately, it is the most comprehensive means of determining the value of an option.

A thorough understanding of volatility requires research and experience, but even a basic understanding can be profitable for the options trader. You may wish to reread this chapter as you work through this book.

5

The Greeks and risk assessment: delta

Because there are several components that contribute to the price of an option, it is essential to understand how each of these components can be affected by changes in the market. Short-term interest rates and dividends, especially with respect to a stock index, are fairly predictable. The three major variables that affect an option's price are:

- a change in the underlying
- the passage of time
- a change in the implied volatility.

Options theory is able to quantify exposure to these variables. The terms that are applied to the calculations are borrowed from other mathematical fields, and they are Greek:

- **delta** and **gamma** express exposure to a change in the underlying
- **theta** expresses exposure to the passage of time
- **vega** expresses exposure to a change in the implied volatility.

'The Greeks', as they are called, are invaluable aides in determining the risk/return potential of an options position. They are the fundamental parameters of risk assessment.

'The Greeks', are invaluable aides in determining the risk/ return potential of an options position

Delta

Delta is the amount that an option changes with respect to a small change in the underlying.

If an option is so deeply in-the-money that it is at parity with the underlying, its price will change one for one with the underlying. Its delta is therefore 1.00. Traders often say that this option has a 'one-hundred delta' because it has a 100 per cent correlation with the underlying.

An option that is at-the-money changes price at half the rate of the underlying, and therefore has a delta of 0.50. Traders often say that this option has a 'fifty delta'.

In an extreme case, an option may be so far out-of-the-money that it is virtually worthless. Practically any change in the underlying can not affect its price. Its delta is therefore 0.00.

Table 5.1 gives a typical example of a set of options with their deltas for one contract month:

December Corn at $3.80

90 days until expiration

Implied volatility at 30 per cent

Interest rate at 3 per cent

Options multiplier at $50, so multiply call and put values times $50.

Table 5.1 December Corn at 380

Strike	Call value × $50	Call delta	Put value × $50	Put delta
320	63.00	0.90	$3^1/_4$	0.10
340	47.00	0.80	7.00	0.20
360	$33^7/_8$	0.67	14.00	0.33
380	22.00	0.53	22.00	0.47
400	15.00	0.40	35.00	0.60
420	$8^5/_8$	0.27	$48^1/_2$	0.73
440	$8^1/_2$	0.19	$65^1/_4$	0.81

If the December futures contract moves up by one point, then the 380 call moves up by $1/_2$ point, to $22^1/_2$; the 380 put then moves down by $1/_2$ point, to $21^1/_2$. If the December futures contract moves down by 1 point, then the 380 call moves to $21^1/_2$ and the 380 put moves to $22^1/_2$.

Note that the 440 call is priced higher than the 320 put even though they are equally out of the money. This is because the model assumes that Corn can rally further than it can break.[1] This is a reasonable assumption, but is it a tradable assumption? In other words, is it true for all price levels? Is it true under any kind of weather? Note as well that a 380 call costs 22 × $50 = $1,100.

As an underlying changes, the delta itself changes. A large move in the underlying can change an option's status from in-the-money to at-the-money or out-of-the-money, or vice versa. The option's delta will change too radically for the purpose of price assessment. The delta calculation therefore only applies to a small change in the underlying.

Delta and time decay

The delta of an out-of-the-money option decreases with time. This is because the probability of the underlying reaching its strike price also decreases with time. The delta of an in-the-money option increases with time. This is because the probability of its strike price remaining in the money also increases with time. The delta of an at-the-money option remains at 0.50. Table 5.2 is another set of options contracts on the above underlying; it is the same contract month with fewer days until expiration:

Table 5.2 December Corn at $3.80 × 5,000 bushels

Strike	Call value × $50	Call delta	Put value × $50	Put delta
320	60$^{1}/_{8}$	0.99	$^{1}/_{8}$	0.01
340	41$^{1}/_{8}$	0.92	1$^{1}/_{4}$	0.08
360	24$^{5}/_{8}$	0.76	4$^{3}/_{4}$	0.24
380	12$^{1}/_{2}$	0.51	12$^{1}/_{2}$	0.48
400	5$^{3}/_{8}$	0.28	25$^{1}/_{4}$	0.72
420	1$^{7}/_{8}$	0.12	41$^{7}/_{8}$	0.83
440	$^{5}/_{8}$	0.04	60$^{1}/_{2}$	0.96

---

[1] The calls here can actually be priced higher than I've given. This is because I have eliminated the volatility skew for the purpose of demonstration. To learn about volatility skews, turn to Chapter 20.

30 days until expiration; implied volatility at 30 per cent; interest rate at 3 per cent; options multiplier at $50.

A comparison of each strike price from Table 5.1 to Table 5.2 demonstrates the effect of time decay on deltas.

Delta position: equivalence to underlying

A delta position corresponds to a long or short position in the underlying. For example, a long call has a long delta position which corresponds to a long underlying position. All the **delta correspondences** are summarised below:

■ long call = long delta = long underlying

■ short call = short delta = short underlying

■ long put = short delta = short underlying

■ short put = long delta = long underlying.

A consequence of these correspondences is that a delta becomes **equivalent to a percentage of the underlying contract**. One short, at-the-money call with a 0.50 delta equals half of a short underlying contract. Four such calls equal two short underlyings, and so on.

All the deltas in an options position can then be summarised into a net delta position. Table 5.3 is an example of a small position.

Table 5.3 Sample options position, December Corn, 90 DTE, implied at 30%

Long	Short	Call/put	Month/strike	Delta per option	Deltas per position at strike (+/–)
	5	P	December 340	0.20	+1.00
10		P	December 380	0.47	–4.70
10		C	December 380	0.53	+5.30
	10	C	December 420	0.27	–2.70
	10	C	December 440	0.19	–1.90
	Net delta position				–3.00

Here, an equivalent long underlying position is given a plus sign (+), and an equivalent short underlying position is given a minus sign (–). The net delta position of –3.00 is equivalent to an underlying position that is short three contracts. Remember that this equivalency only applies to a small move in the underlying.[2]

Hedge ratio

Because a net delta position is an equivalent futures position, it can indicate exposure to an unwanted move by the underlying. This exposure would be hedged simply by buying or selling the number of underlying contracts needed to create a delta neutral position. As a **hedge ratio**, the delta indicates the number of contracts to buy or sell.

For example, an option with a 0.50 delta is hedged by half the amount of underlying contracts. A position of 10 long, 0.50 delta calls is equivalent to a position of long five underlying contracts. This position is exposed to downward move by the underlying, and so may be hedged by selling, or going short, five underlying contracts. The total delta position is then zero, or, as we say, the position is *delta neutral*. For a small move by the underlying in either direction, the profit/loss of the total position changes little, if at all.

The hedge ratio is especially useful to risk managers with large options portfolios. They regularly adjust their exposure to market direction with offsetting transactions in the underlying contracts. Suppose you are a risk manager with the position given in Table 5.3. How do you hedge this position?[3]

The hedge ratio is especially useful to risk managers with large options portfolios

Delta and probability

A useful way to think of delta is that it indicates the probability of an option expiring in-the-money. An option that is at-the-money, with a 0.50 delta, has an even chance of expiring in-the-money. By associating delta with probability, we can determine the market's assessment of the range of the underlying until expiration. This can help us decide how much risk lies in an options position.

---

[2] Occasionally in the options business, the plus sign (+) is used to refer to a call delta and the minus sign (–) is used to refer to a put delta. This practice confuses the process of calculating a net delta position; it is not used in this book.

[3] Buy, or go long, three underlying contracts.

For example, the above December 440 call, with an 0.19 delta, has a 19 per cent probability of expiring in-the-money, and might be considered a low-risk sale. The return on the sale of this call would also be low, but this is a justifiable risk/return scenario for some investors.

On the other hand, a 19 per cent probability of December Corn moving to 440 by expiration may be the point at which another investor wishes to cover a short position in the underlying. Although the market currently indicates that such a move is unlikely, this investor is willing to pay the small premium that would enable him to retain his short position.

As an indicator of probability, a delta is only as good as the current market assessment of price movement until expiration. This assessment is continually subject to new information, and as a result it is continually revised. **Profitable options trading** is often a matter of anticipating, or being one of the first to discern, changes in probability.

Summary of delta

There are four ways to think of delta; the first is the definition, and the following three are the uses:

▪ the rate of change of the option with respect to a small change in the underlying

▪ a percentage of an underlying contract

▪ a hedge ratio

▪ the probability of an option expiring in-the-money.

Delta is discussed further in Part 3.

6

Gamma and theta

It should be apparent after reading the previous chapter that delta is an indispensable tool for understanding an option's behaviour. But because an option's delta changes continually with the underlying, we need to be able to assess its own rate of change. **Gamma** quantifies the rate of change of the delta with respect to a change in the underlying.

Gamma quantifies the rate of change of the delta with respect to a change in the underlying

To understand gamma is to understand how quickly or slowly a delta can change. Suppose XYZ is trading at a price of 100, and there are just two hours until the front-month options contract expires. The typical daily range of XYZ is two points, so we expect it to be between 99 and 101 at the time of expiration.

Now suppose that XYZ starts to move erratically, and for the next two hours it trades between 99 and 101. During this time, what is the delta of the expiring 100 call? If XYZ settles below 100, the 100 call will expire worthless, with a delta of zero. If XYZ settles above 100, the call will close at parity, with a delta of 1.00.

During these last two hours it would have been pointless to calculate the delta because it is changing so rapidly. This rapid and most extreme change of delta, however, is an example of the highest possible gamma that an option can have.

If we consider the out-of-the-money options in the same contract month, such as the 105 calls and the 95 puts, we can be almost certain that they will expire worthless. Their deltas are zero and will not change. They have no gamma. Likewise in-the-money, parity options such as the 90 calls and the 110 puts have no gamma because their deltas will remain at 1.00 through expiration.

The first situation above occasionally occurs, but most options contracts expire well out-of or in-the-money. Nevertheless, several points
about gamma are illustrated. In any contract month, gamma is the highest with the at-the-money options, and it decreases as the strike prices
become more distant from the money, whether they are in-the-money or
out-of-the-money.

As a contract month approaches expiration, the gammas of both the at-
the-money options, and the options near-the-money, increase. The effect
of time decay, however, causes the gammas of the far out-of-the-money
and far in-the-money options to approach zero. Generally speaking, however, time decay least affects the gammas of options in the 0.10 and 0.90
delta ranges. This all becomes complicated, of course, by the fact that
deltas change with time. You should simply remember that as time passes,
the nearer an option is to the underlying, the more its gamma increases.

Table 6.1 is a typical example of a set of options with deltas and gammas
in one contract month:

90 days until expiration; implied volatility at 30 per cent; interest rate
at 3 per cent; options multiplier at $50, so multiply call and put values
times $50.

Table 6.1 December Corn at $3.80

Strike	Call value × $50	Call delta	Put value × $50	Put delta	Gamma
320	63.00	0.90	3¹/₄	0.10	0.003
340	47.00	0.80	7	0.20	0.005
360	33⁷/₈	0.67	14	0.33	0.007
380	22.00	0.53	22	0.47	0.008
400	15.00	0.40	35	0.60	0.007
420	8⁵/₈	0.27	48¹/₂	0.73	0.006
440	5¹/₂	0.19	65¹/₄	0.81	0.005

The gamma-delta calculation is a matter of simple addition or subtraction.
Here, the December 400 call with a 0.40 delta has a gamma of 0.007. This
means that if the December futures contract moves up one point, from
380 to 381, the delta of the call will increase to 0.407, rounded to 0.41.

If the futures contract moves down one point, the delta of the same call will decrease to 0.393, rounded to 0.39. Accordingly, if the futures contract moves up 20 points, then the delta of the 400 call will increase by 0.14, to 0.54, the equivalent delta of the 380 call at present.

If the December futures contract moves down by one point, then the delta of the December 340 put will increase by its gamma of 0.005, from 0.20 to 0.205 (or 0.21 rounded); if the futures contract moves up by one point, the delta will decrease by 0.005.

Note that gamma describes the absolute change in delta, whether increased or decreased.

An option's gamma, like its delta, changes as the underlying changes. If you calculate the new theoretical delta for the December 420 call over an increase of 40 points in the futures contract (corn, like all commodities, can be extremely volatile), the result will be $(0.006 \times 40) + 0.27 = 0.51$. You should instead expect the new delta to be equivalent to that of the present December 380 call at 0.53 This discrepancy is due to the fact that the gamma is increasing from 0.006 to 0.008 as the futures contract moves up. The gamma-delta calculation is therefore best applied to a small change in the delta.

Table 6.2 lists the same set of options but with less time until expiration. If we compare it with Table 6.1, the points previously made about gamma become evident. With the passage of time, the deep in-the-money and far out-of-the-money options have gammas that are unchanged to decreased, while at-the-money and near-the-money options have increased gammas:

Table 6.2 December Corn at $3.80 × 5,000 bushels

Strike	Call value	Call delta	Put value	Put delta	Gamma
320	$60^{1}/_{8}$	0.99	$^{1}/_{8}$	0.01	0.001
340	$41^{1}/_{8}$	0.92	$1^{1}/_{4}$	0.08	0.005
360	$24^{5}/_{8}$	0.76	$4^{3}/_{4}$	0.24	0.01
380	$12^{1}/_{2}$	0.51	$12^{1}/_{2}$	0.48	0.013
400	$5^{3}/_{8}$	0.28	$25^{1}/_{4}$	0.72	0.011
420	$1^{7}/_{8}$	0.12	$41^{7}/_{8}$	0.83	0.006
440	$^{5}/_{8}$	0.04	$60^{1}/_{2}$	0.96	0.003

Gamma can be thought of as the heat of an option. It tells us how fast our option's delta, or our equivalent underlying position, is changing.

30 days until expiration; implied volatility at 30 per cent; interest rate at 3 per cent; options multiplier at $50.

Positive and negative gamma

Because gamma determines the absolute (increased or decreased) change in delta, and delta determines the absolute change in an option's price, gamma helps us determine our exposure to absolute underlying movement.

Gamma helps us determine our exposure to absolute underlying movement

Remember that a long call is an alternative to a purchase of the underlying. It is a hedge for underlying movement in either direction: it gains price appreciation on the upside, and it offers price protection on the downside. A long call yields a benefit when the market moves; its value has a positive correlation with market movement.

The same is true for a long put as an alternative to a sale or short position in the underlying. If you buy a put instead of selling your stock, you'll be very content if the stock makes a large move in either direction.

Positive correlation with market movement is commonly known as **positive gamma**. Just as a long at-the-money option has the most profit/savings potential, a long at-the-money option has the most positive gamma.

Conversely, negative correlation with market movement is known as **negative gamma**. If you sell an at-the-money call instead of selling your stock, you'll be disappointed if the stock moves above or below the amount of the call sale. If you sell an at-the-money put instead of buying stock, you may curse your luck if the stock moves outside the range of the sale price. Should this be unclear, imagine yourself with a potential XYZ position at 100 and with a potential 100 call or put priced at 4.

The following discussion becomes somewhat more advanced. You may return to it later, or have a glance now.

Gamma and volatility trading

The gamma calculation is particularly useful to those who trade volatility, i.e. absolute price movement or price movement in either direction.

Long options can be combined in order to profit from absolute market movement, and short options can be combined to profit from a static market.

If we use the set of options in Table 6.2, a position of long 1 December 380 call plus long 1 December 380 put will have a total positive gamma of +0.013 × 2, or +0.026. This position is known as a **long straddle**, and it will profit from an underlying move in either direction greater that the purchase price of 12.5 + 12.5 = 25. It has two break-even levels, at 405 and 355.

Because this position is long both a call and a put, the gamma figure tells us that its combined delta *increases* by 0.026 for each 1 point increase in the underlying: the call increases its delta by 0.013, and the put decreases its delta by 0.013. The gamma figure also tells us that for each 1 point decrease in the underlying, the combined delta *decreases* by 0.026: the put increases its delta by 0.013, and the call decreases its delta by 0.013.

In other words, as the underlying rallies, this position becomes longer, and as the underlying breaks, this position becomes shorter. As confirmed by the break-even levels, the long straddle profits from increased volatility, or absolute price movement.

Conversely, the opposite position, a *short straddle*, will have a negative gamma position of –0.026, and will profit if December Corn remains between 355 and 405. These two positions are discussed further in the chapter on straddles (Chapter 11).

The gamma calculation is useful to market-makers who carry large positions on their books. The above gamma reading of +/–0.026 indicates more exposure to market movement than, for example, +/–0.0.11, which would be obtained by buying or selling both the December 420 call and the December 340 put. Here, the break-even levels are 423.13 and 336.88. This position is known as the **strangle**, and it is also discussed in Chapter 11.

Positive and negative gamma help to quantify the risk/return potential of a position with respect to absolute market movement.

Theta

Compared to gamma and delta, theta is a straight-forward concept. The **theta** of an option is the amount that the option decays in one day. A short options position receives income from time decay and therefore has **positive theta**. A long options position incurs an expense from time decay and therefore has **negative theta**.

Tables 6.3 and 6.4 are similar to the previous Tables 6.1 and 6.2, but they include the daily theta numbers for all the contracts listed. Here, the theta figures are expressed in actual dollars and cents (they can also be expressed in options ticks):

90 days until expiration; implied volatility at 30 per cent; interest rate at 3 per cent; options multiplier at $50, so multiply call and put values times $50.

Table 6.3 December Corn at $3.80

	Theta in $/day					
Strike	Call value × $50	Call delta	Put value × $50	Put delta	Gamma	Theta ($ per day)
320	63.00	0.90	3.25	0.10	0.003	2.75
340	47.00	0.80	7.00	0.20	0.005	4.5
360	33.88	0.67	14.00	0.33	0.007	5.5
380	22.00	0.53	22.00	0.47	0.008	6.65
400	15.00	0.40	35.00	0.60	0.007	6.0
420	8.63	0.27	48.50	0.73	0.006	5.5
440	5.50	0.19	65.50	0.81	0.004	4.0

30 days until expiration; implied volatility at 30 per cent; interest rate at 3 per cent; options multiplier at $50.

Table 6.4 December Corn at $3.80 × 5,000 bushels

Strike	Call value × $50	Call delta	Purt value × $50	Put delta	Gamma per point	Theta ($ per day)
320	60.13	0.99	0.13	0.01	0.001	0.60
340	41.13	0.92	1.25	0.08	0.005	4.20
360	24.63	0.76	4.75	0.24	0.01	9.00
380	12.50	0.51	12.50	0.48	0.013	11.50
400	5.38	0.28	25.25	0.72	0.011	10.00
420	1.88	0.12	41.88	0.83	0.006	5.50
440	0.63	0.04	60.50	0.96	0.003	2.25

As we said in Chapter 3, all options lose their value at an accelerated rate as they approach expiration. The at-the-money options, the 380s, have the most increase in theta because they contain the most time premium. Those nearest the money, the 360s and the 400s, also have increased theta. The far out-of-the-money and deep in-the-money options can have decreased theta, but this is because they contain only a small amount of time premium with 30 DTE.

Use and abuse of theta

Theta quantifies the expense of owning, or the income from selling, an option for a day of the option's life. You may have an outlook for movement in a particular underlying. What is the cost of a long options position for the duration of your outlook? If your outlook is for a stable market, what is your expected return from a short options position during this time period?

The subject of theta gives rise to a few words of caution. It is tempting to sell options simply to collect money from time decay. This strategy contains a hidden risk. It can become habitual because it often works on a short- and medium-term basis. In the long term, however, it usually fails. The reason is that it ignores the basis of options theory: that

time premium is a fair exchange for volatility coverage. Many traders have gone bust by ignoring this basic principle. To sell options in such a manner is to ignore probability, and to hope that you are out of the market when it eventually moves.

A story about theta

The following story tells what can go wrong with a short options position, but also how trouble can be avoided.

A few years ago I worked for one of the more prominent traders in index options in Chicago. His strategy was to sell index calls and hedge them with long S&P 500 futures contracts. We were in a bear market. Stocks and the index implied volatility were both in a downtrend. The trader I worked for, Bobby, routinely leaned short, i.e. his overall delta position was negative from day to day. He had made substantial profits in this way.

I did then as I do now, follow a number of technical indicators. One of them was the 200-day moving average. The S&P 500 was holding at this level after an extensive decline, and I became worried that Bobby's strategy, which had worked so well for many months, might have run its course, at least for the time being. Because I was new to the business, Bobby would have none of my beginner's advice. After all, he was my boss, and he had recently made a substantial amount of money. He had also substantially increased the size of his positions.

A week or two later, I was on the floor early for a government economic indicator. The report was bullish, bonds were up, and so was the call for stocks. I phoned in my report, and Bobby greeted the news with dead silence. A few minutes later, he joined me in the pit, and the stock market gapped open higher with no chance to cover his position. We stood there for about half an hour just watching the order flow and the indexes amid frenetic trading. Then things started to quiet down. The indexes downticked a little, but they weren't picking up momentum.

Bobby made his first trades, big ones – he sold calls. I tapped him on the shoulder and tried to say, 'Bobby, they're not going down,' but he cut me off by saying, 'Shut up and gimme the count,' meaning calculate his position. Several minutes later, the market made its second move, fast and higher. Again, there was no chance to cover. It levelled off at about half again the distance of the first move. Bobby then covered as best as he could by buying in calls, which were well bid, and by buying futures. He left the pit without saying a word, and I stayed on to tally his position.

A half hour later, I joined him upstairs in his office to give him my report. He was sitting in his chair, staring through his trading screen. He didn't hear a word I was saying; he was speechless and catatonic. He had lost a great deal of money. I knew his position was safe for the moment, so I left the office.

There are a few lessons to be learned from this story. One is to know why your strategy is working. Of course you're talented, astute and you work hard, but is your style of trading or your strategy particularly suited to a certain kind of market? What happens if the market changes its character?

Another lesson is the converse. Perhaps the strategies that you're most comfortable with aren't the ones that profit in the current market. Can you adapt? If you don't feel comfortable with a different style or strategy, then by all means take a break from the market.

Finally, remember that options are derivatives. Once you're in the business a while, it becomes easy to lose touch with the fundamental and technical analyses of underlying contracts. Lack of awareness sooner or later proves costly.

The trader I worked for eventually worked his way back into the market, and has done very well in recent years. We've still never discussed the 200-day moving average.

7

Vega

Often in an options market circumstances arise that cause the volatility of the underlying to increase or decrease suddenly. This may be the result of the inception or conclusion of an unforeseen market event. During such circumstances the implied volatility of each options contract month reacts to a different degree, and this in turn affects the price of each option of each contract month to a different degree. Under these as well as more usual circumstances there is a need to quantify the effect of a change in implied volatility on the price of a particular option. **Vega** is the amount that an option changes if the implied volatility changes by one percentage point.

> **Vega** is the amount that an option changes if the implied volatility changes by one percentage point

Vega itself can be expressed in either options ticks or in an actual currency amount. Table 7.1 shows a set of options with their vegas for one contract month. The vegas are expressed in dollars then rounded into ticks.

30 days until expiration

Implied volatility at 30 per cent

Interest rate at 3 per cent.

An increase in implied volatility leads to an increase in options premiums, while a decrease in implied volatility has the opposite effect. If the current implied volatility increases from 30 per cent to 31 per cent, the value of the December 380 call increases from $12^1/_2$ to 13. If the implied volatility decreases from 30 per cent to 29 per cent, the value of the December 380 call decreases from $12^1/_2$ to 12.

Table 7.1 December Corn at $3.80 × 5,000 bushels

	Options multiplier at $50							
Strike	Call value × $50	Call delta	Put value × $50	Put delta	Gamma per point	Theta ($ per day)	Vega ($ per ivol point)	Vega (ticks)
320	60$^1/_8$	0.99	$^1/_8$	0.01	0.001	0.60	1.4	0
340	41$^1/_8$	0.92	1$^1/_4$	0.08	0.005	4.20	5.7	0.13
360	24$^5/_8$	0.76	4$^3/_4$	0.24	0.01	9.00	18.5	0.38
380	12$^1/_2$	0.51	12$^1/_2$	0.48	0.013	11.50	21.0	0.50
400	5$^3/_8$	0.28	25$^1/_4$	0.72	0.011	10.0	21.5	0.50
420	1$^7/_8$	0.12	41$^7/_8$	0.83	0.006	5.50	15.0	0.38
440	$^5/_8$	0.04	60$^1/_2$	0.96	0.003	2.25	6.5	0.13

Note that the vega, or the number of options ticks, is multiplied by the number of percentage points that the implied volatility changes. The above implied may increase 3 per cent (commonly meaning 3 percentage points), from 30 per cent to 33 per cent. The new value of the December 380 call will then be 14.

For out-of- and in-the-money options, the vega itself increases as the implied increases, and it decreases as the implied decreases. Therefore with these options the vega calculation is most accurate for a small change in the implied. For at-the-money options, the vega remains constant through changes in the implied.

At-the-money options have larger vegas than out-of- and in-the-money options. This is because a change in volatility increases or decreases their range of coverage more than out-of- and in-the-money options. Their value becomes increased or decreased accordingly.

Table 7.2 shows a set of longer-term options, with their vegas, on the same underlying:

90 days until expiration; implied volatility at 30 per cent; interest rate at 3 per cent; options multiplier at $50, so multiply call and put values times $50.

Table 7.2 December Corn at $3.80

							Theta in $/day		
Strike	Call value × $50	Call delta	Put value × $50	Put delta	Gamma per point	Theta ($ per day)	Vega ($ per ivol point)	Vega (ticks)
320	63.00	0.90	$3^1/_4$	0.10	0.003	2.75	25.0	$^1/_2$
340	47.00	0.80	7.00	0.20	0.005	4.50	25.0	$^1/_2$
360	$33^7/_8$	0.67	14.00	0.33	0.007	5.50	35.5	$^3/_4$
380	22.00	0.53	22.00	0.47	0.008	6.65	37.5	$^3/_4$
400	15.00	0.40	35.00	0.60	0.007	6.00	37.5	$^3/_4$
420	$8^5/_8$	0.27	$48^1/_2$	0.73	0.006	5.50	25.0	$^1/_2$
440	$5^1/_2$	0.19	$65^1/_4$	0.81	0.005	4.00	25.0	$^1/_2$

The vega of an option increases with the time until expiration. This is because an increase in implied volatility over a longer term necessitates a greater increase in the options premiums. Consequently, if the implied volatility increases equally for both a near- and a long-term contract, the options in the latter will increase more.

A long options position profits from an increase in implied volatility, and therefore it has a **positive vega**. A short options position profits from a decrease in implied volatility, and therefore it has a **negative vega**.

Vega and implied volatility trends

Practically speaking, the implied volatility of long-term contracts is more stable than those of near-term contracts. Front-month implied volatility is the most reactive to current events, or current non-events.

In quiet markets, the front-month implied can trend lower and lower for months in anticipation of continued conditions. Each point that the implied decreases in turn multiplies, by the vega, the number of options ticks that the options' values decrease. The frustration of, and the risk to, the premium holders becomes almost unbearable as their accounts diminish, while the premium sellers nonchalantly collect their time decay.

If an unexpected event shocks the market, the front-month implied can leap 5, 10, 30 or more percentage points within minutes. As the vegas become multiplied by the increase in the implied volatility, even small positions take on almost unmanageable proportions. The premium holders become vindicated, while the premium sellers see months of profits eliminated.

Risk/return of vega

Because at-the-money options have the largest vegas, they are the most exposed to a change in implied volatility. All options, of course, face this exposure. In quiet markets, a short options position can profit not only from time decay, but also from a decline in the implied. In active markets, a long options position can profit from an increase in the implied that more than offsets the cost of time decay.

It is important to know how much the vegas of options on a particular contract can be affected by changes in volatility, and for that you need to research the past historical and implied volatility ranges. Most data vendors, the exchanges and many websites have this information. For example, if you want to know how the crash of 1987 and the grinding retracement of 1988 affected OEX implieds, how in turn the implieds multiplied the vegas, and how in turn the vegas affected the options prices, consult the CBOE.

Options spreads

Introduction

Spreading risk

'I'm bullish, what do I do?' Occasionally I am asked this question, and I usually begin my response with another question: 'How much risk do you want to take?' In the options business there are many ways of taking a position, and they all have varying degrees of risk. As with all kinds of investments, there is a risk/return trade-off. High risk corresponds to high return, while low risk corresponds to low return. The advantage of options spreads is that each investor can take the amount of risk that he is able to justify and manage. This part outlines the major strategies that spread risk. These strategies can be traded on all the exchanges, and, with few exceptions, they can be traded in one transaction.

At the outset, it is important to know what risks you want to spread. Premiums may be too high to justify an outright options purchase. The potential for unlimited risk from a short call or put position may be unjustified, even though premiums are at a high and declining level. Your outlook may be for a directional move, but it may be uncertain of the extent. The market may be due for a large move but the direction may be difficult to assess. Implied volatilities may be decreasing but they may be subject to frequent, upward spikes. You may want to buy a short-term option, but its cost in terms of time decay may be too great. These are just a few of the reasons for spreading risk.

At the outset, it is important to know what risks you want to spread

Most options spreads can be classified as either directional or volatility spreads. Directional spreads are those that profit from either bullish or bearish market movement. Volatility spreads profit from either increased or decreased *absolute* market movement, regardless of direction.

Any spread has the opposite risk and return potential depending on whether it is bought or sold.

Below is an index of the major spreads. It will serve as a quick reference in selecting strategies. In a few cases the terms that are applied to these spreads vary, but these will be noted. If you are first starting to trade, or if this is your first reading, focus on the spreads marked with an asterisk (*), because they have the least, and most manageable, risk.

Index of spreads

Bull spreads	Bear spreads
* long call spread 74	* short call spread 76
* short put spread 80	* long put spread 78
long 1×2 call spread 85	long 1×2 put spread 88
long call ladder 91	long put ladder 94
long call, short put combo 101	long put, short call combo 104
* long OTM call butterfly 137	* long OTM put butterfly 138
* long OTM call condor 141	* long OTM put condor 144
* long diagonal call spread 160	* long diagonal put spread 160
Volatile market spreads	**Stationary market spreads**
long straddle 110	short straddle 114
long strangle 116	short strangle 118
* long iron butterfly 121	* short iron butterfly 124
short ATM butterfly, call or put 136	* long ATM butterfly, call or put 131, 135
* long iron condor 128	* short iron condor 125
* short ATM put condor 146	* long ATM put condor 145
* short ATM call condor 147	* long ATM call condor 143
	covered write 151
	long calendar spread 157

ATM = at-the-money; OTM = out-of-the-money.

Terms to use when placing spread orders

Whenever you place an order for one of these spreads, **omit the jargon**. It is most important to know the price at which you want to trade the spread. Then, you must know the prices of the individual options, or the pieces, that you want to trade.

When you ring your broker, state that you are placing an order for an options spread, and state the stock or other underlying. Next, specify the following: buy or sell, quantity, month, strike price, and call(s) or put(s). Do this for each options strike. Next, specify the net debit or credit for *one* spread. Then, specify the total debit or credit for the trade. Make sure your broker repeats all the specifications to you. Last of all, use the jargon, but only if you and your broker have previously agreed on the terms. Your conversation with your broker should sound like the following:

> Whenever you place an order for one of these spreads, omit the jargon

You: *Hi, I want to place an options spread order in IBM.*

Broker: *Go ahead.*

You: *On a spread buy 5 July130 calls, and sell 5 July 135 calls for a net debit of 1.27 times 5. Total debit is 6.35. [You should know that 6.35 equals $635.00.]*

Broker: *Checking, in IBM options you are buying 5 July 130 calls, and selling 5 July 135 calls as a spread, for a debit of 1.27 times 5. Your total debit is 6.35.*

You: *Yes, that's correct.*

Broker: *Working, I'll call you back.*

When your broker calls you back to confirm, he or she should specify all of the above plus the prices of each option.

Broker: *Hi, you're filled on your spread.*

You: *Good, read it off.*

Broker: *On a spread in IBM you bought 5 July 130 calls, and sold 5 July 135 calls for a debit of 1.27 times 5. Your total debit is 6.35. You paid 2.87 for 5 of the July 130 calls, and you sold 5 of the July 135 calls at 1.60.*

You: *Yes, that's correct.*

Broker: *Checking, you paid 1.27 for 5 July 130–135 call spreads.*

You: *Yes, I paid 1.27 to go long (to buy) 5 July 130–135 call spreads.*

Broker: *Can you confirm that again?*

You: *Have a nice day, wise guy.*

Note that when reporting the prices of the options, your broker should use the following terms:

■ when buying: price *for* quantity

■ when selling: quantity *at* price.

These terms avoid confusion, and they have been used for many years on most of the major exchanges, including the CBOT and the LIFFE. Learn to use them.

Advice for beginners

Before we begin our discussion of spreading, here are two pieces of advice:

■ The first is not to change your risk/return profile in order to reduce your premium outlay or to pay less commissions. Trade an options position because your outlook tells you it is the best position to take under the current market conditions. Specifically, selling extra options may reduce the cost of your spread, or failing to buy protective options may reduce the amount of your brokerage bill, but in both cases, you incur added and unjustifiable risk.

■ Second, if you are new to trading options, do not take a position that is net short an option or options. There are many ways to trade from the short side without taking unlimited, or practically unlimited, risk. They all involve the purchase of one or more risk limiting options. Each *short* option should be covered by a long option.

Each *short* option should be covered by a long option

It is helpful to discuss the profit/loss potential of spreads in terms of their value at expiration. Practically speaking, however, you will most often close a spread before expiration because you will not want to exercise or be assigned to an underlying contract. You also do not want pin risk.

8

Call spreads and put spreads, or one by one directional spreads

Investors with a directional outlook often find the risks of a straight long or short options position to be undesirable. A stock index may be at a historically high level, and therefore an investor may want to sell calls or buy puts in order to profit from a decline. But perhaps the market is still too strong to sell 'naked' calls, i.e. short calls without a hedge. If premium levels are high, then the investor may not want to risk investing in a straight put purchase. A sensible alternative is to spread the risk of a straight options position by taking the opposite long or short position at a strike price that is more distant from the underlying.

> Spread the risk of a straight options position by taking the opposite long or short position at a strike price that is more distant from the underlying

For example, if XYZ is trading at 100, we may buy the 95 put and simultaneously sell the 90 put, thereby creating a **long put spread**, a bearish strategy. If instead we are bullish, we may sell the 95 put and buy the 90 put, creating a **short put spread.**

Another bullish strategy is to buy the 105 call while selling the 110 call, creating a **long call spread.** If instead we sell the 105 call while buying the 110 call, we create a **short call spread**, an alternative bearish strategy. These four spreads are also known as **vertical spreads.**

In practice, both strikes of the call or put spread are usually placed out-of-the-money. The key to all these spreads is the option that is at, or nearest to, the underlying. We will discuss each of them.

In addition, by spreading one option against the other, you are also spreading cost against cost, so if one option is dear, then it is financed by another that is dear. You also minimise your exposure to the Greeks. I repeat: *you minimise your exposure to the Greeks*.

The profit/loss calculations that form the basis of these spreads can be applied to any underlying in stocks, bonds, commodities or FX. For the purpose of illustration, a set of options on a stock index is given in Table 8.1:

SPDR at 115.22

45 days until June expiration

Contract multiplier of $100

Table 8.1 SPY options

Strike	107	109	111	113	115	117	119	121	123
June calls				5.05	3.80	2.60	1.70	1.00	0.55
June puts	1.75	2.15	2.60	3.10	3.90	4.80			

*Long call spread

Bullish strategy

The SPDR[1] ('Spider') is currently trading at 115.22. You may wish to purchase the 117 call to profit from an upside move. It's close to expiration, time decay is costly, and the implied volatility is higher than it has been recently, so an expenditure of 2.60 × $100, or $260 may seem too great. You could sell the 119 call for 1.70 at the same time as you buy the 117 call, for a total debit of 0.90 or $90. Your short call then effectively finances the purchase of your long call, and minimises your exposure to the Greeks.

---

[1] S&P 500 ETF Trust. The options trade at Chicago's CBOE. The SPDR is a mutual fund based on the S&P 500. Just think of it as the S&P 500. The current open interest on this options contract is a massive 13 million. In other words, everybody and his uncle trade it. Because it's 1/10th the size of the Spu's, it's affordable.

With this spread, you have a potential buy at 117 and a potential sell at 119, for which you pay a premium. Your analysis may indicate that the near-term price gain for the SPDR is expected to be 119. You are willing to trade unlimited upside potential for a reduced risk in your premium exposure.

This position is known as the **long call spread** because it is similar to a long call.[2] In order to assess the profit/loss potential of the spread at expiration, first the price of the spread is considered as a unit, 0.90.

The maximum profit is gained if the stock is at or above the higher strike, or 119, at expiration. This is calculated as the difference between the strike prices minus the cost of the spread, or $(119 - 117) - 0.90 = 1.10$.

The maximum loss of the spread is equal to its cost, or 0.90. This loss is incurred if the stock is at or below the lower strike, or 117, at expiration.

The break-even level is the level at which an increase in the stock pays for the spread. This is calculated as the lower strike price plus the cost of the spread, or $117 + 0.90 = 117.90$. Here is a summary of this spread's profit/loss at expiration:

Debit from long June 117 call: –2.60
Credit from short June 119 call: 1.70
Total debit: –0.90

Maximum profit: difference between strikes – cost of spread: $(119 - 117) - 0.90 = 1.10$

Maximum loss: cost of spread: 0.90

Break-even level: lower strike + cost of spread: $117 + 0.90 = 117.90$

The risk/return potential of this spread is maximum loss divided by maximum profit, or $0.90/1.10 = 0.82$. In other words, a risk of 0.82 has a potential gain of 1.00, or 1.6 to 2.[3]

Table 8.2 shows the expiration profit/loss for this spread.

In graphic terms, the expiration profit/loss can be illustrated as shown in Figure 8.1.

---

[2] This spread is also known as the **bull call spread** and the **long vertical call spread**.

[3] In practice, I prefer to have a risk/return ratio of 0.5 or better unless I'm very bullish, which I was when I looked at this spread. We'll talk about R/R as we move on.

Table 8.2 Long SPY June 117–119 call spread

SPDR	115	116	117	117.90	118	119	120	121
Spread debit	−0.90							
Value of spread at expiration	0	0	0.00	0.90	1.00	2.00	2.00	2.00
Profit/loss	−0.90	−0.90	−0.90	0.00	0.10	1.10	1.10	1.10

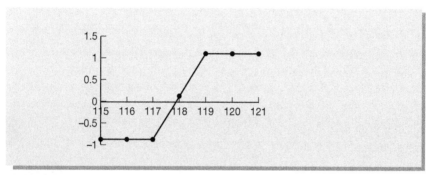

Figure 8.1   Expiration profit/loss relating to Table 8.2

*Short call spread
Neutral to bearish strategy

Suppose you are neutral to bearish on the S&P 500. With 45 days till expiration, June time decay is beginning to accelerate. You would like to collect premium if the index stays in its current range or if it declines, but you don't want to risk the unlimited loss from a short call. You may then sell the June 117 call at 2.60, and in the same transaction pay 1.70 for the June 119 call, for a net credit of 0.90 Your position is known as the **short call spread** because it is similar to a short call.[4]

The advantage of your spread is that it has a built-in stop-loss cover at the higher strike, or 119. You may think of this spread as a potential sale of the stock at 117, and a potential buy of the stock at 119. For this risk, you collect a premium.

---

[4] This spread is also known as the **bear call spread** and the **short vertical call spread**.

The expiration profit/loss of this spread is opposite to the above long call spread, but the break-even level is the same. Here, the maximum profit is the credit received from the spread, or 0.90. This profit is earned if the stock is at or below the lower strike, or 117.

The maximum loss occurs if the stock is at or above the higher strike. This is calculated as the difference between strike prices minus the income from the spread, or (119 – 117) – 0.90 = 1.10.

The break-even level is the same as the long call spread. This is the level at which a loss due to an increase in the stock price matches the income from the spread. The calculation is the lower strike price plus the price of the spread, or 117 + 0.90 = 117.90. Below is a summary of this spread's expiration profit/loss:

Credit from short June 117 call:	2.60
Debit from long June 119 call:	–1.70
Total credit:	0.90

Maximum profit: credit from spread: 0.90

Maximum loss: (difference between strikes) – credit from spread: (119 – 117) – 0.90 = 1.10

Break-even level: lower strike + credit from spread: 117 + 0.90 = 117.90

The risk/return potential from this spread is also opposite to the long call spread, or maximum loss divided by maximum return at 1.10/0.90. Here, a risk of each $110 offers a potential return of $90.

Table 8.3 shows the expiration profit/loss for this short call spread.

Table 8.3 Short SPY June 117–119 call spread

SPDR	115	116	117	117.90	118	119	120	121
Spread credit	0.90	-----	-----	-----	-----	-----	-----	-----
Value of spread at expiration	0	0	0.00	0.90	1.00	2.00	2.00	2.00
Profit/loss	0.90	0.90	0.90	0.00	–0.10	–1.10	–1.10	–1.10

The expiration profit/loss for this spread is graphed in Figure 8.2.

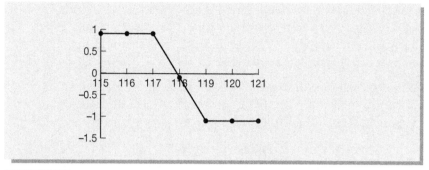

Figure 8.2   Expiration profit/loss relating to Table 8.3

*Long put spread

Bearish strategy

The SPDR is currently trading at 115.22, and you are bearish, short term, on the S&P 500 index. You may wish to purchase the June 113 put to profit from a downside move. With 45 days till expiration, time decay is accelerating and the implied volatility is higher than it has been recently, so an expenditure of 3.10 or $310, may seem too great.

Instead, you could sell the June 111 put at 2.60, and in the same transaction pay 3.10 for the June 113 put, for a total debit of 0.50. Your short put then effectively finances the purchase of your long put, and minimises your exposure to the Greeks.

The trade-off is that your downside profit is limited by the 111 put, but at that point you have probably captured the best part of the move. Your analysis may tell you that the SPX is supported below 111, in which case your 111 put would effectively be the level at which you take the profit from your 113 put.

In this case, you are buying the June 113–111 put spread. This position is known as the **long put spread** because it is similar to a long put.[5] You may simply think of this spread as a potential sale of the index (the ETF) at 113, and a potential buy of the index at 111. For this profit potential you pay a premium.

In order to assess the profit/loss potential of the spread at expiration, first the price of the spread is considered as a unit: 0.50.

---

[5] This spread is also known as the **bear put spread** and the **long vertical put spread**.

At expiration, the maximum profit is gained if the stock is at or below the lower strike, or 111. This is calculated as the difference between strike prices minus the cost of the spread, or $(113 - 111) - 0.50 = 1.50$.

The maximum loss is taken if the stock is at or above the higher strike, or 113, at expiration. This is calculated simply as the cost of the spread, or 0.50.

The break-even level is the level at which a decline in the stock pays for the cost of the spread. This is calculated as the higher strike minus the cost of the spread, or $113 - 0.50 = 112.50$. The expiration profit/loss is summarised as follows:

Debit from long June 113 put: –3.10
Credit from short June 111 put: 2.60
Total debit: –0.50

Maximum profit: difference between strikes – cost of spread:
$(113 - 111) - 0.50 = 1.50$

Maximum loss: cost of spread: 0.50

Break-even level: higher strike – cost of spread: $113 - 0.50 = 112.50$

The risk/return potential of this spread is maximum loss divided by maximum profit, or 0.50/1.50. In other words you are risking $0.33 for each potential profit of $1.00, or a risk/return ratio of 1/3.[6]

In tabular form the expiration profit/loss is as in Table 8.4.

Table 8.4 Long SPY June 113–111 put spread

Microsoft	109	110	111	112	112.50	113	114	115
Spread debit	–0.50							
Value of spread at expiration	2	2	2	1	0.50	0	0	0
Profit/loss	1.50	1.50	1.50	0.50		0	–0.50	–0.50	–0.50

[6] This is a more justifiable R/R than we had with the 117–119 call spread. The reason why this put spread is cheaper than the call spread is because of the steep put skew. We'll discuss this later.

In graphic terms, the profit/loss of this spread is illustrated in Figure 8.3.

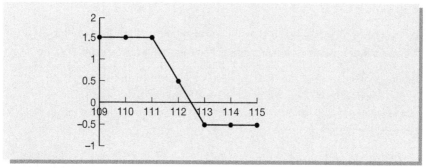

Expiration profit/loss relating to Table 8.4

*Short put spread

Neutral to bullish strategy

On the other hand, suppose that you are neutral to bullish on the SPX or the SPDR. Your analysis tells you that it is oversold, or that earnings prospects are better than expected. You would like to sell a put in order to profit either from time decay if the index stabilises or from a decline in the put's value if the index rallies. At the same time, you do not want the exposure of a naked short put.

You may then sell the June 113 put at 3.10, and in the same transaction pay 2.60 for the June 111 put, for a net credit of 0.50. This position is known as the **short put spread** because it is similar to a short put.[7] The advantage of this spread is that if the stock declines, a possible loss is cut at the lower strike, or 111. You may think of this spread as a potential buy of the stock at the higher strike, or 113, and a potential sale of the stock at the lower strike, or 111. For this potential risk you collect a premium.

The expiration profit/loss of this short put spread is exactly opposite to the former long put spread. The maximum profit is earned if the stock is at or above the higher strike, or 113. This amount is simply the premium collected for the spread, or 0.50.

The maximum loss occurs if the stock is at or below the lower strike, or 111. This is calculated as the difference between the strike prices minus the income from the spread: $(113 - 111) - 0.50 = 1.50$.

---

[7] This spread is also known as the **bull put spread** and the **short vertical put spread**.

The break-even level is the level at which a decline in the stock matches the spread income. This is calculated as the higher strike minus the price of the spread, or $113 - 0.50 = 112.50$.

The profit/loss at expiration is summarised as follows:

Credit from short June 113 put:	3.10
Debit from long June 111 put:	–2.60
Total credit from spread:	0.50

Maximum profit: credit from spread: 0.50

Maximum loss: difference between strikes – credit from spread:
$(113 - 111) - 0.50 = 1.50$

Break-even level: higher strike – credit from spread: $113 - 0.50 = 112.50$

The risk/return potential for this spread is also opposite to the long put spread, at maximum loss divided by maximum profit, or 1.50/0.50. Here, you risk 3.0 to make 1.00.[8]

In tabular form the expiration profit/loss is shown in Table 8.5.

Table 8.5 Short SPY June 113–111 put spread

SPY	109	110	111	112	112.5	113	114	115
Spread credit	0.50	-----	-----	-----	-----	-----	-----	-----
Value of spread at expiration	–2	–2	–2	–1	–0.50	0	0	0
Profit/loss	–1.50	–1.50	–1.50	–0.50	0	0.50	0.50	0.50

The graph of the profit/loss position at expiration is shown in Figure 8.4.

Long versus short call and put spreads

So far we have seen that both a long call spread and a short put spread profit from an upside move. Likewise both a long put spread and a short

---

[8] I wouldn't, but many do because supposedly 'It'll never happen'.

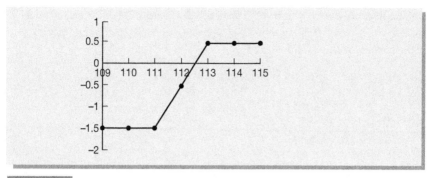

Figure 8.4 Expiration profit/loss relating to Table 8.5

call spread profit from a downside move. The question may arise as to which one is preferable. The basic difference is that of buying or selling premium, and the trade-offs are similar to straight long or short positions in calls or puts.

If a long and a short spread are both out-of-the-money and equidistant from the underlying, the maximum profit of the long spread is greater than the maximum profit of the short spread, but the short spread has the greater probability to profit.

The probability of either spread expiring in the money can be approximated by the delta of the strike that is nearest the underlying. In the above examples, both the 117 call and the 113 put have a delta that is approximately 0.40. If the index has a 40 per cent probability of moving to a strike in either direction, then the direction which is short has a 60 per cent probability of collecting its premium. The maximum loss, however, is greater with the short spread. The maximum profit, of course, favours the long spread, and this is a fair return for an outcome that is less probable.

Premium sellers often short out-of-the-money spreads that are at a safe distance from the underlying because these spreads have limited risk. Premium buyers, however, can afford to place their position closer to the underlying because the cost of the spread is less than the cost of a straight call or put.

Which strikes?

Call spreads and put spreads can be created with any two strikes. Of course, there are trade-offs. (They don't call them 'options' for nothing.)

If you spread the strikes, then you get a greater profit range but you pay more. You need to do technical analysis to determine which strikes to spread. Also, call spreads and put spreads can be any *distance* from the underlying. The trade-offs are similar to those between straight out-of-the-money and at-the-money calls or puts. The further a spread is from the underlying, the less cost or income it has, and the less probability it has of becoming in-the-money.

1×1s and volatility skews

In the stock or bond markets, the out-of-the-money put spread often costs less than the equidistant out-of-the-money call spread. This is because the lower strike put is priced higher than the higher strike call, although they are the same distance from the underlying. In the above example, the 111 put is 2.60 while the 119 call is 1.70. This is a function of what are known as volatility skews, which are discussed in Part 3.

In commodities, however, the call spreads are often cheaper than the equidistant put spreads because there is a positive call skew.

But don't be bewildered at this point. If you spread 1×1s then you minimise your exposure to the skews. Long call spreads and long put spreads are the safest way to trade options.

> Long call spreads and long put spreads are the safest way to trade options

A final note

The difference between a spread and a straight call or put is that the spread's maximum profit/loss can be quantified at the outset. For the longs, the cost of the spread is the maximum loss, and if the trader is good with technicals, he can pick his levels. For the shorts, these spreads allow for premium selling with a built-in stop-loss order. On a risk/return basis they can be recommended to everyone, especially beginners.

9

One by two directional spreads

There are other ways of financing the purchase of a directional position. Those that we will discuss in this chapter are variations of the long call and put spreads. Again, they involve buying an option to take advantage of a chosen market direction. But instead of selling one, they sell two options at the strike price that is more distant from the underlying.

The spreads in this chapter are suitable for slowly trending markets, and they are unsuitable for markets that are trending rapidly higher or lower, or volatile markets that are subject to sudden shifts in direction.

Long one by two call spread
Bullish strategy

The **long one by two call spread** is a long call spread with an additional short call at the higher strike. If XYZ is at 100, you could buy one 105 call and sell two 115 calls in the same transaction. This spread is also known as the one by two ratio call spread or the one by two vertical call spread.

In order to trade this spread, your outlook should call for the underlying to increase to a level that is near, but not substantially above, the higher strike. This spread, like the long call spread, has its maximum profit if the underlying is at the higher strike at expiration. It is less costly than the long call spread because it is financed by an extra short call. But because of the extra short call, this spread has the potential for unlimited loss if the underlying rallies substantially. The extra short call includes added exposure to the Greeks.

With Coca-Cola at 52.67, examine the August options on offer[1](60 days until expiration):

Strike		40	42.50		45	47.50		50	52.50		55	57.50		60
August calls								4.04	2.52		1.45	0.79		0.34
August puts		0.34	0.47		0.82	1.30		2.05	2.90					

Here, you could pay 1.45 for one August 55 call and sell two August 60 calls at 0.34 for a net debit of 0.77. At expiration, the maximum profit occurs if the stock closes at the higher strike; this is the same level as with a long call spread at the same strike. This profit is calculated as the difference between the strike prices less the cost of the spread, or $60 - 55 - 0.77 = 4.23$.

Because of the extra short call there are two break-even levels. The lower break-even level is, like the long call spread, the lower strike price plus the cost of the spread, or $55 + 0.77 = 55.77$.

The upper break-even level is the maximum profit plus the higher strike price, or $60 + 4.23 = 64.23$.

Above the upper break-even level this spread takes a loss equivalent to the amount that the stock increases. A summary of the profit/loss at expiration is as follows.

Debit from August 55 call:	1.45
Credit from two August 60 calls: $2 \times 0.34 =$	–0.68
Total debit:	–0.77

Maximum profit: (difference between strikes) minus cost of spread: $(60 - 55) - 0.77 = 4.23$

Lower break-even level: lower strike plus cost of spread: $55 + 0.77 = 55.77$

Upper break-even level: maximum profit plus higher strike: $60 + 4.23 = 64.23$

Maximum loss: unlimited upside

In order to evaluate the risk/return potential of this spread, you must consider the upside potential of the stock or underlying. Remember that the maximum loss is potentially unlimited.

---

[1] Data courtesy of the Chicago Board Options Exchange, CBOE.

In tabular form, the expiration profit/loss is as shown in Table 9.1.

Table 9.1 Coca-Cola long August 55-60 one by two call spread

Coca-Cola	50.00	52.50	55.00	55.77	60.00	64.23	67.50	70.00	72.50
Spread debit	–0.77	--------	--------	--------	--------	--------	--------	--------	-------
Value of one by one spread at expiration	0.00	0.00	0.00	0.77	5.00	5.00	5.00	5.00	5.00
Value of extra short call at expiration	0.00	0.00	0.00	0.00	0.00	–4.23	–7.50	–10.00	–12.50
Profit/loss	–0.77	–0.77	–0.77	0	–4.23	0	–3.27	–5.77	–8.27

In graphic form, the expiration profit/loss of this spread is as shown in Figure 9.1.

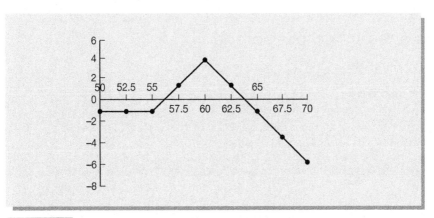

Figure 9.1 Expiration profit/loss relating to Table 9.1

Long one by two call spread for a credit

Bearish to slightly bullish strategy

With adjacent strikes, or strikes that are close to each other, the long one by two call spread can often be done for a credit. Effectively, then, there is no lower break-even level, and the spread will profit from a downside market move. The upper break-even level, however, becomes much closer to the underlying. But there is a hidden danger in this spread.

For example, using the above strikes, you could pay 1.45 for one Auggie 55 call and sell two Auggie 57.50 calls at 0.79 for a net credit of 0.13 on the spread.

The upper break-even level is calculated as the higher strike plus the maximum profit, or $57.50 + 0.13 = 57.63$.

Remember that above the upper break-even level this spread has the potential for unlimited loss.

This spread may look like easy money, but *don't be misled*. If the one by two call (or put) spread can be done for a credit, the market is probably telling you that the underlying is sufficiently volatile to be above the upper break-even level at expiration. Perhaps for this reason the one by two spread for a credit is not often traded. If, after considering these factors, your outlook still calls for the stock to remain below the upper break-even level through expiration, then the long one by two call spread for a credit is a justifiable strategy. This is not recomended for beginners.

Long one by two put spread

Bearish strategy

The **long one by two put spread** is a long put spread with an extra short put at the lower strike. It is also known as the one by two ratio put spread or the one by two vertical put spread. If XYZ is at 100, you could by one 95 put and sell two 85 puts in the same transaction.

The **long one by two put spread** is a long put spread with an extra short put at the lower strike

In order to trade this spread, your outlook should call for the underlying to decline to a level that is near, but not substantially below, the lower strike. At expiration the maximum profit is earned if the stock closes at the lower strike, but because of the extra short put, the maximum downside loss is potentially great. The extra short put includes added exposure to the Greeks. This spread is less costly than the long put spread because it is financed by the extra short put.

With Coca-Cola at 52.67, examine the August options on offer[2] (60 days until expiration):

Strike	40	42.50	45	47.50	50	52.50	55	57.50	60
August calls					4.04	2.52	1.45	0.79	0.34
August puts	0.34	0.47	0.82	1.30	2.05	2.90			

With Coca-Cola at 52.67, in the August options, you could pay 2.05 for the 50.00 put and sell two 45.00 puts at 0.82 for a net debit of 0.41 ($41). At expiration, the maximum profit occurs if the stock closes at 45.00. This profit is calculated as the difference between strikes minus the cost of the spread, or $(50.00 – 45.0) – 0.41 = 4.59$.

Like the long one by two call spread, there are two break-even levels. The upper break-even level is calculated as the higher strike minus the cost of the spread, or $50.00 – 0.41 = 49.59$ The lower break-even level is calculated as the lower strike minus the maximum profit, or $45.00 – 4.59 = 40.41$.

Below the lower break-even level the spread loses point for point with the decline of the stock.

A summary of the expiration profit/loss is as follows:

Debit from long August 50.00 put:	–2.05
Credit from two short August 45.00 puts: 2 × 0.82 =	1.64
Total debit:	–0.41

Maximum profit: (difference between strikes) minus cost of spread: $50.00 – 45.00 – 0.41 = 4.59$

Upper break-even level: higher strike minus cost of spread: $50.00 – 0.41 = 49.59$

Lower break-even level: lower strike minus maximum profit: $45.00 – 4.59 = 40.41$

Maximum loss: amount of stock decline below lower break-even level

[2] Data courtesy of the Chicago Board Options Exchange, CBOE.

The risk/return potential of this spread must consider that the potential loss is the full amount that the stock may decline below the lower break-even level.

In tabular form, the expiration profit/loss is as shown in Table 9.2.

Table 9.2 Coca-Cola long August 50–45 one by two put spread: Coca-Cola at 52.67, 100 days until expiration

Coca-Cola	(below)	35.00	37.50	40.41	42.50	45.00	47.50	49.59	50.00
Spread debit	–0.41	------	------	------	------	------	------	------	------
Value of one by one spread at expiration		5.00	5.00	5.00	5.00	5.00	5.00	2.50	0.41	0.00
Value of extra short put at expiration	– full amt	–10.00	–7.50	–4.59	–2.50	0.00	0.00	0.00	0.00
Profit/loss	– full amt	–5.41	–2.91	0.00	2.09	4.59	2.09	0.00	–0.41

In graphic form, the expiration profit/loss of this spread is shown in Figure 9.2.

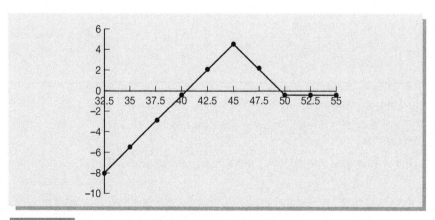

Figure 9.2 Expiration profit/loss relating to Table 9.2

How to manage the risk of the long one by two spreads

The return scenario for these spreads is a gradual underlying move from the long towards the short strike. If, however, the underlying makes a sudden move to the short strike, with no sign of a retracement, the spread becomes subject to the delta and vega risk of the extra short option. It is then advisable to cover the risk of this option. There are two practical solutions:

■ The first is simply to buy back the extra short. This cuts the loss on the position and leaves a net long call or put spread with limited risk.

■ The second solution is less costly, and it is to buy an out-of-the-money option that is the same distance from the two short options as they are from the long option. For example, if the spread is long one 105 call and short two 115 calls, and if XYZ rallies to 115, then the solution is to buy one 125 call. Likewise, if the spread is long one 95 put and short two 85 puts, and if XYZ breaks to 85, then the solution is to buy one 75 put.

In the first case, the resulting position is a long call butterfly, and in the second case, the resulting position is a long put butterfly. Both positions have limited risk because they have covered the naked short option. They also have the potential to recoup some of the loss through time decay. The butterfly spread is discussed in a separate chapter.

Before you trade any spread that is net short an option, you should *have a contingency plan* as part of your risk scenario. At the same time as you place your spread order, you should also place a buy-stop, market order for a covering option that is activated at a predetermined level of the underlying.

Long call ladder (UK), or long call Christmas tree (US)

Bullish strategy

A variation of the long one by two is a spread that places the two short options at different strikes. The **long call ladder** is a long call spread with an extra short call at a third strike that is above the lower two strikes. If XYZ is at 100, then you can buy one 105 call, sell one 110 call,

> **Long call ladder** is a long call spread with an extra short call at a third strike that is above the lower two strikes

and sell one 115 call in the same transaction. This spread is also known as the long Christmas tree, or simply, the 'tree'.[3] In practice, it is placed out-of-the-money.

In August, with the Coca-Cola stock at 52.67, you could pay 1.45 for one 55.00 call, sell one 57.50 call at 0.79, and sell one 60.00 call at 0.34 for a net debit of 0.32.

At expiration, the maximum profit for the ladder is earned when the stock closes at the two upper strikes, 57.50 and 60. This profit is calculated as the difference between the two lower strikes minus the debit, or 57.50 – 55.00 – 0.32 = 2.18. The lower break-even level is calculated as the lowest strike plus the spread debit, or 55.00 + 0.32 = 55.32.

The upper break-even level is the highest strike plus the maximum profit. In this case, the calculation is 60.00 + 2.18 = 62.18. Above the upper break-even level the spread loses point for point with the stock, and faces the possibility of unlimited loss. The expiration profit/loss is as follows:

Debit from long August 55.00 call:	–1.45
Credit from short August 57.50 call:	0.79
Credit from short August 60.00 call:	0.34
Total debit:	–0.32

Maximum profit: (middle strike minus lower strike) minus debit from spread: here, (57.50 – 55.00) – 0.32 = 2.18

Lower break-even level: lowest strike plus spread debit: 55.00 + 0.32 = 55.32

Upper break-even level: highest strike plus maximum profit: 60.00 + 2.18 = 62.18

Maximum loss: potentially unlimited

Note again the potential for unlimited loss compared to a maximum profit of 2.18. The expiration profit/loss of this spread is shown in Table 9.3.

---

[3] This term probably signifies that the options are placed at higher and higher levels, like ornaments on a Christmas tree. Remember that this spread is net short an option, so you will want to put out the fire before it reaches the top.

Table 9.3 Coca-Cola long August 55.00–57.50–60.00 call ladder

Coca-Cola	52.50	55.00	55.32	57.50	60.00	62.18	65.00	(above)
Spread debit	–0.32 ---							
Value of one by one spread at expiration	0.00	0.00	0.32	2.50	2.50	2.50	2.50	2.50
Value of extra short call at expiration	0.00	0.00	0.00	0.00	0.00	–2.18	–5.00	(– unlimited)
Profit/loss	–0.32	–0.32	0.00	2.18	2.18	0.00	–2.82	(– unlimited)

Figure 9.3 is a graph of this spread at expiration.

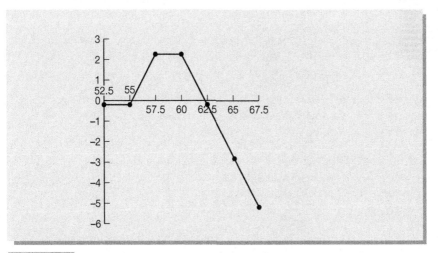

Figure 9.3   Expiration profit/loss relating to Table 9.3

You can compare this ladder to the 55–60 one by two. It would cost 0.75, and the break-even levels are 55.75 and 64.25. The maximum profit of the 1 × 2 is 4.25, but this profit level is 60.00. This ladder is a fair alternative in terms of risk/return.

Long put ladder (UK), or long put Christmas tree (US)
Bearish strategy

The long put ladder is a long put spread with an extra short put at a third strike below the put spread

The **long put ladder** is a long put spread with an extra short put at a third strike below the put spread. If XYZ is at 100, then you could buy one 95 put, sell one 90 put and sell one 85 put in the same transaction. This spread is also known as the long put Christmas tree.

With Coca-Cola at 52.67 you could pay 2.05 for one August 50 put, sell one August 45 put at 0.82 and sell one August 40 put at 0.34. Here, the spread trades for a net debit of –0.89.

At expiration, the maximum profit is earned when the stock closes between the lower two strikes, 45–40. In this case, because of the small spread debit, this profit is calculated as the difference between the higher two strikes minus the cost of the spread, or $(50 – 45) – 0.89 = 4.11$.

The upper break-even level is the highest strike minus the cost of the spread, or $50 – 0.89 = 49.11$. The lower break-even level is the lowest strike minus the maximum profit, or $40 – 4.11 = 35.89$.

The maximum loss can be significant; it is the full amount that the stock declines below the lower break-even level. The expiration profit/loss for this spread is as follows:

Debit from long August 50 put:	–2.05
Credit from short August 45 put:	0.82
Credit from short August 40 put:	0.34
Total debit:	–0.89

Maximum profit/loss: (highest strike minus middle strike) minus cost of spread: $(50 – 45) – 0.89 = 4.11$

Upper break-even level: highest strike – cost of spread: $50 – 0.89 = 49.11$

Lower break-even level: lowest strike minus maximum profit: $40 – 4.11 = 35.89$

Maximum loss: amount of stock decline below lower break-even level

The risk/return potential of this spread should account for a decline in the stock below the lower break-even level. The expiration profit/loss in tabular form is shown in Table 9.4.

Table 9.4 Coca-Cola long August 50–45–40 put ladder

Coca-Cola	30.00	35.00	35.89	40.00	45.00	49.11	50.00	55.00
Spread debit	−0.89							
Value of one by one spread at expiration	5.00	5.00	5.00	5.00	5.00	0.89	0.00	0.00
Value of extra short call at expiration	−10.00	−5.00	−4.11	0.00	0.00	0.00	0.00	0.00
Profit/loss	−5.89	−0.89	0.00	4.11	4.11	0.00	−0.89	−0.89

Figure 9.4 is a graph of the expiration profit/loss.

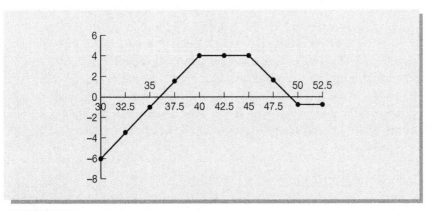

Figure 9.4 Expiration profit/loss relating to Table 9.4

You might compare this put ladder to the Coca-Cola call ladder. Here, we have split strikes, while the call ladder has adjacent strikes. For the put ladder we paid 0.82, while for the call ladder we paid 0.30. With the put ladder, however, we have doubled our profit range from 2.50 points to 5.00 points. We have also placed our break-even point further from the underlying.

How to manage the risk of the long ladder

The risk of the long ladder is managed similarly to that of the long one by two. If the underlying suddenly moves to the short strike that was formerly furthest out-of-the-money, the first solution is to buy back that strike.

The second solution is to buy the out-of-the-money option that is as far from the ladder as the three options in the ladder are from each other. For example, if the ladder is long one 105 call, short one 110 call and short one 115 call, and if XYZ quickly rallies to 115, then the solution is to buy one 120 call. Likewise, if the ladder is long one 95 put, short one 90 put and short one 85 put, and if XYZ suddenly breaks to 85, then the solution is to buy one 80 put. In the first case, the resulting position is a **long call condor**, and in the second case, the resulting position is a **long put condor**. Both of these spreads have limited risk; they are discussed in Chapter 13.

Ladders at different strike prices

With the ladder the consecutive strike prices are usually equidistant from each other. The equidistance[4] may vary, however, from adjacent to any number of non-adjacent strikes. For example, if XYZ is at 100, a call ladder may have strike prices at 105, 110 and 115, or it may have strike prices at 105, 115 and 125. The second ladder costs more because the sum of the options sold is less. Its profit potential, however, is 10 points instead of 5, less cost. Its upper break-even level, or point of potential unlimited risk, is further from the underlying. With ladders, the major risk consideration is that the strike furthest out-of-the-money should be at a safe distance from the underlying.

---

[4] i.e., the distance that is equal. This word, found in the Lenny Jordan Dictionary, will come in handy when we discuss spreads with four components.

Asymmetric or broken ladder

Finally, there is no reason why the strikes of a ladder need to be equidistant from each other. Asymmetric ladders are occasionally traded, and they have different risk/return profiles. For example, you may wish to place the second short strike further from the underlying. If XYZ is at 100, instead of placing your call ladder at 105, 110 and 115, you may place it at 105, 110 and 120. The second spread costs more and therefore has less profit potential, but it has less risk because its upper break-even level is further from the underlying.

Alternatively, you may place your ladder at 105, 115 and 120. This spread costs more than the two above because the two options sold are the least expensive, but it has the greatest profit potential. It also has the least potential risk because its upper break-even level is the furthest from the underlying. Just remember that the major risk of the ladder lies with the extra short option.

Comparing call spreads, 1×2s and ladders

At this point, it will be constructive to compare the data from the spreads already discussed. We want to examine costs, profit potentials, risks and break-even levels. If we examine the call spreads, then we can apply the conclusions to the put spreads. Refer to the table of Coca-Cola options above.

Coca-Cola at 52.67

August options, 100 days until expiration

Try to develop your options awareness by taking a few minutes to analyse the data in Table 9.5. Compare the costs or incomes to the potential profits, and compare the potential profits to the upper break-even levels, etc.

The most risk averse spreads are obviously the two one by one call spreads. Concerning the others, if the market moves in the direction of your short strike you may have to cover simply out of worry. It is much easier to make trading decisions when your judgement is not impaired by proximate risk.

An analysis procedure such as the above should always be used when deciding which spread to trade.

Table 9.5 Comparing call spreads, 1×2s and ladders

Coca-Cola call spreads	Cost/income	Max. profit	Max. loss	Lower break-even	Upper break-even (point of unlim. loss potential)
55–57.50 call spread	0.66 debit	1.84	0.66	55.66	none
55–60 call spread	1.11 debit	3.89	1.11	56.11	none
55–60, one by two	0.77 debit	4.23	unlim.	55.77	64.23
55–57.50–60 ladder	0.32 debit	2.18	unlim.	55.32	62.18

A story about 1×2s and ladders

Several years ago I was a client strategist for a boutique London brokerage firm. I would give lectures to clients about the same strategies that you are learning. My job was to get the clients up to speed with options so that when our brokers phoned them they would know what our brokers were talking about.

We covered the fundamental spreads, the risk/return trade-offs, the use of technical analysis, etc: in other words, the basics of options.

I also increased our brokers' knowledge, but mostly in terms of applications. (Brokers seldom want to know about theory.) Then together we devised trade recommendations which the brokers passed on to their clients.

The clients did well. One of them took one of our recommendations and bought a Bund put ladder at just the right time. The Greeks and the levels worked in her favour. Another did well in the Euribor for the same reasons.

But later, one of the brokers falsely assumed that he had mastered what I had taught him, and he began to recommend 1×2s and ladders without consulting me. It led to disaster.

One of our clients was a a trader for a major hedge fund who got caught out on a put 1×2. He began to cover their risk by selling futures. Then the other players in the market needed to sell futures in order to cover *their* risk. The market went down and down. Traders were ringing us up, asking 'What's going on? This don't make sense.' Finally the spread-arbs stabilised the market, but our client had lost big, and he was furious.

There were phone calls and meetings, but fortunately it didn't get ugly. In the end he forgave us our sins because he accepted that the broker made an honest mistake. (Like not knowing what he was doing.) The lesson is: either you work with an options strategist or you stick to 1×1s, long vanillas, and butterflies or condors.

Either you work with an options strategist or you stick to 1×1s, long vanillas, and butterflies or condors

10

Combos and hybrid spreads for market direction

Long call, short put combo or cylinder

Bullish strategy

Still another way of financing a long call position is to sell a put. Usually both strikes are out-of-the-money, and this spread is called the long call, short put **combo**. It is also called the **cylinder**. If XYZ is at 100, you may buy the 110 call and sell the 85 put in the same transaction. In order to trade this spread, you must be reasonably certain that

Another way of financing a long call position is to sell a put

the underlying is due to increase in value, because the short put incurs the potential obligation to buy the underlying. The downside risk is great, but so is the upside potential.

This spread is often traded by professionals who want to *buy the underlying*. The long call serves as a buy-stop order, while the short put serves as a resting buy order where value is estimated to be.

Consider the following:

Coca-Cola at 52.67

60 days until August expiration

Contract multiplier of $100

The August options are shown in Table 10.1.

Table 10.1 Coca-Cola August options

Strike	40.00	42.50	45.00	47.50	50.00	52.50	55.00	57.50	60.00
June calls					4.04	2.52	1.45	0.79	0.34
June puts	0.34	0.47	0.82	1.30	2.05	2.90			

Based on data from Chicago Board Options Exchange, CBOE.

Here, you could pay 0.79 for one August 57.50 call, and sell one August 45.00 put at 0.82 for a net *credit* of 0.03.[1] On the upside, the spread behaves like a long 57.50 call sold for 0.03. The break-even level is the call strike price minus the cost of the spread, or 57.50 − 0.03 = 57.47. You are long a call, so you have unlimited upside potential.

On the downside, the spread behaves like a short 45 put for which you receive a credit of 0.03. If at expiration, the stock closes below the put strike, or 45, you will be assigned on the short put, and you will be obligated to buy the stock at the strike price, or 45. The cost of your stock purchase will be effectively *reduced by the credit* of the spread. For example, if the stock closes at 45 and you are assigned on the put, the purchase price of Coca-Cola would be 45 − 0.03 = 44.97. If the stock continues to decline, you are still obligated to make purchase for an effective price of 44.97. Because of the naked, short put, the potential loss is large.

It is advisable to place the put at a greater distance from the underlying than the call, unless you are convinced that the stock has bottomed out. Use the technicals to find a support area.

If at expiration the stock closes between 45 and 57.50, the credit from the spread, or 0.03 in this case, is earned. The expiration profit/loss is summarised as follows:

Debit from August 57.50 call:	−0.79
Credit from August 45 put:	0.82
Total credit:	0.03

Because you have traded this spread for a credit, there is no upside break-even level.

---

[1] The credit earned from this spread is possible because of the positive put volatility skew. This is often the case. But beware of taking too much credit from this spread.

Maximum upside profit: potentially unlimited

Downside potential purchase price: lower strike price minus credit from spread: 45.00 – 0.03 = 44.97

Maximum downside loss: decline of stock below downside potential purchase price: 44.97

Profit/loss between strikes: credit from spread: 0.03 profit between 45 and 57.50

The risk/return potential is, practically speaking, equal and great. In tabular form, the expiration profit/loss is shown in Table 10.2.

Table 10.2 Coca-Cola long August 57.50 call, short 45 put combo

Coca-Cola	(below)	40.00	44.97	45.00	50.00	55.00	57.50	62.50	(above)
Spread credit	0.03								
Value of spread at expiration	(– full amt)	–5.00	0.00	0.00	0.00	0.00	0.00	5.00	(unlimited)
Profit/loss	(– full amt)	–4.97	0.00	0.03	0.03	0.03	0.03	5.03	(unlimited)

In graphic terms, the expiration profit/loss is shown in Figure 10.1.

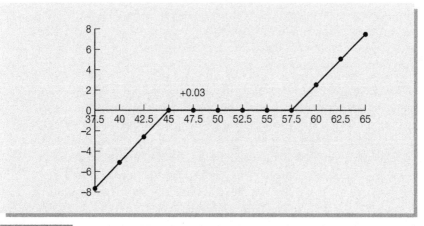

Figure 10.1 Expiration profit/loss relating to Table 10.2

The long call, short put combo is often traded in bull markets, and especially bull markets in commodities that are starting from long-term support levels.

Long put, short call combo, or fence

Bearish strategy

A long out-of-the-money put coupled with a short out-of-the-money call, known as the long put, short call **combo**

A more common use of this spread is with a long out-of-the-money put coupled with a short out-of-the-money call, known as the long put, short call **combo**. It is also called the **cylinder** or the **collar**. If XYZ is at 100, you could buy one 95 put and sell one 110 call in the same transaction. Both options positions are a potential sale of the underlying.

This spread is often used as a hedge by investors who own or are long an underlying contract. They want their cash back if the market declines, but they want to take their profit if the market rallies. The long put acts as a stop-loss order on their underlying position while the short call acts as a resting sell order at a favourable price. When used in this manner this spread is called the **fence**.[2]

The call and the put can be placed at whatever levels are desirable, but often 10 per cent out-of-the-money levels are used as a reference.

In Coca-Cola you could pay 1.30 for one Auggie 47.50 put and sell one Auggie 60 call at 0.34 for a net debit of 0.96. On the downside, your spread behaves like a long 47.50 put purchased for 0.96. Your break-even level is the put strike minus the cost of the spread, or 47.50 – 0.96 = 46.54. Below this level you profit one to one with the decline of the stock, or you hedge your investment one to one.

On the upside, your spread behaves like a short 60 call for which you have *paid* 0.96. If the stock closes above 60 at expiration, you will be assigned on your short call, and you will be obligated to sell the stock at 60. The spread was traded for a debit of 0.96, so your effective sale price would be the call strike minus the spread debit, or 60 – 0.96 = 59.04. No matter how far the stock rises above 60, you will still be obligated to sell it for an effective purchase price of 59.04. The loss, as with any short call position, is potentially unlimited. You had better own the stock.

---

[2] I've even heard of this spread referred to as the 'collar'. Again, omit the jargon. Instead say 'I want to buy [this] option and sell [that] option as a spread.'

At expiration, if the stock closes between the strike prices, the spread debit is taken as a loss. Here, if the stock closes between 47.50 and 60, the loss on the position is 0.96.

A summary of the expiration profit/loss is as follows:

Debit from long August 47.50 put:	–1.30
Credit from short August 60 call:	0.34
Total debit:	–0.96

Downside break-even level: put strike minus cost of spread:
$47.50 – 0.96 = 46.54$

Maximum downside profit: decline of stock below lower break-even level:
46.54

Upside potential sale price: higher strike minus debit from spread:
$60 – 0.96 = 59.04$

Maximum upside loss: potentially unlimited

Profit/loss if stock closes between strikes: loss of spread debit: 0.96

Again, the risk/return potential, practically speaking, is equal and great. The expiration profit/loss is shown in Table 10.3.

Table 10.3 Coca-Cola August long 47.50 put, short 60 call combo

Coca-Cola	(below)	42.50	46.54	47.50	60.00	62.50	65.00	(above)
Spread debit	–0.96							
Value of spread at expiration	(full amt)	5.00	0.96	0.00	0.00	–2.50	–5.00	(–unlimited)
Profit/loss	(full amt)	4.04	0.00	–0.96	–0.96	–3.46	–5.96	(–unlimited)

Figure 10.2 shows a graph of this combo.

If you were the owner of Coca-Cola stock, and if you applied this spread as a fence, then your effective selling levels at expiration would be either 46.54 or 59.04.

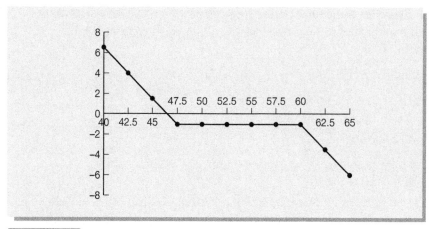

Figure 10.2 Expiration profit/loss relating to Table 10.3

Directional hybrid spreads

The directional spreads that we have discussed are the most common, but they are not the only choices available. Many investors create spreads that

Many investors create spreads that combine components of the standard spreads to suit a particular outlook and strategy

combine components of the standard spreads to suit a particular outlook and strategy. There are no special terms for these hybrid spreads, but they can be traded in one transaction on most, if not all, open-outcry exchanges. You may not trade these spreads, but you might review them in order to improve your options awareness.

As with all spreads, a hybrid can be created provided your outlook accounts for:

■ direction

■ level of support

■ level of resistance.

The risk/return potential should also be assessed, and any contingency plans prepared. The following is just one example of a hybrid spread.

Bullish strategy

If a call purchase can be financed by the sale of a put, then a call spread purchase can be financed by the sale of a put. If XYZ is at 100, you could buy the 105–115 call spread and sell the 85 put. On most open-outcry exchanges, this three-way can be traded in one transaction, and the bid–ask spread for it will be marginally greater than with a single option.

The advantage of this spread is that the long call is financed with two options, but the disadvantage is that the short put contains the potential obligation to purchase the underlying if the market declines. Also, the upside is limited.

With Coca-Cola at 52.67, you could pay 1.45 for one August 55 call, sell one August 60 call at 0.34, and sell one August 45 put at 0.82 in the same transaction for a net debit of 0.29. The profit range is 5 points at a cost of 0.29. Compare this to the August 55–60 spread, which has the same profit range at a cost of 1.11. The three-way must account for the naked short put, however. Here, your technical analysis tells you that there is support at 45.

The upside of this spread behaves like a long 55–60 call spread purchased for a cost of 0.29. The break-even level at expiration is the lower strike plus the cost of the spread, or 55 + 0.29 = 55.29.

The maximum upside profit is the difference between the call strikes minus the cost of the spread, or (60 − 55) − 0.29 = 4.71.

The downside of this spread behaves like a short 45 put traded for a *debit* of 0.29. If the stock closes below 45 at expiration, you will be assigned on the short put, and you will be obligated to pay 45 for the stock. Because your spread was traded for a debit of 0.29 your effective purchase price will be the strike price of the put *plus* the cost of the spread, or 95 + 0.29 = 95.29. No matter how far the stock declines below 95, you will still be obligated to purchase it for an effective cost of 95.29. Because of the naked short put, the potential loss is great.

If at expiration the stock closes between the middle strikes of the spread, or 45–55, a loss is taken equal to the cost of the spread, or 0.29. A summary of the profit/loss at expiration follows.

Debit from long August 55 call: −1.45

Credit from short August 60 call: 0.34

Credit from short August 45 put: 0.82
_____
Total debit: −0.29

Upside break-even level: lower call strike plus cost of spread: 55 + 0.29 = 55.29

Maximum upside profit: difference between strikes minus cost of spread: (60 − 55) − 0.29 = 4.71

Potential downside purchase price: put strike plus cost of spread:
45 + 0.29 = 45.29

Maximum downside loss: full extent of the stock's decline below 45.29

Profit/loss if stock closes between the middle two strikes (55–60) is the cost of the spread, or 0.29 loss

Like the combo, this three-way is occasionally traded at the beginning of bull markets in commodities, when long-term support levels are well established. There are many other hybrids which are traded less often. The more sophisticated traders are continually inventing new ways to spread options.

11

Volatility spreads

Market volatility

Options differ from most other investment products because they address market volatility.[1]
Volatility is a function of absolute price movement, i.e. price fluctuations in either direction.
Options can be traded to profit from either

Options can be traded
to profit from either
increasing or decreasing
absolute movement

increasing or decreasing absolute movement. Often the price trend of an
underlying is more difficult to assess than its volatility trend. When this is
the case, volatility spreads are preferable.

If the volatility is increasing, we can often assume that the underlying
is expanding its range, and that it will be significantly higher or lower
at expiration than it is at present. The risk of our assumption is that the
underlying may increase its range but that at expiration it may settle at
the midpoint.

If the volatility is decreasing, we can often assume that the underlying will
be within its recent range at expiration. The risk of our assumption is that
the underlying may decrease its range but that by expiration the range
itself may shift to a higher or lower level.

If we wish to trade volatility, we can take positions that profit from either
increasing or decreasing absolute movement. In more conventional terms,
we say that we can take positions to profit from either volatile or stationary markets. By convention, the word 'volatile' means high volatility, and by

---

[1] This chapter should be read in conjunction with Chapter 4, 'Volatility and pricing
models'.

convention, the word 'stationary' means low volatility. These conventional terms may not be precise, but now that we know their limitations, we can use them. Therefore, for our purpose we can set out the following definitions:

- **Volatile** means increasing absolute price movement, high absolute price movement, increasing historical and implied volatility, and high historical and implied volatility.

- **Stationary** means decreasing absolute price movement, low absolute price movement, decreasing historical and implied volatility, and low historical and implied volatility.

Spreads for volatile markets, such as the long straddle, profit from increased volatility, both historical and implied. They incur a cost from time decay. They may or may not be net long options. They have net positive vega, positive gamma and negative theta. These spreads are best opened when the market is quiet, or emerging from quiet conditions, and when absolute movement is expected to increase.

Spreads for stationary markets, such as the long at-the-money butterfly, profit from decreased volatility, both historical and implied. They profit from time decay. They may or may not be net short options. They have net negative vega, negative gamma and positive theta. These spreads are best opened when the market has been active, and when absolute movement has started to decrease.

The same spread can often be traded in either volatile or stationary markets, depending on whether it is bought or sold. Practically speaking, some of these spreads are more suitable for the first or the second type of market, and some have more inherent risks. All beginners should trade the spreads with the least risk, and these are marked with an asterisk (*).

At some point, you may benefit from reviewing this introduction.

Long straddle

For volatile markets

The **long straddle** is a simultaneous purchase of the at-the-money call and put. This spread profits when the underlying, at expiration, has increased or decreased to a level that more than compensates for its cost. If XYZ is at 100, you could buy the 100 call and the 100 put in the same transaction. The maximum risk of the spread is its cost,

> The **long straddle** is a simultaneous purchase of the at-the-money call and put

and the potential return is the full amount that the underlying increases or decreases above the upside, or below the downside, break-even levels.

Consider the following April options on Marks and Spencer:

Marks and Spencer at 350.60

30 days until April expiry

Contract multiplier is £1,000

Table 11.1 Marks and Spencer April options

Strike	310.00	320.00	330.00	340.00	350.00	360.00	370.00	380.00
Apr calls				17.00	11.25	6.75	3.75	2.00
Apr puts	1.00	2.00	3.75	6.25	10.25	16.25		

Based on data from NYSE Euronext Liffe.

Here, you could purchase the April 350 straddle by paying 11.25p for the 350 call and 10.25p for the 350 put in a single transaction, for a total debit of 21.50p (£215). This debit is your maximum risk. With this spread you have the right to buy the shares at 350; also the right to sell the shares at 350.

At expiry, the upside break-even level is the strike price plus the cost of the spread, or 350 + 21.50 = 371.50. The downside break-even level is the strike price minus the cost of the spread, or 350 – 21.50 = 328.50.

Above 371.50 the spread profits point for point with an increase in the stock price, and the maximum return is potentially unlimited. Below 328.50 the spread profits point for point with a decline in the stock price, and the maximum return is the full extent of the shares' decline. (There are probably buyers for Marks and Spencer before it gets to zero.)

Between the break-even levels, a partial loss is taken. On the upside, this equals the share price, minus the strike price, minus the cost of the spread.

In this case, if the shares at expiry close at 370, the loss would be (370 – 350) – 21.50 = –1.50. On the downside, the partial loss equals the strike price, minus the share price, minus the cost of the spread. In this case, if the shares close at 330, the loss would be (350 – 330) – 21.50 = –1.50.

The expiry profit/loss is summarised as follows:

Debit from long April 350 call: –11.25
Debit from long April 350 put: –10.25
Total debit: –21.50

Upside break-even level: strike price plus cost of spread: 350 + 21.50 = 371.50

Downside break-even level: strike price minus cost of spread:
350 – 21.50 = 328.50

Maximum upside profit: potentially unlimited

Maximum downside profit: amount that stock declines below lower break-even level: 328.50

Maximum risk : cost of spread: 21.50

In order to determine the risk/return potential of this spread, you must consider the cost of the spread versus the potential for absolute price movement of the stock. In tabular form, the expiration profit/loss is as in Table 11.2.

Table 11.2 Marks and Spencer long April 350 straddle

M&S	(below)	320.00	328.50	340.00	350.00	360.00	371.50	380.00	(above)
Spread debit	–21.50	--------	--------	--------	--------	--------	--------	--------	--------
Value of spread at expiry	(full amt)	30.00	21.50	10.00	0.00	10.00	21.50	30.00	(unlimited)
Profit/ loss	(full amt)	8.50	0.00	–11.50	–21.50	–11.50	0.00	8.50	(unlimited)

A profit/loss graph of this spread at expiry is as shown in Figure 11.1.

The long straddle has the total positive vega of the call plus the put. It is extremely sensitive to a change in the implied volatility. If the underlying starts to move, and the implied volatility starts to increase, this spread profits on two accounts: direction and increased implied.

This spread has double the gamma of a single at-the-money call or put. If the market rallies, the increase of the call delta accelerates, the decrease of the put delta accelerates, and the spread gets longer quickly. If the market breaks, the spread gets shorter quickly for the opposite reasons.

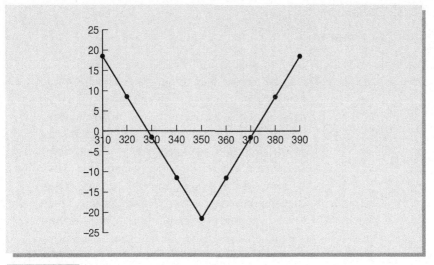

Figure 11.1   **Expiration profit/loss relating to Table 11.2**

The risk, or the trade-off, of the long straddle is that the market may stay in its present range, and that the implied volatility may decrease while time decay depreciates the investment. Remember that with at-the-money options time decay accelerates in the period of 60–30 days until expiration. The risk here is double that of a single at-the-money option, and even greater than with an out-of-the-money option. It is therefore advisable to take a long straddle position that is *half the size* of your usual position.

The long straddle is the most expensive options spread, and so it requires a great deal of market movement in order to profit. It can pay off handsomely, or it can result in a big let-down.

Many traders buy straddles in anticipation of a short-term spike in volatility – for example, if an event is foreseen. Then a bit of market movement is a bonus. They sell their straddle quickly after the event, before time decay reduces their profit.

In this example, time decay is severe with 30 days until expiry, so in order to buy this straddle, you would need to be confident that Marks and Spencer is due for a big move, and that the options were due for an increase in implied volatility.

A spread that profits from volatile markets but that has less risk than the long straddle is the **long iron butterfly** (discussed in Chapter 12).

Short straddle

For stationary markets

The **short straddle** is the opposite position of the long straddle, i.e. a simultaneous sale of the at-the-money call and put. If XYZ is at 100, you could sell both the 100 call and the 100 put. The risk/return characteristics are also opposite to the long straddle. The maximum return is the amount of the premium collected; the potential loss is unlimited. In order to sell the straddle, you must be convinced that the underlying will not exceed the range covered by the premium income, or the break-even levels, at expiration. You must also be prepared to meet large margin calls if the position goes against you. Because the potential risk is unlimited *it is not advisable to sell the straddle* until you are an experienced options trader.

> The short straddle is the opposite position of the long straddle, i.e. a simultaneous sale of the at-the-money call and put

Because the straddle is the most expensive options spread, it is often a tempting sale, and it is often profitable. It is justifiable only when probability is on the seller's side. Assessing probability is difficult, but the volatility trends are the most helpful guides.

The expiry profit/loss for the short straddle can be summarised by making the opposite calculations of the previous long straddle. This summary is as follows:

Credit from long April 350 call: 11.25

Credit from long April 350 put: 10.25

Total credit: 21.50

Upside break-even level: strike price plus credit from spread:
350 + 21.50 = 371.50

Downside break-even level: strike price minus credit from spread:
350 – 21.50 = 328.50

Maximum upside loss: potentially unlimited

Maximum downside loss: amount that stock declines below lower break-even level: 328.50

Maximum profit: income from spread: 21.50

The risk/return potential of this spread must be evaluated in terms of its income versus a loss that is potentially unlimited. In tabular form, the expiry profit/loss is as shown in Table 11.3.

Table 11.3 Marks and Spencer short April 350 straddle

M&S	(below)	320.00	328.50	340.00	350.00	360.00	371.50	380.00	(above)
Spread credit	21.50								
Value of spread at expiry	(full amt)	−30.00	−21.50	−10.00	0.00	−10.00	−21.50	−30.00	(unlimited)
Profit/ loss	(full amt)	−8.50	0.00	11.50	21.50	11.50	0.00	−8.50	(unlimited)

In graphic form, the expiry profit/loss is as shown in Figure 11.2.

Again, many traders sell the straddle to profit from a short-term decline in volatility. Their view is that a forthcoming event will be a non-event. For example, if the US non-farm payrolls are reported as expected, then volatility may get crushed, and the straddle sellers quickly buy their straddles back.

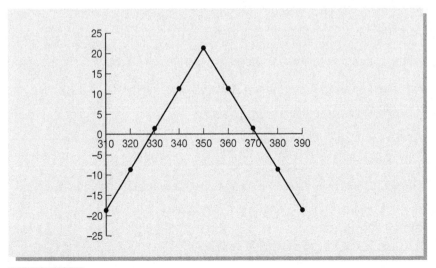

Figure 11.2 Expiration profit/loss relating to Table 11.3

Two similar spreads that profit from stationary markets but that have limited risk are the **long at-the-money butterfly** (discussed in Chapter 13) and the **short iron butterfly** (discussed in Chapter 12). They are among the spreads recommended for stationary markets.

Long strangle

For absolute market movement

The **long strangle** is the simultaneous purchase of an out-of-the-money call and put. Both the options are equidistant from the underlying. If XYZ is at 100, you could buy the 90 put and buy the 110 call in the same transaction. This spread is similar to the long straddle but costs less. The break-even levels are more distant from the underlying, and while there is less potential profit, there is also less risk.

The **long strangle** is the simultaneous purchase of an out-of-the-money call and put

Using the preceding set of Marks and Spencer April options, you could pay 6.75 for one 360 call and pay 6.25 for one 340 put in the same transaction for a total debit of 13p (£130) This debit is your maximum risk.

At expiry, the upside break-even level is the higher strike price plus the cost of the spread, or 360 + 13 = 373. The downside break-even level is the lower strike price minus the cost of the spread, or 340 − 13 = 327.

Like the long straddle, this spread profits the full amount that the stock closes outside the break-even levels at expiration. If the stock closes between the strike prices, the cost of the spread is taken as a loss. Between the strike prices and the break-even levels, a partial loss is taken.

The expiry profit/loss for this spread is summarised as follows:

Debit from long April 360 call:	−6.75
Debit from long April 340 put:	−6.25
Total debit:	−13.00

Upside break-even level: upper strike price plus cost of spread: 360 + 13 + 373

Downside break-even level: lower strike price minus cost of spread:
340 − 13 = 327

Maximum upside profit: potentially unlimited

Maximum downside profit: amount of stock decline below lower break-even level: 327

Maximum risk: cost of spread: 13

In order to determine the risk/return potential of this spread, you must weigh its cost against the potential for the shares to move outside the break-even levels. The expiry profit/loss is as shown in Table 11.4.

Table 11.4 Marks and Spencer long April 340–360 strangle

M&S	(below)	320.00	327.00	340.00	350.00	360.00	373.00	380.00	(above)
Spread debit	13.00	--							
Value of spread at expiry	(full amt)	20.00	13.00	0.00	0.00	0.00	13.00	20.00	(unlimited)
Profit/ loss	(full amt)	7.00	0.00	–13.00	–13.00	–13.00	0.00	7.00	(unlimited)

The expiry profit/loss is shown in Figure 11.3.

As a spread for volatile markets, the long strangle can be placed at any distance from the underlying. The closer both strikes are to the underlying, the more this spread behaves like a long straddle, with increased exposure

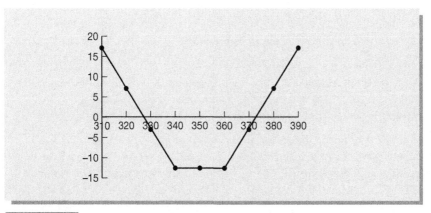

Figure 11.3 Expiration profit/loss relating to Table 11.4

to time decay (via negative theta), and increased exposure to a decline in implied volatility (via positive vega). Because the maximum risk of this spread is known at the outset, it is not inadvisable to trade it, but because of the premium exposure, and because only one of the strikes is likely to profit, the risk may be unjustifiable for some investors. A similar spread with less premium risk is the **long iron condor**, discussed in Chapter 12.

The long strangle is preferable as a trade to profit from increasing implied volatility. If the current implied is low and/or increasing, this spread has an additional return scenario. It is therefore justifiable in itself, regardless of direction, and the wings, or each strike, can be placed far-out-of-the-money. As with all long volatility positions, the days until expiration should be more than 60.

Short strangle

For stationary markets

The strangle is more often used as a short spread to profit from decreasing implied volatility. The short strangle is too often traded simply to gain income from time decay, which is a dangerous misapplication, as we have already seen.

> The strangle is more often used as a short spread to profit from decreasing implied volatility

The short strangle has, like the short straddle, theoretically unlimited risk, but because the two strikes are at greater distances from the underlying, it is more manageable strategy. The positive theta, or the daily income from time decay, is not as great, but the negative vega, or exposure to increased implied volatility, is also not as great.

Because of the two short, naked options, it is advisable not to trade this spread until you have gained experience. A similar spread for stationary markets with less risk is the **short iron condor**, which is also discussed in Chapter 12.

Using the set of Marks and Spencer April options, a typical short strangle would be a sale of the 330 put at 3.75 and a sale of the 370 call at 3.75 in the same transaction, for a total credit of 7.50 (£75).

At expiry, the upside break-even level is the upper strike price plus the income from the spread, or 370 + 7.50 = 377.50. Above this level the potential loss is unlimited. The downside break-even level is the lower strike price minus the income from the spread, or 330 − 7.50 = 322.50. Below this level the potential loss is the full value of the stock. The expiry profit/loss is summarised as follows:

Credit from April 370 call: 3.75
Credit from April 330 put: 3.75
Total credit: 7.50

Upside break-even level: higher strike plus income from spread:
370 + 7.50 = 377.50

Downside break-even level: lower strike minus income from spread:
330 – 7.50 = 322.50

Maximum loss: potentially unlimited

Maximum profit: income from spread: 7.50

The expiry profit/loss is shown in Table 11.5.

Table 11.5 Marks and Spencer short April 330–370 strangle

M&S	(below)	310.00	322.50	330.00	350.00	370.00	377.50	390.00	(above)
Spread credit	7.50								
Value of spread at expiry	(full amt)	–20	–7.50	0.00	0.00	0.00	–7.50	–20.00	(unlimited)
Profit/ loss	(full amt)	–12.50	0.00	7.50	7.50	7.50	0.00	–12.50	(unlimited)

Figure 11.4 is a graph of the profit/loss at expiry.

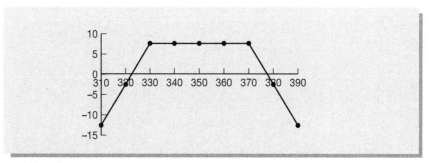

Figure 11.4 Expiration profit/loss relating to Table 11.5

12

Iron butterflies and iron condors: combining straddles and strangles for reduced risk

Often the risk of unlimited loss from being short two naked options cannot be justified. This is especially true for new traders. Occasionally, the risk of premium loss from being long two options cannot be justified. By combining straddles and strangles, you can take the same approaches to volatile or stationary markets, but you can quantify and limit your risks. Your poten-

Occasionally, the risk of premium loss from being long two options cannot be justified

tial returns may not be as great, but you can sleep more soundly, and you'll be easier to live with. The following spreads all have more manageable risk.

Again, all these spreads can be traded in one transaction on most exchanges. Their bid–ask market should be marginally greater than that of a single option.

* Long iron butterfly
For absolute market movement

A long straddle can be financed by the sale of a strangle. If XYZ is at 100, you could buy the 100 straddle and simultaneously sell the 90–110 strangle in order to create the **long iron butterfly.** You can also think of this spread as a long at-the-money call spread at the 100 and 110 strikes, plus a long at-the-money put spread at the 100 and 90 strikes.

Compared to the long straddle, this spread has reduced premium exposure, but it also has reduced potential return.

Using the previous set of Marks and Spencer April options:

M&S at 350.60

30 days until April expiry

Strike	310.00	320.00	330.00	340.00	350.00	360.00	370.00	380.00
April calls				17.00	11.25	6.75	3.75	2.00
April puts	1.00	2.00	3.75	6.25	10.25	16.25		

Here, you could pay 21.50 for the 350 straddle, and sell the 330–370 strangle at 7.50, for a net debit of 14. This is similar to paying 7.5 for the 350–370 call spread plus paying 6.5 for the 350-330 put spread.

Like the long call spread and the long put spread, the distance between strikes of the long iron butterfly can be varied in order to adjust the risk/return potential. Practically speaking, underlyings do not move to zero or infinity within the life of an options contract; there are always levels of support and resistance. It is realistic to place the short wings of this spread at these levels. The above choice of strikes views support/resistance at approximately 6 per cent below or above the current price. This is a large but very possible move for Marks and Spencer. If you choose this strategy in the first place, then you are expecting something out of the ordinary to happen.

Note that the above strikes are widely separated, and as a result the straddle component has a large exposure to the Greeks. This spread has a better return potential when the implied is increasing. A profit/loss summary at expiry is as follows:

Debit from April 350 straddle:	–21.50
Credit from April 330–370 strangle:	7.50
Total debit:	14.00

Upside break-even level: straddle strike plus spread debit:
350 + 14 = 364

Downside break-even level: straddle strike minus spread debit:
350 – 14 = 336

Maximum upside profit: highest strike minus middle strike minus spread debit: 370 – 350 – 14 = 6

Maximum downside profit: middle strike minus lowest strike minus spread debit: 350 – 330 – 14 = 6

Maximum loss: cost of spread: 14

The risk/return ratio of this spread is 14/6, or 2.3/1, or £2.30 potential risk for each potential return of £1. Admittedly, this is not an optimum risk/return ratio, but it is better than that of the long 350 straddle if you expect the stock to range at a maximum of 6 per cent.

And when a risk/return ratio looks this unfavourable, then you need to consider doing the opposite side of the trade (see below).

The expiry profit/loss for this spread is shown in Table 12.1.

Table 12.1 Marks and Spencer long April 330–350–370 iron butterfly

M&S	310	320	326	340	350	360	364	370	380
Spread debit	−14								
Value of spread at expiry	20	20	14	1 0	0	10	14	20	20
Profit/loss		6	6	0	−4	−14	−4	0	6	6

In graphic form, the profit/loss at expiry is as shown in Figure 12.1.

Suppose you think that the upside potential for the stock is greater than its downside potential. You might create a long *broken* iron butterfly by substituting a short April 380 call at 2 for the short April 370 call at 3.75. Your spread debit increases to 15.75, but your profit potential is now 8.25 greater.

Alternatively, you might create a three-way spread by paying 21.5 for the April 350 straddle, and selling only the April 340 put at 6.25 for a total debit of 15.25. Here, your upside profit potential is unlimited.

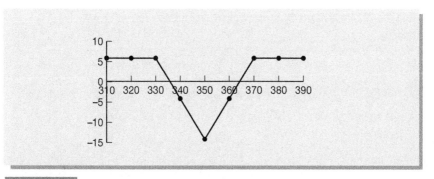

Figure 12.1 Expiration profit/loss relating to Table 12.1

*Short iron butterfly

For stationary markets

Suppose premium levels are high and trending downward. You would like to sell a straddle but you don't want the risk of unlimited loss. Instead, you could sell the above iron butterfly. You are then short the April 350 straddle and go long the April 330–370 strangle, which acts as two stop-loss orders at guaranteed levels. You are effectively short the 350–370 call spread and short the 350–330 put spread. The profit/loss summary and table at expiry for this spread are exactly opposite to those of the above, while the expiry graph is the inverse.

Credit from April 350 straddle:	21.50
Debit from April 330–370 strangle:	7.50
Total credit:	14.00

Upside break-even level: straddle strike plus spread credit:
$350 + 14 = 364$

Downside break-even level: straddle strike minus spread credit:
$350 - 14 = 336$

Maximum profit: credit from spread: 14

Maximum upside loss: (highest strike minus middle strike) minus spread credit: $(370 - 350) - 14 = 6$

Maximum downside loss: (middle strike minus lowest strike) minus spread credit: $(350 - 330) - 14 = 6$

Note that the risk/return ratio is also opposite to the former spread, at 1/2.3. This is a preferred ratio, provided volatility is declining. The profit/loss table at expiry is shown in Table 12.2.

Table 12.2 Marks and Spencer short April 330–350–37 iron butterfly

M&S	320	330	336	340	350	360	364	370	380
Spread credit	14								
Value of spread at expiration	-20	-20	-14	-10	0	-10	-14	-20	-20
Profit/loss	-6	-6	0	4	14	4	0	-6	-6

The profit/loss at expiry is shown in Figure 12.2.

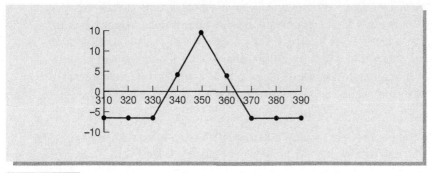

Figure 12.2   Expiration profit/loss relating to Table 12.2

Looking ahead (for those who already know the fundamentals) we will learn that the profit/loss characteristics of this spread are identical to the long April 330–350–370 call or put butterfly. Personally, I would rather trade the above spread because the out-of-the-money call and put are usually more liquid than either the corresponding in-the-money put and call of the straight butterfly. In other words the April 370 call is probably more liquid than the April 370 put. This usually results in a tighter bid–ask market for the spread as a whole.

Lastly, there is every reason to vary the wings of the short or long iron butterfly depending on your outlook. For example, you may sell the April 350 straddle at 21.50 and instead pay 13 for the April 340–360 strangle, resulting in a net credit and maximum profit of only 8.5. Your break-even levels are then 358.5 and 341.5. Your maximum loss is only 1.5, bringing your risk/return ratio down to 1/5.6. The trade-off is that your profit range is reduced from 28 points (twice the credit from the spread) to 17 points.

*Short iron condor

For stationary markets

The risks of the short strangle can be limited by buying a long strangle at strikes that are further out-of-the-money. If XYZ is at 100, you could sell the 90–110 strangle, and buy the 85–115 strangle in the same transaction. You might think of this four-way spread as a short out-of-the-money call spread at 110–115, plus a short out-of-the-money put spread at 90–85. This spread is known as the **short iron condor**.

The risks of the short strangle can be limited by buying a long strangle at strikes that are further out-of-the-money

The maximum profit here is the combined credit from the short call and put spreads. Like the short call and put spread, the maximum loss here is quantifiable and limited at the outset. Like all premium selling strategies, this spread is most profitable when used with accelerated time decay. Declining implied and historical volatilities are also profitable scenarios for this spread. If your outlook calls for lower market volatility, this spread is one of the best choices.

Using the previous set of Marks and Spencer options, you could sell the April 340–360 strangle at 13, and pay 7.5 for the April 330–370 strangle, for a net credit of 5.5.

On the upside, this spread behaves like a short 360–370 call spread for which you have collected 5.5. At expiry, the upside break-even level is the strike price of the lower call plus the total income from the spread, or 360 + 5.5 = 365.5. The maximum upside loss is the difference between call strikes minus the income from the spread, or (370 – 360) – 5.5 = 4.5.

On the downside, this spread behaves like a short 340–330 put spread for which you have collected 5.5. At expiry, the downside break-even level is the strike price of the higher put minus the total income from the spread, or 340 – 5.5 = 334.5. The maximum downside loss is the difference between put strikes minus the income from the spread, or (340 – 330) – 5.5 = 4.5. The profit/loss at expiration is summarised as follows:

Credit from short April 340 put:	6.25
Credit from short April 360 call:	6.75
Debit from long April 330 put:	–3.75
Debit from long April 370 call:	–3.75
Total credit:	5.50

Maximum profit: income from spread: 5.5

Upside break-even level: lower call strike plus spread credit:
360 + 5.5 = 365.5

Downside break-even level: higher put strike minus spread credit:
340 – 5.5 = 334.5

Maximum upside loss: difference between call strikes minus spread credit: (370 – 360) – 5.5 = 4.5

Maximum downside loss: difference between put strikes minus spread credit: (340 – 330) – 5.5 = 4.5

The risk/return ratio for this spread is maximum loss divided by maximum profit, or 4.5/5.5 = 0.82 or 0.82 at risk for each potential return of 1.[1] Although the profit potential of this spread is not spectacular, neither is the maximum loss. Also consider that the profit range is 365.5 – 334.5 = 31 points. The stock would need to settle more than +/– 4.4 per cent at expiry before a loss would result. Remember, you are trading this spread because you expect the stock to range, and for volatility to come down.

The expiry profit/loss is shown in Table 12.3.

Table 12.3 Marks and Spencer short April 330–340–360–370 iron condor

M&S	320.0	330.0	334.5	340.0	360.0	365.5	370.0	380.0
Spread credit	5.5							
Value of spread at expiration	−10.0	−10.0	−5.5	0.0	0.0	−5.5	−10.0	−10.0
Profit/loss	−4.5	−4.5	0.0	5.5	5.5	0.0	−4.5	−4.5

The expiration profit/loss is graphed as in Figure 12.3.

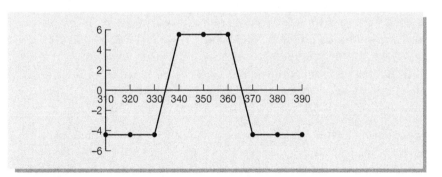

Figure 12.3 Expiration profit/loss relating to Table 12.3

---

[1] It can be easier to think in terms of the risk as the number 1. Here, you could calculate the R/R ratio as 5.5/4.5 = 1.22, or risking 1 to make 1.22.

Again, there are asymmetric possibilities. If you are range-bullish, you might sell the 350–340 put spread at 4 and sell the 360–380 call spread at 4.75 for a total credit of 8.75. Here, your maximum loss is 1.25 on the downside and 11.25 on the upside. Your break-even levels are 341.25 and 368.75, with a profit range of 27.5 points.

*Long iron condor

For volatile markets

The opposite form of the above four-way spread is occasionally used as a way of financing the long strangle. If XYZ is at 100, you could buy the 95–105 strangle and sell the 90–110 strangle in one transaction. You might think of this as a long out-of-the-money call spread at 105–110, plus a long out-of-the-money put spread at 100–95. This spread is known as the **long iron condor**. As with long call and put spreads, the long options here can be placed closer to the underlying because they are financed by short options that are further out-of-the-money. There is less potential return than with the long strangle, but there is also less cost and less premium risk.

With the previous set of Marks and Spencer options, you could trade this spread with non-adjacent strikes on both the call and put sides in order to extend the profit range. You could pay 13 for the April 340–360 strangle, and sell the April 330–370 strangle at 7.5, for a net debit of 5.5.

On the upside, this spread behaves like a long April 360–370 call spread for which you have paid 5.5. At expiration, the upside break-even level is the lower call strike plus the cost of the spread, or 360 + 5.5 = 365.5. The maximum upside profit is the difference between call strikes minus the cost of the spread, or (370 – 360) – 5.5 = 4.5. The maximum risk is the cost of the spread, or 5.5.

On the downside, this spread behaves like a long April 340–330 put spread for which you have paid 5.5. At expiration, the downside break-even level is the higher put strike minus the cost of the spread, or 340 – 5.5 = 334.5. The maximum downside profit is the difference between put strikes minus the cost of the spread, or (340 – 330) – 5.5 = 4.5. The maximum risk is again the cost of the spread, or 5.5. The expiration profit/loss is summarised as follows:

Debit from long April 360 call: –6.75

Debit from long April 340 put: –6.25

Credit from short April 370 call: 3.75

Credit from short April 330 put: 3.75

Total debit: –5.50

Upside break-even level: lower call strike plus spread debit:
360 + 5.5 = 365.5

Downside break-even level: higher put strike minus spread debit:
340 – 5.5 = 334.5

Maximum upside profit: difference between call strikes minus spread debit: (370 – 360) – 5.5 = 4.5

Maximum downside profit: difference between put strikes minus spread debit: (340 – 330) – 5.5 ≈ 4.5

Maximum loss: cost of spread: 5.5

The risk/return potential is maximum loss/maximum profit: 5.5/4.5 = 1.2 at risk for each potential profit of 1.[2] Table 12.4 shows the expiration profit/loss.

Table 12.4 Marks and Spencer long April 330–340–360–370 iron condor

M&S	320.0	330.0	334.5	340.0	360.0	365.5	370.0	380.0
Spread debit	–5.5							
Value of spread at expiration	10.0	10.0	5.5	0.0	0.0	5.5	10.0	10.0
Profit/loss	4.5	4.5	0.0	–5.5	–5.5	0.0	4.5	4.5

A graph of the expiration profit/loss is shown in Figure 12.4.

---

[2] The opposite side of this trade is preferable.

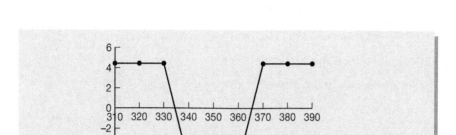

Figure 12.4   Expiration profit/loss relating to Table 12.4

13

Butterflies and condors: combining call spreads and put spreads

The spreads in this chapter are used most often to profit from stationary or range-bound markets. All combine a long one by one spread with a short one by one spread that is further out-of-the-money. For one example, if XYZ is at 100, you could buy the 95–100 call spread and sell the 100–105 call spread to create a **long call butterfly**.

All these spreads have four components. They are most commonly bought, and they are used to profit from declining volatility and/or premium erosion. There are directional uses as well, which we will discuss.

All these spreads are able to be traded in one transaction on most, if not all, exchanges. Their bid–ask markets are only marginally greater than those of single options. When purchased, they have minimal risk, and are therefore *recommended for new traders*.

*Long at-the-money call butterfly

For stationary markets

The **long at-the-money call butterfly** is most easy to understand as the combination of a long call spread whose higher strike is at the money, plus a short call spread whose lower strike is also at the money. For example, if XYZ is at 100, the long at-the-money call butterfly would be a long 95–100 call spread plus a short 100–105 call spread. The combined spread is long one 95 call, short two 100 calls, and long one 105 call.

The spread is done for a debit, usually small, and the debit is the maximum potential loss. The profit/loss graph at expiration resembles a butterfly. If the following discussion seems complicated, keep in mind that this spread is basically two call spreads combined.

The return scenario is for the underlying to close at the middle strike at expiration. There, the long, lower call spread is worth its maximum, or the difference between the lower two strikes, and the short, upper call spread expires worthless. Taking the example above, if XYZ closes at 100, then the 95–100 call spread is worth 5, and the 100–105 call spread is worth zero. The cost of the butterfly is then subtracted from 5 to calculate the profit.

There are two common risk scenarios.

■ The first is that at expiration the underlying closes at or below the lowest strike, leaving all options out-of-the-money and worthless. If XYZ closes at 93, then all the above options will settle at zero. The cost of the butterfly is then taken as a loss.

■ The second risk scenario is that at expiration the underlying closes at or above the highest strike. There, both call spreads expire at full and equal value, making their sum zero. For example, with the long 95–100–105 call butterfly above, if XYZ closes at 108, both call spreads are worth 5. The profit on the long 95–100 call spread pairs off against the loss on the short 100–105 call spread. The butterfly is then worthless, and the cost of the butterfly is taken as a loss.

There are other, less common risks, and they are discussed at the end of the section on butterflies.

A long at-the-money butterfly increases in value as it approaches expiration and when the underlying remains between the outermost strikes. Because it is a premium selling strategy, it is best opened when the options contract has 60 days or less till expiration. Because there is minimum risk to the butterfly, it can be opened close to expiration, for example, under 30 days, and it can be held until several days before an options contract expires. The risk remains mimimal provided the spread remains at the money, i.e. with no short strike deeply in the money and therefore subject to early assignment.

> A long [ATM] butterfly increases in value as it pproaches expiration and when the underlying remains between the outermost strikes.

Taking again the set of Marks and Spencer options:

M&S at 350.60

40 days until April expiry

Strike	310.00	320.00	330.00	340.00	350.00	360.00	370.00	380.00
April calls				17.00	11.25	6.75	3.75	2.00
April puts	1.00	2.00	3.75	6.25	10.25	16.25		

Here, you could pay 17 for one April 340 call, sell two April 350 calls at 11.25 and pay 6.75 for the April 360 call for a net debit of 1.25 You are then long the April 340–350–360 call butterfly. The premium outlay is small, but so is the possibility of the shares closing at 350, 30 days from now. On the other hand, the potential profit is 8.75, and the profit range is 8.75 × 2 = 17.5 points. The value of the spread grows as expiry approaches and as the shares remain centred at approximately 350.

At expiration, the maximum profit occurs if the shares close at 350. There, the lower call spread is worth its maximum, 10, and the upper call spread is worth its minimum, 0. The profit is calculated as the difference between the lower two strikes minus the cost of the butterfly, or (350 – 340) –1.25 = 8.75. The maximum loss is the cost of the butterfly, or 1.25.

At expiry, there are two break-even levels with the call butterfly. The lower level is where the value of the long call spread pays for the cost of the butterfly. This is calculated as the lowest strike price plus the spread debit, or 340 + 1.25 = 341.25.

The higher break-even level is where the profit on the long call spread equals the loss on the short call spread. This could be calculated as the difference between the lower two strikes, minus the butterfly debit, plus the middle strike, or (350 – 340) – 1.25 + 350 = 358.75. However, it is more easily calculated as the highest strike minus the butterfly debit, or 360 – 1.25 = 358.75. At this level, the value of the 340–350 call spread at 10, less the butterfly debit of 1.25, equals the value of the 350–360 call spread at 8.75.

The profit range of this butterfly is then 358.75 – 341.25 = 17.50. It is important to think about profit ranges when trading volatility because, in essence, we are trading a range of probable outcomes for the underlying at expiry.

The expiry profit/loss is summarised as follows:

Debit from one long April 340 call:	–17.00
Debit from one long April 360 call:	–6.75
Credit from two short April 350 calls: 2 × 11.25 =	22.50
Total debit:	–1.25

Downside break-even level: lowest strike plus cost of butterfly: 340 + 1.25 = 341.25

Upside break-even level: highest strike minus cost of butterfly: 360 – 1.25 = 358.75

Maximum profit: difference between lower two strikes minus cost of butterfly: (350 – 340) – 1.25 = 8.75

Level of maximum profit: middle strike: 350

Maximum loss: cost of butterfly: 1.25

The risk/return ratio for this spread, at expiry, is 1.25/8.75, or 0.14 at risk for each potential profit of 1, or 1 at risk for a return of 7.[1] This low ratio is the particular advantage of the long butterfly.

You don't want to hold this spread until expiry, however. Instead you want to take your profit after a reasonable amount of time decay. Be glad if you double your money.

The expiry profit/loss is shown in Table 13.1

Table 13.1 Marks and Spencer long April 340–350–360 call butterfly

M&S	330.00	340.00	341.25	350.00	358.75	360.00	370.00
Spread debit	−1.25						
Value of long 340–350 call spread at expiry	0.00	0.00	1.25	10.00	10.00	10.00	10.00
Value of short 350–360 call spread at expiry	0.00	0.00	0.00	0.00	−8.75	−10.00	−10.00
Profit/loss	−1.25	−1.25	0	8.75	0	−1.25	− 1.25

The graph of the expiry profit/loss is as shown in Figure 13.1.

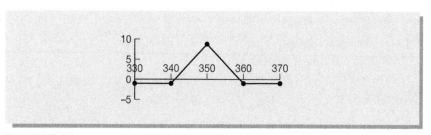

Figure 13.1   Expiration profit/loss relating to Table 13.1

---

[1] 8.75/1.25 = 7/1, and flip it over.

*Long at-the-money put butterfly

For stationary markets

The **long at-the-money put butterfly** has the identical profit/loss characterisitics of a long at-the-money call butterfly. (This fortunate occurrence has brought relief to many options trainers.) If both spreads are at-the-money, their cost is nearly the same. The same strikes are used, but with puts instead of calls. For example, if XYZ is at 100, you could buy one 105 put, sell two 100 puts, and buy one 95 put to create the butterfly. You can think of this spread as a long in-the-money put spread at the 105 and 100 strikes, plus a short at-the-money put spread at the 100 and 95 strikes.

At expiration the maximum profit occurs if the underlying closes at the middle strike. The maximum loss is the cost of the spread.

With the above Marks and Spencer options, you could pay 16.25 for the April 360 put, sell two April 350 puts at 10.75, and pay 6.25 for the April 340 put order to go long the April 340–350–360 put butterfly. Your total debit is 1.00,[2] and this is your maximum potential loss.

At expiration, the upside break-even level is the highest strike minus the cost of the butterfly, or 360 – 1 = 359. The downside break-even level is the lowest strike plus the cost of the butterfly, or 340 + 1 = 341. Note that the profit range is 359 – 341 = 18.

The maximum profit is the difference between the two higher strikes minus the cost of the spread, or (360 – 350) – 1 = 9 The expiration profit/ loss is summarised as follows:

Debit from one long April 360 put:	–16.25
Debit from one long April 340 put:	–6.25
Credit from two short April 350 puts: 2 × 10.75 =	21.50
Total debit:	–1.00

Maximum profit: difference between two higher strikes minus spread debit: (360 – 350) – 1 = 9

Level of maximum profit: middle strike: 350

Upside break-even level: highest strike minus cost of spread: 360 – 1 = 359

Downside break-even level: lowest strike plus cost of spread: 340 + 1 = 341

Maximum loss: cost of spread: 1

---

[2] Bear in mind that the prices in Table 13.1 above are settlements, and settlement prices can occur on or between the bid and the offer. You would expect to pay less for an ATM put fly that is further from the money than the ATM call fly.

The risk/return ratio of this spread is maximum loss ÷ maximum profit, or 1/9. In tabular form the expiry profit/loss is summarised in Table 13.2.

Table 13.2 Marks and Spencer 340–350–360 long put butterfly

M&S	330	340	341	350	359	360	370
Spread debit	−1						
Value of long 360–350 put spread at expiry	10	10	10	10	1	0	0
Value of short 350–340 put spread at expiry	−10	−10	−9	0	0	0	0
Profit/loss	−1	−1	0	9	0	−1	−1

The graph of the expiration profit/loss (see Figure 13.2) is almost identical to the one shown in Figure 13.1 for the call butterfly.

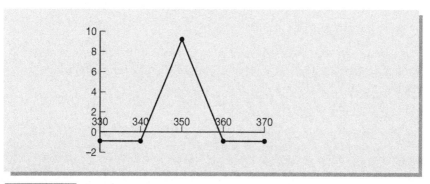

Figure 13.2   Expiration profit/loss relating to Table 13.2

Short at-the-money call and put butterflies
For volatile markets

For each spread traded there are two opposing outlooks. Intsead of buying an at-the-money butterfly in order to profit from a stationary market, a trader may sell the same butterfly because his outlook calls for the underlying to be outside the spread's range at expiration. This is usually not done by investors because the risk/return ratios are unfavourable.

For example, instead of buying, you could sell the above put butterfly at 1. This is your maximum profit at expiry if the stock closes at or below 340, or at or above 360. Practically spreaking, this 1p income is small, but in a volatile market so is the risk of the stock expiring within the butterfly's range. Your position would be short one April 340 call, long two April 350 calls, and short one April 360 call. Your risk is 9p, however, if the shares settle at 350 at the options' expiry.

Figure 13.3 below illustrates the risk/return profile.

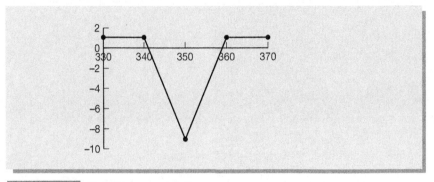

| Figure 13.3 | The risk/return profile |

You can see why only a market-maker will sell you this butterfly, so don't begrudge him one tick while he risks nine.

*Long out-of-the-money call butterfly
For upside direction followed by stationary market

A butterfly can be used with a directional outlook. Suppose you think that a stock has recently become oversold because of an unfavourable analyst's report, or because of less than expected earnings. You know, however, the stock is fundamentally sound, and it will most likely rally back to its former level. In order to profit from your outlook, you could buy an out-of-the-money call butterfly. This spread costs less than an at-the-money butterfly, and its price will increase as the stock enters its range. All the better if the rally is slow and time consuming, because the butterfly, when it finally becomes at-the-money, will be worth more through time decay.

A butterfly can be used with a directional outlook

For example, if you expect Marks and Spencer to increase from its current price of 350.60 into the 360 range, you could pay 1 for the April 350–360–370 call butterfly. You do this by paying 11.25 for one 350 call, selling two 360 calls at 7, and paying 3.75 for one 370 call.[3] If the shares increase to 360 in 40 days' time your butterfly will be worth 3.25. You know this because the current March at-the-money butterfly, the 340–350–360, with 10 days to go, is worth 3.25. If the shares then settle into a range centred on 360, you have a profitable and low-risk options position. You may decide to take your profit at this point.

The expiration profit/loss for this butterfly is as follows.

Debit from one long April 350 call:	−11.25
Debit from one April 370 call:	−3.75
Credit from two short April 360 calls: 2 × 7 =	14.00
Total debit:	−1.00

Maximum profit: difference between two lower strikes minus spread debit: $(360–350) –1 = 9$

Level of maximum profit: middle strike of spread: 360

Lower break-even level: lowest strike price plus spread debit: $350 + 1 = 351$

Upper break-even level: highest strike price minus spread debit: $370 – 1 = 369$

Profit range: $369 – 351 = 18$

Maximum loss: cost of spread: 1

The risk/return ratio is 1/9.

Through knowing the basics of butterflies, the table and graph of the profit/loss at expiration can be constructed.

*Long out-of-the-money put butterfly
For downside direction followed by stationary market

Just as the long out-of-the-money call butterfly can profit from oversold conditions, the long out-of-the-money put butterfly can profit from overbought conditions. This situation often occurs in commodities, but it is common to all markets, especially bear markets.

---

[3] These prices are realistic.

For example, if you expect Marks and Spencer to retrace to 330, you could pay 0.75 for the April 320–330–340 put butterfly. You do this by paying 6.25 for the 340 put, selling two 30 puts at 3.75, and paying 2.00 for one 320 put. If the shares eventually settle into a range centred at 330, then you have a low-risk profit opportunity. The expiry profit/loss is summarised as follows.

Debit from one April 340 put:	–6.25
Debit from one April 320 put:	–2.00
Credit from two April 330 puts: 2 × 3.75 =	7.50
Total debit:	–0.75

Maximum profit: difference between two higher strikes minus spread debit: $(340 - 330) - 0.75 = 9.25$

Level of maximum profit: middle strike: 330

Upper break-even level: highest strike minus spread debit: $340 - 0.75 = 339.25$

Lower break-even level: lowest strike plus spread debit: $320 + 0.75 = 320.75$

Profit range: $339.25 - 320.75 = 18.5$

Maximum loss: cost of spread: 0.75

The risk/return ratio of this butterfly is $0.75/9.25 = 0.08$ at risk for each potential profit of 1. ($1/0.08 = 12.5$, or 1 at risk for a return of 12.5). Again, note the excellent risk/return ratios for this group of spreads.

A story about OTM flies

One of out clients was head of fixed income at a London major. He was a very astute trader, having traded successfully over the years.

On this occasion, he thought that the Euribor was due for a rally during the next few weeks, and then to range at a higher level. He bought an OTM call fly before travelling to a meeting in Tokyo.

While he was on the plane, the market suddenly rallied, and he doubled his money. As usual, he was right.

But when he arrived in Tokyo he unfortunately decided to hold his fly in the hope of getting time decay through a stationary market. After all, his view called for the Euribor to range. To be fair, his trading sense was probably distracted by his admin duties.

The question for the trader was, had the market made its move to a new level earlier than expected, or had the market simply made a temporary upward spike? Either way, he knew that with the butterfly his maximum risk was his outlay.

When back in London, he found that new information had hit the market, and it retraced to its former level. He was back to break-even. Wisely, he sold his fly without a loss.

I have made this mistake many times in my career, and the lesson is: *take a gift.*

Additional risks with the butterfly

There are other risks with the butterfly. The first is pin risk, which is unlikely, but possible. The two short strikes may expire at-the-money. It is best to close the butterfly several days before expiration. You may refer to the section on pin risk in Part 1.

Another risk is that of early exercise with American-style options such as the OEX, and most options on individual stocks in the US and UK. If your short strike becomes deep in-the-money close to expiration, you may be assigned to cash in the indexes, therefore leaving your long options unhedged. With a long call butterfly in stocks, you may be assigned an unwanted short stock position, and with a long put butterfly in stocks, you may be assigned an unwanted long stock position. In all these cases, if your butterfly becomes deep in-the-money close to expiration, it will have lost its value, and you should close the position.

If you hold the long butterfly until expiration there are two additional risks. For a call butterfly, if the underlying settles between the two higher strikes, then you will be assigned one more short underlying contract than the one to which you will exercise. Most likely you will not want this position.

Second, if the underlying settles between the two lower strikes, then you or your clearing firm will exercise to one long underlying contract, which you may not want.

For the long put butterfly, if the underlying settles between the two lower strikes, then you will be assigned one more long underlying contract than the one to which you will exercise. If the underlying settles between the two higher strikes, then you or your clearing firm will exercise one short underlying contract.

There is an additional risk in that the deep in-the-money puts on stocks and American-style stock indexes generally have more early exercise premiums, and are more frequently subject to early exercise and assignment. Perhaps for this reason the at-the-money call butterfly is more often traded than the put butterfly, especially in stocks.

The most prudent way to avoid these risks is to close your butterfly position if it becomes deeply in-the-money, or close it several days before expiration.

*Long out-of-the money call condor
For upside direction followed by stationary market

If the expected upside range of an underlying is too difficult to assess for the use of an out-of-the-money call butterfly, then you can increase the range of the spread by shifting the short call spread to the next two higher strikes that are out of the money. This creates a **long out-of-the-money call condor**. For example, if XYZ is at 100 you could buy one 105 call, sell one 110 call, sell one 115 call, and buy one 120 call. While the maximum profit is the same as with the butterfly, *the profit range is extended* by five points. This spread costs more, but it has an increased probability of profit. It is similar to the long call ladder or Christmas tree, but it has the protection of the extra long call at the highest strike.

For example, in Marks and Spencer options you could pay 11.25 for one 350 call, sell one 360 call at 6.75, sell one 370 call at 3.75, and pay 2.00 for one 380 call. Your debit is 2.75. Here, the maximum profit is taken if the shares are between 360 and 370 at expiry. The break-even levels are 352.75 and 377.25. The profit/loss calculations are practically the same as with the call butterfly. The expiration profit/loss for this condor is summarised as follows:

Debit from one long April 350 call:	–11.25
Debit from one long April 380 call:	–2.00
Credit from one short April 360 call:	6.75
Credit from one short April 370 call:	3.75
Total debit:	2.75

Maximum profit: difference between lowest two strikes minus spread debit: $(360 - 350) - 2.75 = 7.25$

Lower break-even level: lowest strike plus spread debit:
$350 + 2.75 = 352.75$

Upper break-even level: highest strike minus spread debit:
380 − 2.75 = 377.25

Profit range: 377.25 − 352.75 = 24.50

Maximum loss: cost of spread: 2.75

The risk/return ratio of this long call iron butterfly is 2.75/7.25 = 0.38 at risk for each potential profit of 1. A table of the profit/loss at expiration is shown in Table 13.4.

Table 13.4 Marks and Spencer long April 350–360–370–380 call condor

M&S	340.00	350.00	352.75	360.00	370.00	377.25	380.00	390.00
Spread debit	−2.75	--------	--------	--------	--------	--------	--------	--------
Value of long 350–360 call spread at expiry	0.00	0.00	2.75	10.00	10.00	10.00	10.00	10.00
Value of short 370–380 call spread at expiry	0.00	0.00	0.00	0.00	−0.00	−7.25	−10.00	−10.00
Profit/loss	−2.75	−2.75	0.00	7.25	7.25	−0.00	−2.75	−2.75

A profit/loss graph of this condor at expiration appears in Figure 13.4.

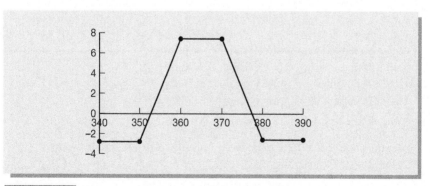

Figure 13.4   Expiration profit/loss relating to Table 13.4

*Long at-the-money call condor

For stationary markets

Like the butterfly, the call condor can be placed at many different strikes, depending on your outlook for the price range of the underlying. If you think that the underlying has made its move for the near future, then you might trade the at-the-money call condor. For example, if XYZ is at 100, you could buy one 95 call, sell one 100 call, sell one 105 call,

> The call condor can be placed at many different strikes, depending on your outlook for the price range of the underlying

and buy one 110 call. This spread costs more than the at-the-money butterfly, and consequently its maximum profit is less than the at-the-money butterfly, but its profit range is greater.

Using our now familiar set of Marks and Spencer April options, you could pay 17 for one 340 call, sell one 350 call at 11.25, sell one 360 call at 6.75, and pay 4.00 for one 370 call. Your net debit is 3.00. The expiration profit/loss is summarised as follows:

Debit from one April 340 call: −17.00
Debit from one April 370 call: −4.00
Credit from one April 350 call: 11.25
Credit from one April 360 call: 6.75
Total debit: −3.00

Maximum profit: difference between two lowest strikes minus spread debit: $(350 - 340) - 3.00 = 7.00$

Range of maximum profit: 350 – 360

Lower break-even level: lowest strike plus spread debit: $340 + 3.00 = 343.00$

Upper break-even level: highest strike minus spread debit: $370 - 3.00 = 367.00$

Profit range: 367.00 – 343.00

Maximum loss: cost of spread: 3.00

The risk/return ratio for this spread is $3/7 = 0.43$ for 1, or 1/2.64. By knowing how the condor works, you can devise a table and a graph of the profit/loss at expiry.

*Long out-of-the-money put condor
For downside direction followed by stationary market

If the profit range of an out-of-the-money put butterfly is too limited, it can be extended by shifting the short put spread to the next two lower strikes. If XYZ is at 100, you could buy one 100 put, sell one 95 put, sell one 90 put, and buy one 85 put. The resulting spread is the **long out-of-the-money put condor.** This spread costs more than the butterfly and its maximum profit is consequently less, but its profit range is greater. It is similar to the long put ladder or long put Christmas tree, but it has the protection of the long put at the lowest strike.

For example, in Marks and Spencer April options you could pay 10.25 for one 350 put, sell one 340 put at 6.25, sell one 330 put at 3.75, and pay 2.00 for one 320 put. Your total debit is 2.25.

The expiration profit/loss for this put condor is summarised as follows.

Debit from long April 350 put:	–10.25
Debit from long April 320 put:	–2.00
Credit from short April 340 put:	6.25
Credit from short April 330 put:	3.75
Total debit:	–2.25

Maximum profit: difference between highest two strikes minus spread debit: $(350 - 340) - 2.25 = 7.75$

Range of maximum profit: $340 - 330$

Upper break-even level: highest strike minus spread debit: $350 - 2.25 = 347.75$

Lower break-even level: lowest strike plus spread debit: $320 + 2.25 = 322.25$

Profit range: $347.75 - 322.25 = 25.50$

Maximum loss: cost of spread: 2.25

The risk/return ratio is again favourable at $2.25/7.75 = 0.29$ for 1, or 1/3.44. The profit/loss at expiration is shown in Table 13.5.

The graph of the profit/loss at expiration is shown in Figure 13.5.

Table 13.5 Marks and Spencer long April 320–330–340–350 put condor

M&S	310.00	320.00	322.25	330.00	340.00	347.75	350.00	360.00
Spread debit	−2.25	----	----	----	----	----	----	----
Value of long 350–340 put spread at expiry	10.00	10.00	10.00	10 .00	10.00	2.25	0.00	0.00
Value of short 330–320 put spread at expiration	−10.00	−10.00	−7.75	0.00	0.00	0.00	0.00	0.00
Profit/loss	−2.25	−2.25	0.00	7.75	7.75	0.00	−2.25	−2.25

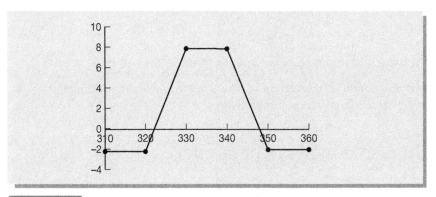

Figure 13.5   Expiration profit/loss relating to Table 13.5

*Long at-the-money put condor

For stationary markets

Put condors, like call condors, can be placed at many different strikes, depending on your near-term outlook for the underlying. If your out-look calls for a stationary market, but you wish to leave room for error on the downside, you can substitute the long at-the-money put condor for the at-the-money put butterfly. You might, for example, buy the above April 360–350–340–330 put condor for a debit of 3.5 The downside profit potential of this spread is

> Put condors, can be placed at many different strikes, depending on your near-term outlook for the underlying

the same as the upside profit potential of the long April 340–350–360–370 call condor. The profit/loss at expiration is summarised as follows:

Debit from long April 360 put: –16.25
Debit from long April 330 put: –3.75
Credit from short April 350 put: 10.25
Credit from short April 340 put: 6.25
Total debit: –3.50

Maximum profit: difference between highest two strikes minus spread debit: $(360 – 350) – 3.5 = 6.5$

Range of maximum profit: 350 – 340

Upper break-even level: highest strike minus spread debit: $360 – 3.5 = 356.5$

Lower break-even level: lowest strike plus spread debit: $330 + 3.5 = 333.5$

Profit range: $356.5 – 333.5 = 23$

Maximum loss: cost of spread: 3.5

The risk/return ratio is again favourable at $3.5/6.5 = 0.54$ for 1, or 1/1.85.

By now you should be an expert at tabulating and graphing the expiration profit/loss levels of condors and butterflies.

* Short at-the-money put condor
For volatile markets

Like the butterfly, the condor can be sold in order to profit from a volatile or trending market. Although this is more of a market-maker's trade,

> Like the butterfly, the condor can be sold in order to profit from a volatile or trending market

you might consider trading it during volatile markets. For example, you could sell the above April 360–350–340–330 put condor at 3.5. If Marks and Spencer closes above 360 or below 330 at expiration, you earn the credit from the spread. In this case you are taking a slightly bullish position.

The profit/loss figures are exactly the opposite of the above long put condor.

* Short at-the-money call condor for volatile markets

If instead your outlook is for volatile conditions and you are slightly bear-ish, you might sell the April 340–350–360–370 call condor at 2.75. (Don't be surprised if you earn your profit on the upside.) If at expiration Marks and Spencer closes below 340 or above 370, then you earn the credit from the spread. Again, this is a market-maker's trade, but you might learn about it to increase your market awareness. Your profit/loss summary is as follows.

Credit from short April 340 call:	17.00
Credit from short April 370 call:	3.75
Debit from long April 350 call:	–11.25
Debit from long April 360 call:	–6.75
Total credit:	2.75

Maximum profit: spread credit: 2.75

Range of maximum profit: below 340 and above 370

Lower break-even level: lowest strike plus spread credit:
340 + 2.75 = 342.75

Upper break-even level: highest strike minus spread credit:
370 – 2.75 = 367.25

Maximum loss: difference between lowest two strikes minus spread credit: (350 – 340 – 2.75 = 7.25

Price range of shares for potential loss: 367.25 – 342.75 = 24.5 points

The risk/return ratio is 7.25/2.75 = 2.64 to 1.

*Butterflies and condors with non-adjacent strikes

Butterflies are flexible spreads which can profit from a variety of trading ranges. You can extend the profit range of a butterfly by extending the distance of the strikes. If XYZ is at 100, and you expect it to rally into a range of between 105 and 115, then you can buy the 100–110–120 call but-terfly. This spread costs more than the adjacent strike, 105–110–115 call butterfly, but it has a greater profit range.

> Butterflies are flexible spreads which can profit from a variety of trading ranges

Using the set of Marks and Spencer April options, you could pay 11.25 for the 350 call, sell two 370 calls at 3.75, and pay 1 for the 390 call, for a net debit of 4.75. Your profit range is then 354.75 to 385.25, or 30.5 points, or 8.7 per cent of the share's value.

Condors can also increase their profit ranges by increasing the distance of the strikes. This is especially feasible while that stock indexes and, as a result, options premiums, are at high levels. Consider the set of FTSE options below.

June FTSE-100 options

June Future at 6250[4]

106 days until expiry

ATM implied at 26 per cent

Strike	6225.0	6325.0	6425.0	6525.0	6625.0	6725.0	6825.0	6925.0
Calls	359.5	303.0	253.5	205.0	165.0	131.0	102.5	80.0

If you discern that the path of least resistance is up, or if you're simply bullish, you may wish to take a long call position in the UK market. But if the thought of spending £2,000 to £3,000 for one options contract gives you pause, then you may instead consider financing your call purchase with a spread.

For £470, the 6325–6525–6725–6925 call condor can be purchased without taking out a second mortgage. The maximum profit is $200 - 47 = 153$ ticks. The break-even levels, at 6372 and 6878, provide a profit range of 506 points. The risk/return for this spread is favourable, at $^{47}/_{153} = 0.31$.

The trade-off with this spread is that if the FTSE rallies quickly, then the spread will show only a modest profit. Like all butterflies and condors, this spread needs time decay to work for it.

Non-adjacent strike butterflies and condors are preferred alternatives in the OEX or SPX and SPY (SPDRS) as well. They are sensible ways of reducing premium exposure while minimising risk. Some exchanges have reduced the tick size of these contracts in order to accommodate the individual investor, and to improve liquidity and price discovery.

---

[4] If and when the FTSE reaches this level again. The point is to use butterflies and condors when options premiums are expensive.

Volatility, days until expiration, and butterflies and condors

Likewise when volatilities are high, you can often find inexpensive adjacent strike butterflies and condors, such as in the above FTSE example. This is because the underlying is trading in a wide range, and the probability of it settling near a particular strike at expiration is small. The same factors apply to these spreads when there are many days until expiration. At times like these, it is preferable to trade butterflies and condors with non-adjacent strikes.

The advantages

In this chapter we have covered butterflies and condors in depth. The reasons for this are twofold: when purchased, these spreads have low risk/return ratios; also, they can easily be opened and closed in one transaction. They are therefore justifiable trading strategies under many market conditions. It is worth learning how to use them.

14

The covered write, the calendar spread and the diagonal spread

The diagonal spread for trending markets

There are two additional spreads that profit from stationary markets. The **covered write** involves selling a call against a long underlying position, and the **calendar** or **time spread** involves selling a near-term at-the-money option, usually a call, and buying a further-term at-the-money option, again usually a call. Both spreads profit from time decay.

The covered write or the buy-write

If an investor owns or is long an underlying contract, he may sell or write a call on it to earn additional income. This strategy is known as the **covered write** and it is often used by long-term holders of stocks that are temporarily underperforming. It is often traded in bear markets.

When the underlying is bought and the call is sold in the same transaction, this spread is also known as the buy-write

When the underlying is bought and the call is sold in the same transaction, this spread is also known as the **buy-write.**

For example, if you own XYZ at a price of 100, or hopefully less, you may sell one 105 call at 3. The maximum profit is the premium earned from the sale of the call plus the amount that the underlying appreciates to the strike price of the call. Here, this would be 5 + 3 = 8. The downside break-even level is the price of the underlying at the time of the call sale less the call income. Here, this would be 100 – 3 = 97.

There are two risks:

▪ The first is that the underlying may decline below the downside break-even level, and that you will take a loss on the total position.

▪ The second is that the underlying may advance above the call strike price, the underlying will be called away, and you will relinquish the upside profit from the underlying.

This spread is best used by investors who have purchased the underlying at significantly lower levels, who think that there is little or no upside potential, and who can tolerate short-term declines in the underlying.

Consider Coca-Cola at 52.67; August options with 60 days until expiration:

Strike	40.00	42.50	45.00	47.50	50.00	52.50	55.00	57.50	60.00
August calls					4.04	2.52	1.45	0.79	0.34
August puts	0.34	0.47	0.82	1.30	2.05	2.90			

For example, Coca-Cola is currently trading at 52.67, and the August 60 calls, with 60 days until expiration, are priced at 0.34. You may sell one call on each 100 Coca-Cola shares that you own. Alternatively, you may pay 52.67 for 100 shares, while selling the call, as a spread.

At expiration, the maximum profit for your spread occurs at the strike price of the call. There, you gain the price appreciation of the stock plus the full income from the call. The maximum profit is calculated as the strike price minus the purchase price of the stock plus the income from the call, or $(60 - 52.67) + 0.34 = 7.67$.

Above the call strike price, the profit from the stock is offset by the loss on the call, on a point for point basis. The maxium profit is earned, no more, no less. The stock will be called away from you at expiration.

The lower break-even level for your position is the price at which the call income equals the decline in the stock price. This is calculated as the price of the stock minus the income from the call, or $52.67 - 0.34 = 52.33$. Below this level the spread loses point for point with the stock.

The expiration profit/loss for this covered write is summarised as follows.

Maximum profit: strike price minus stock price, plus income from call: $(60 - 52.67) + 0.34 = 7.67$

The maximum profit occurs at or above the strike price of the call

Break-even level: stock price minus income from call: 52.67 – 0.34 = 52.33

Maximum loss: full amount of stock price decline below break-even level: 52.33

The expiration profit/loss is summarised in Table 14.1.

Table 14.1 Coca-Cola covered write: with Coca-Cola at 52.67, sell August 60 call at 0.34

Coca-Cola	(below)	45.00	50.00	52.33	52.67	55.00	60.00	65.00
Credit from 60 call	0.34	---						
Value of call at expiration	0.00	0.00	0.00	0.00	0.00	0.00	0.00	–5.00
Stock profit/loss at expiration	(–full amt)	–7.67	–2.67	–0.34	0.00	2.33	7.33	12.33
Total profit/loss	(–full amt)	–7.33	–2.33	0.00	0.34	2.67	7.67	7.67

The expiration profit/loss is shown in Figure 14.1.

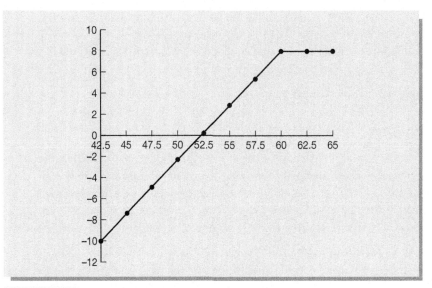

Figure 14.1   Expiration profit/loss for Coca-Cola

Two comments

First, if this chart looks like a naked short put, then you're absolutely right. The buy write is no more than a synthetic short put. (Refer to Chapter 21 on synthetics.)

So why bother with the complications? Make it simple: if you want to buy stock and write the call, and if there are no dividends involved, and if you're a short-term investor, then just sell the in the money put and save yourself commissions. You'll have the same risk profile. (Obviously, I'm not a fan of selling naked puts.)

Second, and more importantly, there is currently a lot of common advice which tells you to initiate buy-writes for tempting yields. Well-meaning advisers usually tell you that you could pay 52.67 for Coca-Cola and sell the August 55 call at 1.45. Your annualised return would be 1.45/52.67 × 360/60 = 16.5% But this yield projects that the stock stays where it is for a year while you write more calls.

True, if Coca-Cola rallies then you've made a bit, but then you're making the classic mistake of trading on hope. Instead, if Coca-Cola declines past 52.67 – 1.45 = 51.22 then you're a loser. This is why I don't recommend the buy-write as an initiating trade.

On the other hand, if you've inherited the stock from your father, who bought it for $20 or thereabouts, and we're at the start of a bear market, or maybe we're in a bull market, and Coca-Cola is looking toppy, and you can't afford to sell it because you'll pay capital gains tax, then, in either of these cases you might consider writing a call.

But only do it once or twice.

And a story

Several years ago, I gave a lecture at a major London bank. During the interval, a trader confided to me that they had recently done very well with a buy-write on shares. He also stated that they were disappointed because the shares had rallied past the cut-off level, or the short call level, and that they had missed out on a good deal of profit.

Knowing what they had done, I suggested that there were better ways of capturing the upside. These are outlined in the examples at the end of Chapters 1 and 2, and they are called substitution trades.

If you really like the 'stuff' (as we called it at the Chicago Board of Trade), and by this I mean soybeans, wheat, bonds, or whatever, then *just buy it* with a sell stop order. You don't need options.

On the other hand, if you have ever been stopped out two or three times in one trade, then options are the way forward for you.

How to manage the risk of the covered write

The covered write is best suited to long-term stock-holders who can tolerate a decline in the stock price below the current price.

There are two solutions to the upside risk. Using the above spread, first note that with Coca-Cola at 52.67, the August 55 calls are priced at 1.45. Let's assume that Coca-Cola immediately rallies $5, to 57.67. At this point, your short 60 calls will be worth approximately 1.45, and you may simply buy them back. Your profit/loss is as follows:

Sale of 60 call:	0.34 credit
Purchase of 60 call:	1.45 debit
Profit on stock:	5 credit
Profit/loss:	3.89 credit

With this solution you have revised your outlook. You have concluded that there is significant upside potential for Coca-Cola.

The second solution is to maintain your outlook. You conclude that you have erred in your estimate for Coca-Cola's upside potential, but that the stock's new level is the top for the time being. Your strategy is to write calls for the next two expirations, and you expect to profit in the end.

With Coca-Cola at 57.67, the value of the 60 call will be, as we said, approximately 1.45. The 65 call will then be approximately 0.34. The 60–65 call spread will be approximately 1.45 – 0.34 = 1.11. You can then buy this spread, and by doing so, roll your short call to the 65 strike.

The options summary is as follows:

Sale of 60 call:	0.34
Purchase of 60 call:	–1.45
Sale of 65 call:	0.34
Total options debit:	–0.77

Here, the profit equals the five points appreciation on the stock minus the total options debit, or 5 – 0.77 = 4.23.

The total profit/loss summary at expiration is as follows:

Maximum profit: new strike price minus stock purchase price, minus debit from call position: (65 – 52.67) – 0.77 = 11.56

The maximum profit occurs at or above the strike price, 65, of the open August call

Break-even level: stock purchase price plus total options debit: 52.67 + 0.77 = 53.44. Note that this level is 1.11 points above the former break-even level, which was 52.44.

Maximum loss: full amount of stock price decline below break-even level: 53.44

The risk here is that at the new price level, 57.67, Coca-Cola contains five points of downside loss potential for which you have received a credit of only 4.23. The potential return, of course, is improved.

The expiration profit/loss is summarised in Table 14.2.

Table 14.2 Expiration profit/loss for Coca-Cola

Coca-Cola	(below)	45.00	47.50	50.00	52.67	53.44	60.00	62.50	65.00
Total options debit	–0.77	–0.77	–0.77	–0.77	–0.77	–0.77	–0.77	–0.77	–0.77
Value of 65 call at expiration	0.00	0.00	0.00	0.00	0.00	0.00	0.00	0.00	0.00
Stock profit/ loss at expiration	(–full amt)	–7.67	–5.17	–2.67	0.00	0.77	7.33	9.83	12.33
Total profit/loss	(–full amt)	–8.44	–5.94	–3.44	–0.77	0.00	6.56	9.06	11.56

A story and a bit of advice

With the covered write, it is important *not* to think in terms of the short call as 'downside protection'. Remember 'portfolio insurance'? A form of this now discredited strategy was a variation of the covered write. During the 1980s portfolio insurance was sold to investors as a means of 'downside protection', in other words, calls were written against a stock portfolio in order to compensate for a price decline, and in the meantime, to earn income.

Have you ever heard of an insurance policy that *paid* you to be insured? On 19 October 1987, no amount of calls sold protected stockholders from the enormous loss of their assets' values. With options, the only form of full downside protection is the purchase of a put.

The long calendar spread or long time spread

Calendar spreads in particular can be complicated, and their return potentials can in many cases be duplicated by other stationary market spreads. However, learning about them is an excellent way to improve your understanding of options, and to improve your risk awareness.

Because an option's decay accelerates with time it is possible to sell a near-term option and buy a further-term option at the same strike in order to profit from the different rates of decay. The resulting position is termed either the **long calendar spread** or the **long time spread**. Usually this spread is traded with both options at-the-money. For example, if XYZ is at 100, you could sell one June 100 call and buy one September 100 call in the same transaction. Apart from extraordinary circumstances, this spread is done for a debit. Your outlook should call for a stationary market with both options remaining at-the-money.

This spread is best opened when the near-term option has between 60 to 30 days till expiration. The time distance between the two options can vary. A greater distance increases the cost of the spread, and reduces the hedge value of the further-term option, while a shorter distance reduces the difference in rates of decay, which in turn lowers the profit potential. Optimally, there should be 30 to 90 days between options. This spread should be closed before the near-term option expires.

A preferable opportunity is when the relationship between the near-term implied volatility and the further-term volatility is at a discrepancy, i.e. the near-term volatility is at a higher level than usual in comparison to the further-term volatility. This often occurs when the underlying has reacted suddenly to an event that is of short-term significance, or perhaps when the longer-term significance of an event is not fully accounted for. The underlying has moved to a level at which it is expected to remain for the near term.

Consider the following set of options on Rolls-Royce:

Rolls-Royce at 223.5

November options with nine days until expiry, November implied at 52 per cent

February options with 98 days until expiry, February implied at 46 per cent (Feb–Nov = 89 days)

May options with 188 days until expiry, May implied at 44 per cent (May–Feb = 90 days)

Strike	180.0	(CS)	220.0	(CS)	260.0	(CS)
November calls	44.0		8.5		Cab	
		(7)		(17)		(10.5)
February calls	51.0		25.5		10.5	
		(5)		(7)		(6.5)
May calls	56.0		32.5		17.0	

The values of the calendar spreads are given in parentheses (CS). Note that the calendar spread with the most value is the February–November 220 call calendar spread. There the characteristic of at-the-money, accelerated time decay is most in evidence. By comparing the February–November 220 call calendar spread to the February–November 180 and 260 call calendar spreads it can be seen that as the underlying moves away from the strikes, the calendar spreads have less value.

Because of this latter fact, many traders buy calendar spreads that are out of the money. Their outlook calls for the underlying to approach the strike of the spread as the front month option reaches 30 or fewer days until expiration. For example, you could pay 6.5 for the May–February 260 call calendar, and if the stock rises to 260 at the point when February has nine days until expiration, then the spread will be worth approximately 17, or the present value of the February–November 220 call calendar.

To get an accurate profit/loss assessment at expiration requires simulation by computer, which can determine the value of the calendar at various points in time and at various price levels of the underlying. The above set of options, however, indicate the basic profit/loss behaviour of this spread.

Except under unusual circumstances, the maximum loss is the debit of the spread.

Risks of calendar spreads

Because the calendar spread includes options on two contract months there are several risk scenarios, and these are different for options on stocks, interest rate contracts and commodities. Calendar spreads must often be evaluated as two separate positions, and therefore a proper risk/return profile can only be obtained with the aid of a risk analysis program. However, the major risks can be noted.

Calendar spreads must often be evaluated as two separate positions, a proper risk/return profile can only be obtained with a risk analysis program

One risk common to all is that the implied volatility may increase more for the short, near-term option than for the long, further-term option, causing the spread to lose its value. This is usually due to an unforeseen event. The underlying may then move away from the strikes before profit is made from time decay.

Another possible risk is that the historical volatility of the underlying may decrease, bringing the implied volatilies of all the options contracts down with it. Because the long, further-term contract has the greater vega, the spread will lose its value.

If a stock makes a large upside move, both calls may go to parity, and the spread will become worthless. If a stock makes a large downside move, both calls, and the spread, will become worthless.

With stocks and stock indexes, takeovers, changes in dividends or a change in the current level of interest rates can affect the delta spread between the two options contracts.

Short-term interest rate and other interest rate contracts have their own risks. A central bank may unexpectedly announce a change in interest rates, or the change may be greater or less than expected. Economic indicators may change the market's assessment of the interest rate outlook. This will cause the spreads between the underlying futures contracts, and consequently the options spreads, to change. Caution must be exercised when spreading options between contracts with different delivery months.

There is significant risk in spreading agricultural commodities from old crop to new crop. For example, with CBOT corn early in the growing season you should avoid selling September calls against December calls. This is because a shortage may develop in September which will cause its underlying futures contract to rally while the December underlying remains practically unchanged. Many commodities have seasonal volatility trends which should be studied.

Most calendars traded are call calendars, but there is no reason not to trade put calendars. The profit/loss characteristics are practically identical, except in the OEX and other American styled contracts, where the calls and puts have different behaviour due to early exercise. Puts on stocks are more likely to be exercised early if trading at parity, because a put is the right to sell the stock and raise cash.

Because there are more variables with a calendar spread, it is simpler to buy a butterfly or condor if your outlook calls for decreased volatility and for the underlying to close near a particular strike. A better reason to trade the long calendar as opposed to the long butterfly is to profit from a discrepancy in the implied volatilities from month to month.

Long diagonal call spread for a bullish market followed by a stationary market

It is possible to alter the strikes of the calendar spread. The most common variation is to sell a near-term, out-of-the-money call and buy a far-term at-the-money call. For example, you might pay 32.5 for the May 220 call above, while selling the February 260 call at 10.5, for a net debit of 22.

The return scenario for this spread is for the shares to rally gradually to 260 towards February expiration. At nine days until February expiration, the value of the spread would be similar to the current February 180–November 220 call calendar, at 42.5. The diagonal calendar is a combination of the long, far-term, at-the-money call spread plus the long, out-of-the-money call calendar spread:

(long May 220 call + short May 260 call) + (long May 260 call + short February 260 call) = long May 220 call + short February 260 call

Diagonal spreads may also be traded with puts. Here, you can buy a far-term put and sell a near-term put that is at a strike further out-of-the-money.

Thinking about options

Introduction

Part 3 describes the finesse of options. There's a lot involved here and it takes you way past 1×1s.

This part guides you through advanced topics such as how the Greeks interact. Bear in mind that the Greeks have non-linear variables, and so you need to read about them and work with them. In other words, reading this part will give you a head start on experience.

Part 3 also discusses volatility skews. It talks about why a 10 per cent out-of-the-money put costs more that a 10 per cent OTM call in the financials. It discusses common problems in trading options, such as leverage (gearing), as well as practical issues such as liquidity.

One of these days you'll ask youself why such and such happened, and it will probably be because of a topic covered in Part 3. So, read or skim this part once each year I do.

15

The interaction of the Greeks

The Greeks, the time until expiration and the implied volatility interact with each other in ways that work together and in ways that trade off. They work differently for each options position. By knowing how they interact you can test your position for market scenarios. You can anticipate what may happen under the best, or return, scenario, or under the worst, or risk, scenario. You can know what to expect.

This chapter summarises what you have previously learned about the Greeks. It places them all into perspective and describes their interaction.

Comparing options 1: the Greeks and time

Let's look again at December Corn options. Tables 15.1 and 15.2 show two sets of options with different days until expiration, and with the corresponding deltas, gammas, thetas and vegas. The price of the underlying is held constant.

You may compare the effect of time on options with the same strike, and on options with different strikes. Note, for example, the 400 call, a two-strike out-of-the-money option. As it approaches expiration, its delta becomes smaller, its gamma becomes greater, its theta becomes greater and its vega becomes smaller. Note the 340 put, whose delta, theta and vega become less, but whose gamma remains practically the same. Note that with time passing the gamma of the at-the-money option increases significantly more than the out-of and the in-the-money options. These are all consequences of the characteristics discussed in previous chapters.

Table 15.1 December Corn options, 90 days until expiration

Strike	Call value × $50	Call delta	Put value	Put delta	Gamma per point	Theta ($ per day)	Vega ($ per implied volatility point)
320	63.00	0.90	$3^1/_4$	0.10	0.003	2.75	22.5
340	47.00	0.80	7.00	0.20	0.005	4.50	23.0
360	$33^7/_8$	0.67	14.00	0.33	0.007	5.50	35.5
380[a]	22.00	0.53	22.00	0.47	0.008	6.65	37.5
400	15.00	0.40	35.00	0.60	0.007	6.00	36.5
420	$8^5/_8$	0.27	$48^1/_2$	0.73	0.006	5.50	25.0
440[b]	$5^1/_2$	0.19	$65^1/_4$	0.81	0.005	4.00	23.5

December Corn at $3.80; 90 days until expiration; implied volatility at 30 per cent; no volatility skews; interest rate at 3 per cent; options multiplier at $50, so multiply call and put values times $50

[a] The 380 call is actually 22 × $50 = $1,100.
[b] Note that the 440 call is priced higher than the 320 put even though they are equally out-of-the-money. This is because the model assumes that Corn can rally further than it can break.

Table 15.2 December Corn options, 30 days until expiration

Strike	Call value × $50	Call delta	Put value × $50	Put delta	Gamma per Corn point	Theta ($ per day)	Vega ($ per ivol point)
320	$60^1/_8$	0.99	$^1/_8$	0.01	0.001	1.0	1.4
340	$41^1/_8$	0.92	$1^1/_4$	0.08	0.005	4.0	9
360	$24^5/_8$	0.76	$4^3/_4$	0.24	0.01	9	19.5
380	$12^1/_2$	0.51	$12^1/_2$	0.48	0.013	11.5	21.5
400	$5^3/_8$	0.28	$25^1/_4$	0.72	0.011	10	21.5
420	$1^7/_8$	0.12	$41^7/_8$	0.87	0.006	5.2	15
440	$^5/_8$	0.04	$60^1/_2$	0.96	0.003	2.25	6.5

December Corn at $3.80 × 5,000 bushels; 30 days until expiration; implied volatility at 30 per cent; no volatility skews; interest rate at 3 per cent; options multiplier at $50

Table 15.3 is a generalised summary of the effect of time on the Greeks. Again, the underlying is held constant. The terms 'in-the- money' (ITM), 'at-the-money' (ATM) and 'out-of-the-money' (OTM) are used in abbreviated form.

Table 15.3 The effect of time passing on the Greeks

			Delta	Gamma	Theta	Vega
Time forward:	OTM	call	down	up	up	down
		put	down	up	up	down
	ATM	call	unch'd	up	up	down
		put	unch'd	up	up	down
	ITM	call	up	up	up	down
		put	up	up	up	down

These relationships hold true for all options, but they become more exaggerated as the underlying has less value, and less implied volatility, with less time until expiration, and with strike prices that are more widely separated. Conversely, they become less exaggerated if, as the strike prices narrow, the underlying increases in value, and time and the implied increases.

Imagine a stock index at 4000 and an implied at 50 per cent. (I've seen it.) The Greeks between the 4000 and 4050 strikes will be very similar. When Corn was at $2.20 per bushel (for those of us with a memory), and with 60 days until expiration, the Greeks between the 220 and 180 strikes were very different.

The exceptions to Table 15.3 are the deep in-the-money and far out-of-the-money options, such as the December 320 calls and puts, and the December 440 calls and puts. When these options have 30 DTE, most of their time premium has been expended, and changes in the Greeks are of little consequence (except when you're short them).

A long options position has positive gamma, negative theta and positive vega

Remember that a long options position has positive gamma, negative theta and positive vega. As time passes, it benefits more from price movement, it costs more in time decay, and it benefits less from an increase in implied volatility. A short options position has the opposite profile with respect to the Greeks.

By knowing how the Greeks interact, we can evaluate a position from just two variables. Traders often do this with delta and the number of days until expiration. 'I'm long a hundred, twenty-delta calls with thirty days out', has a very different meaning from 'I'm long a hundred, twenty-delta calls with ninety days out'. The former call position has a strike price that is closer to the money, higher (positive) gamma, greater (negative) theta and smaller (positive) vega (see Table 15.4). It indicates that the trader is looking for a large move in the underlying, soon. The latter position indicates that the trader is looking for a large eventual move and/or an increase in implied volatility.

Table 15.4 December Corn options with approx 0.28 deltas

December Corn at 380			
90 DTE December 420 calls		**30 DTE** December 400 calls	
Delta	0.27	Delta	0.28
Gamma	0.006	Gamma	0.011
Theta	$5.5	Theta	$10.0
Vega	$25.0	Vega	$21.5

Understandably, traders seldom discuss their positions except with their risk managers. Consider the
characteristics of the Greeks and the outlook of the
traders who have positions opposite to those above.

Understandably, traders
seldom discuss their
positions except with
their risk managers

Comparing options 2: delta versus gamma, theta and vega

The above tables also summarise what we already know about the relationship between delta and the other Greeks. Gamma, theta and vega are all
greatest with 0.50 delta options. Therefore, as the underlying moves, the
Greeks of all options increase or decrease together, although not at the
same rate. This simplifies the risk/return analysis of gamma, theta and
vega with respect to delta, or the underlying price movement.

Traders often speak of gamma, theta and vega when discussing how their
positions have fared with a change in the underlying. 'Everything was
fine until my gammas started kicking in, and now vol's getting pumped',
means the opposite of 'I was getting hammered on time decay but now
my gammas and vegas are helping me out'. (Traders are fond of complain-
ing, even while they are making money.)

The first trader has positive theta and he has been collecting time decay.
He has been short out-of-the-money options that have now become at-
the-money options. His deltas are changing rapidly because of his negative
gamma, making his position difficult to manage. In addition, he has negative vega and the implied volatility is increasing.

The second trader has been long out-of-the-money options and his negative theta has cost him in time decay. Now his options are at-the-money.
His positive gamma has caused his deltas, and therefore the value of his
options, to increase rapidly. Because the implied is increasing, his positive
vega is paying off.

In both cases, the market has behaved the same. It was formerly quiet,
it recently moved to a new price range, and now it is more volatile. This
change of underlying level and corresponding change of options characteristics is illustrated in Table 15.5. It happens every day with all options
contracts to a greater or lesser degree.

Table 15.5 December Corn with 30 DTE, position: December 420 calls

Position: December 420 calls			
Position then		**Position now**	
December corn at 380		December corn at 420	
December 420 calls:		December 420 calls:	
Delta	0.12	Delta	0.51
Gamma	0.006	Gamma	0.013
Theta	$5.20	Theta	$11.50
Vega	$15.00	Vega	$21.00

The easiest way to know how an option behaves when the market moves is to compare two options at different strikes. Here, we can say that if Corn rallies from 380 to 420, then the 420 calls will resemble the 380 calls.

But if Corn makes a *sudden* move upward, then most likely the implied volatility will increase. Read on.

Comparing options 3: implied volatility versus the Greeks

Because the implied volatility often trends, or occasionally makes a sudden change, it is essential to know how an options position can change accordingly. The interaction between implied volatility and the Greeks has some unusual characteristics which take time to fully understand. To know how the deltas change is the priority, because a change in the implied often changes the options position with respect to the underlying.

Table 15.6 is our now familiar set of December Corn options. The underlying is again at 380 and there are 90 days until expiration. The implied volatility, however, is increased to 40 per cent. This table should be compared with Table 15.1 on page 166, where the implied is 30 per cent.

Table 15.6 December Corn options with 90 DTE

Strike	Call value × $50	Call delta	Put value	Put delta	Gamma per point	Theta ($ per day)	Vega ($ per ivol point)
320	67$^1/_2$	0.83	7$^3/_4$	0.17	0.003	5.0	28.0
340	52$^1/_2$	0.75	12$^3/_4$	0.25	0.004	7.0	30.5
360	41.00	0.65	21.00	0.35	0.005	7.8	35.5
380	29$^3/_8$	0.54	29$^3/_8$	0.46	0.006	9.0	37.5
400	22$^5/_8$	0.44	42$^3/_8$	0.55	0.005	8.3	37.5
420	15$^7/_8$	0.34	55$^5/_8$	0.65	0.005	8.0	32.5
440	10$^3/_4$	0.26	70$^1/_2$	0.74	0.004	7.0	30.0

With an increase in the implied volatility, we can make the following observations.

The deltas of out-of the-money options increase while the deltas of in-the-money options decrease. The reason is that with an increase in implied volatility, out-of-the-money options have a greater probability of becoming in-the-money, while in-the-money options have less of a probability of staying in-the-money. Similar changes occur when options have more days until expiration.

Gammas decrease. Note that with increased volatility, the difference between the deltas from strike to strike is decreased. This indicates that the underlying passes through strikes more readily and, as a consequence, the deltas of these strikes change less radically. Their corresponding gammas are therefore lowered. This occurrence is also similar in options with more days until expiration.

There is a serious exception to the above. Far out-of- and in-the-money options, such as the $3.00 puts and $4.60 calls increase their gamma. They have low gammas to begin with because their deltas change very little when the underlying is at a low volatility. But if volatility suddenly increases, they wake up. This characteristic becomes more pronounced with approximately 30 days until expiration. *Many traders have gone bust by not understanding this.*

Thetas increase. Because options premiums increase while the time until expiration continues to decrease, there is increased time decay per day. Theta is therefore greater.

The vegas of the out-of-the-money and the in-the-money options increase. As the underlying increases its range, these options are more likely to become at-the-money. Their vegas approach that of the at-the-money options, and they become more sensitive to a change in the implied volatility.

The principle here is that an increased implied signifies that the underlying is increasing its range. This makes the distinctions between strikes less, and therefore the Greeks become more alike.

Table 15.7 is a generalised summary of the effect of increased implied volatility on the Greeks.

Table 15.7 Effect of increased implied volatility on the Greeks

			Delta	Gamma	Theta	Vega
Implied volatility up:	OTM	call	up	down	up	up
	OTM	put	up	down	up	up
	ATM	call	unch'd	down	up	unch'd
	ATM	put	unch'd	down	up	unch'd
	ITM	call	down	down	up	up
	ITM	put	down	down	up	up

Like all generalisations, the above are subject to modifications. Note the set of options shown in Table 15.8 with 30 DTE at 30 per cent implied. You may compare this data with that shown in Table 15.2 which has the December Corn implied at 20 per cent.

The exceptions to the generalised summary are that now the gammas at the 320 and 440 strikes are increased. This is a function of the wake-up effect discussed above. With volatility at 30 per cent and 30 DTE these strikes were marginally in play, but now with volatility at 40 per cent they are showing signs of life. Suppose it's mid-October and the new crop is plentiful and on its way, what could possibly go wrong?

Table 15.8 December Corn options with 30 DTE, implied at 40 per cent

			December Corn at 380				
Strike	Call value × $50	Call delta	Put value	Put delta	Gamma	Theta ($)	Vega ($)
320	61 1/8	0.94	1 1/8	0.06	0.003	4.0	5.5
340	43 3/4	0.85	3 7/8	0.15	0.006	8.5	13.5
360	29.00	0.70	9.00	0.30	0.008	12.5	20.5
380	17.00	0.53	17.00	0.47	0.01	15.5	21.5
400	9 7/8	0.35	29 7/8	0.65	0.009	13.5	22.0
420	5.00	0.21	45.00	0.79	0.007	10.5	15.0
440	2.00	0.10	61 7/8	0.90	0.004	6.5	13.0

A few practical observations on how implied volatility changes

Most of the time an increase in the implied volatility is the result of an increase in the historical volatility, but often it is not. Shortly before the publication of government economic reports, crop forecasts, earnings announcements and the results of central bank meetings, the prices of options often rise in anticipation of market movement. The resulting changes to the Greeks change the exposure of a position, and therefore change the risk/ return profile.

> Most of the time an increase in the implied volatility is the result of an increase in the historical volatility

Occasionally, the implied increases because the options market suspects that there is trouble brewing, and this situation of expectancy can last for months, even though there is no significant change in the underlying's daily price action.

Occasionally, an underlying may increase its volatility over the course of one or two days after a published earnings report or other event, but the implied will exhibit little change. This is because the options market views the event as falling within the range of expectations, and having no significance beyond a few trading sessions.

More troublesome, and at the same time potentially rewarding, is a change of implied volatilty due to an unexpected event. For example, a trader may be comfortably short out-of-the-money calls in stocks or a stock index when a central bank suddenly lowers its overnight lending rate. His position is similar to that in Table 15.5.

If the stock market rallies, as it usually does with an unexpected rate cut, this position becomes shorter in deltas not only because it is trending towards the money but also because the deltas are being given an added push by the increase in the implied. In addition, this trader's formerly manageable, negative vega position suddenly grows with the implied. The price of, and loss on, his short calls is therefore increasing by three factors:

- the increasing deltas
- the increasing implied volatility
- the increasing vegas.

The options are growing teeth.

Meanwhile, the trader who has patiently held the opposite position, paying time decay for his long calls, is rewarded manifoldly.

An out-of-the-money put position behaves in a similar manner if the market takes a sudden hit on the downside. Suppose the central bank suddenly raises its rate. If the market breaks downward, and if, as usual, the implied increases, what is the effect on the out-of-the-money puts?

The other Greeks

There are additional Greeks which some trading firms use to monitor their positions. They are all based on the four that we have discussed, and are more useful in assessing the risk of large hedge funds or institutional portfolios. One of these is **rho** which is the change of an option's value with respect to a change in the interest rate. With the current low levels of interest rates this is not a significant factor unless you have a very large portfolio. It will become significant if, in the future, interest rates reach 5 per cent or more.

The Greeks, implied volatility and the options calculator

You can calculate the Greeks of most options by using an options calculator. With this device you input the strike price, price of the underlying, time until expiration, volatility, interest rate, and dividends if applicable, and it uses the pricing model to calculate the theoretical value of the option with the Greeks.

The options calculator is an invaluable device, especially for beginners. It is advisable to spend at least a few hours with it.

With the options calculator you can also determine the implied volatility of an option from the option's price. Suppose you're reading the closing options prices over the internet. The closing prices of the options and the underlyings are often listed. The near-term eurodollar or short sterling interest rate can be used. In the US, the amount and date of the dividends are consistant and widely reported, but in the UK this requires more of an estimate. The days until expiration are also often listed and, when not, you can check them on the exchange website. For stocks you can generally use the third Friday of the expiration month. The strike price you know.

The options calculator is an invaluable device, especially for beginners

If you plug these five variables into the options calculator, it produces the implied volatility of the option.

Nowadays, options calculators are easy to find with a search engine. Many options websites and some exchange websites have options calculators. Data vendors include the Greeks with their price reports, and most brokerage firms subscribe to one or more data services. Many brokerage and trading firms also have options calculators on their websites.

A story about the Greeks

I once had a discussion with a quant (someone who practises quantitative analysis of the financial markets) about deltas. Very authoritatively, he told me that he was working on a new model to calculate deltas. I replied that I totally approved because of my experience as a market-maker.

I said that when I was trading in a fast market, the underlying would gap up or down, volatility would explode, the skews would take off and the skew crux would shift, and my delta hedge would be practically useless. Then I could only rely on my experience. (Which paid off.)

I told him that what traders really needed was a real-time delta model.

He looked at me with a blank stare, muttered something I can't remember, and then walked away. When I next met him, he wasn't very friendly.

The lesson is that the Greeks can react in complicated ways, so study them and work with them until you get an intuitive feel for how they work. Then you'll have an edge.

16

The cost of the Greeks

So far, we have discussed a number of different ways of analysing straight options and options spreads. We can take this a step further by examining which options are preferable choices given a specific amount to invest. In this chapter we look at a group of straight options and compare their risk-return potentials to their price. We can do this with the help of the Greeks.

Delta/price ratio

The cost of trading price movement

Another way to think of delta is that it indicates the potential for price change in the option. If you compare the delta to the price of the option itself, you can determine the option's potential price change given the amount that you wish to invest. Table 16.1 shows a set of Dow Jones Eurostoxx 50 options at 57 DTE with their deltas. Let's assume that we have an upside directional outlook; only the calls are listed.

In the last column the delta of each option is divided by its price. The ratio is then expressed as a percentage. My term for this figure is the delta/price ratio. If the index moves plus or minus one point, then the 2700 call increases or decreases by plus or minus 0.70 of a point. 0.70 is 0.38 per cent of 185.40, the amount invested.

Dow Jones Eurostoxx 50

June future 2831

57 days until expiration

Interest rate 1 per cent

Table 16.1 June DJ Eurostoxx options, with delta/price ratio

Strike	Call value	Call delta	D/P (%)
2700	185.40	0.70	0.38
2750	149.40	0.64	0.43
2800	116.80	0.56	0.48
2850	88.10	0.48	0.54
2900	63.80	0.40	0.63
2950	44.20	0.32	0.72
3000	29.20	0.24	0.82
3050	18.40	0.17	0.92

By comparing the delta/price ratios we find that the out-of-the-money options have the greatest potential for price movement per amount invested. Note that this potential is for increased as well as decreased price movement. Here, both risk and return increase. But because the amount invested is less than with in- or at-the-money options, investors often find this risk worth taking.

The trade-off is with time decay. The delta/price ratio increases as options move closer to expiration, but eventually an out-of-the-money option has very little probability of profiting from underlying price movement. (But it can cause serious damage if you sell it.)

The option's delta and the number of days until expiration are the best guides to this trade-off. A short-term, 0.30 delta option of less than 30 days, for example, has a greater delta/price ratio than a 0.30 delta option of more than 100 days, but the former is in a rapid decay time period.

Theta/price ratio

The cost of trading time

We have previously discussed the time decay variable, or theta. We said that an option's time decay accelerates as expiration approaches. Before you decide which option to buy or sell, it is important to know the time decay of the option as a percentage of the option's value. You can then better choose the strike to trade. Table 16.2 shows our set of Eurostoxx options, each followed by its theta/price ratio expressed in percentage terms.

Here, the price of the 3050 is 18.40. The daily decay of this option is 0.46, making the theta price ratio 0.46/18.40 × 100 = 2.50%. In percentage terms the 3050 call is the most expensive to hold, while in absolute terms it is the least expensive.

Table 16.2 June Eurosroxx options with theta/price ratios

June Eurostoxx future at 2831 with 57 DTE					
Strike	Call value	Call delta	D/P (%)	Call theta	T/P (%)
2700	185.40	0.70	0.38	0.81	0.44
2750	149.40	0.64	0.43	0.84	0.56
2800	116.80	0.56	0.48	0.85	0.73
2850	88.10	0.48	0.54	0.83	0.94
2900	63.80	0.40	0.63	0.76	1.19
2950	44.20	0.32	0.72	0.68	1.54
3000	29.20	0.24	0.82	0.57	1.95
3050	18.40	0.17	0.92	0.46	2.5

Vega/price ratio

The cost of trading volatility

In Chapter 7 we discussed implied volatility and its relation to vega, and we noted that an option's vega increases with more days until expiration. Table 16.3 compares the vega of an option to its price in order to determine how an investment may perform in percentage terms due to a 1 per cent change in the implied. The vega/price ratio, as a percentage, is listed in the last column.

Table 16.3 June Eurostoxx options with vega/price ratios

DJ Eurostoxx 50 June future at 2831, June options with 57 DTE

Strike	Call value	Call delta	D/P (%)	Call theta	T/P (%)	Call vega	V/P (%)
2700	185.40	0.70	0.38	0.81	0.44	3.9	2.1
2750	149.40	0.64	0.43	0.84	0.56	4.2	2.8
2800	116.80	0.56	0.48	0.85	0.73	4.5	3.9
2850	88.10	0.48	0.54	0.83	0.94	4.5	5.1
2900	63.80	0.40	0.63	0.76	1.19	4.4	6.9
2950	44.20	0.32	0.72	0.68	1.54	4.0	9.0
3000	29.20	0.24	0.82	0.57	1.95	3.5	12.0
3050	18.40	0.17	0.92	0.46	2.50	2.8	15.2

Again, the largest percentage trade-off is with the 3050 calls. They may increase or decrease 15.2 per cent of their value with a 1 per cent change in the implied.

For the purpose of comparison, the same table of figures is given in Table 16.4, but with 30 DTE.

Table 16.4 Eurostoxx June options, 30 DTE, June future at 2831

Strike	Call value	Call delta	D/P (%)	Call theta	T/P (%)	Call vega	V/P (%)
2700	158.80	0.76	0.49	1.02	0.64	2.46	1.55
2750	121.00	0.68	0.56	1.14	0.94	2.86	2.36
2800	87.60	0.58	0.66	1.20	1.37	3.12	3.56
2850	59.80	0.47	0.79	1.17	1.96	3.18	5.32
2900	37.70	0.35	0.93	1.04	2.76	2.97	7.88
2950	22.00	0.24	1.09	0.85	3.86	2.49	11.32
3000	11.50	0.15	1.30	0.61	5.30	1.86	16.17
3050	5.60	0.08	1.43	0.39	6.96	1.23	21.96

As we might expect with time passing, most of the delta/price ratios, theta/price ratios and vega/price ratios have increased for all the options that contain time premium. Note that the vega/price ratio for the ATM call remains at approximately 5 per cent. The risk/return trade-off with all the other options is clear.

Two approaches

In this chapter we have examined risk and return in terms of delta/price, theta/price and vega/price ratios. We have found that both the risk and return per amount invested increase as the option becomes further out-of-the-money and as the option approaches expiration. These ratios vary with options on each underlying contract, and you will need to examine them for the contracts that you wish to trade.

> In all cases, be clear about your market assessment and your goals

There are two approaches to consider:

▣ The first is obviously to limit your risk by limiting the number of contracts you wish to trade. There may be a greater amount at risk by paying 88.10 for one June 2850 call with 57 DTE than there is by paying 11.50 for one June 3000 call, but the latter has greater percentage risk. Perhaps you are a natural risk-taker, often taking long odds. Then the 3000 call has the advantage of greater potential return, and 11.50 is the smaller loss to take if your investment fails to succeed.

▣ The second approach is to limit the amount you wish to invest. For example, If you have €88 to invest (times the multiplier) you may pay 88.10 for one of the 2850 calls, or you may pay 80.50 for seven of the 3000 calls. In this case the percentage risk is greater with the 3000 call position.

Given a fixed amount to invest, we can draw the following conclusions:

▣ If the market is accelerating to the upside, then your best choice is the D/P ratio of the 3000s.

▣ If the market is trending up, but volatility is stable or perhaps declining, then you'll prefer the lower V/P ratio of the 2850s.

▣ If volatility is increasing but it's getting close to expiration, you may prefer the T/P ratio of the 2900s or 2950s.

▣ You might also use the above tables to evaluate risk/return for selling options.

▣ In all cases, **be clear about your market assessment and your goals**.

17

Options talk 1: technical analysis and the Vix

Chapters 17 through 19 are more informal than those previously; their purpose is to provide a general insight. As stated in the introduction to this book, it may be impossible to coach you via long distance, but the more knowledge you have, the more resources you'll have. What follows is not gospel, but it is based on a good deal of experience.

Analysis of a trade

In previous chapters we have referred to the use of technical analysis when trading options. Here, we have an example of one trade. This was a real trade, with a lot of real money behind it. I made this trade recommendation with the help of our brokers, and it was traded by one of our clients.

At one point, it came close to losing, but in the end it went *really* right. Because it was a good trade.

End of Sep 06
Dec Schatz at 104.12
Schatz 104.00 – 103.90 – 103.80 put ladder
Pay 1 tick (0.01)
Maximum profit: (104 – 103.90) – 0.01 = 0.09 (9 ticks)
Upper break-even level: 104 – 0.01 = 103.99
Lower break-even level: 103.80 – 0.09 = 103.71
Technical support at 103.80

> **Schatz put ladder**
>
> End Sep 06   Dec Schatz 104.12
>
> Dec 104.00 – 103.90 – 103.80 put ladder pay 1 tick
>
> risk below 103.71
> but we see support at 103.80
>
> End Oct 06   Dec Schatz at 103.80 sell at 8.5

Background

Our client was cash-flow trader at one of the London majors. She was thinking that the Schatz had made a short-term low. We agreed. The market had bounced off the technical lows at 103.80, but we thought that the lows would hold unless the European Central Bank did something funny, like raise interest rates. Our view of the economic reports told us that they wouldn't.

I analysed this trade forward, back, and upside down. I estimated that the Greeks and the technicals made this a good trade. Being an ex-risk manager, I preferred to sell the naked 103.70 put instead of the 103.80 put, but that would have increased the cost of the spread to 4 ticks.

Anyway, I agreed to sell the 103.80s if we all agreed on a covering plan, which was to buy the 103.70s if the market broke support at 103.80. We would then turn the put ladder into a condor and cut our risk. All agreed.

Several weeks later the market retraced to the 103.80 area. This was a difficult ride for the trader because the 103.80s were in play. Still, we gave her the confidence to know that her break-even level lay at 103.71, and that we had a plan to cover.

We figured that we were seeing a two-test support scenario, which is common in the technicals. We were concerned that if the market tested the low once again, then it would break through.

The trader had a profit, so we advised her to close the trade, which she did for 8.5 ticks. So we paid 1 for the spread and sold it at 8.5. Not a bad rate of return.

Although we came close to being forced to cover, we were never in danger of taking a big hit. But if you want to know what can go seriously wrong with this trade, then refer to the story on page 98.

To conclude, let me reiterate what I've said it before. New traders should not sell naked short options. But as I tell my son:

You shouldn't do it

But you prob'ly will do it

So before you do it

Take some advice.

The Vix

The Vix is a very straightforward idea. It's the projected volatility of the S&P 500. Actually, it's the implied volatility of the near-term, at-the-money and one strike above and below the at-the-money options on the S&P 500. It is a product of the Chicago Board Options Exchange (CBOE).

Remember that options tell you what investors think that the market will do. Options try to anticipate. Options are indicators. And the Vix is an excellent indicator of market sentiment.

Lately, with the aid of the quants, the CBOE has revised the Vix, and so now there are two Vix's: the old and the new. But if you're using the Vix as an *indicator*, there's not much difference between them.

Personally, I think that there are more profitable ways of trading volatility than as a futures contract. You could trade straddles, strangles, butterflies and condors. But if trading the Vix suits your style, then go for it.

Still, the Vix is a very useful indicator. It tells you how volatility can hibernate for a long time, but that when it wakes up, it rears up and roars like a grizzly bear. For example, you don't sell volatility with the Vix at 10 per cent. Don't even think about it.

Trade volatility just like you trade any other underlying contract. Follow the trends, use technical analysis, don't try to catch a falling knife, etc. As we used to say in Chicago: trade the *stuff*.

18

Options talk 2: trading options

Trading delta and time decay

By knowing that delta indicates the probability of an option expiring in-the-money, you can assess the effect of time decay on probability. This can help you decide whether to open or close a position, and which strike prices to consider trading in the first place.

Buying an option

For example, if your outlook is for a large, directional move, you might consider buying a 0.30 delta option, call or put, with 90 to 120 days until expiration. You know that if time passes and the underlying remains stable, the delta decreases. This implies that the large move you are looking for becomes less probable as well. Remember that an option's time decay accelerates as it approaches expiration. You may consider, at some point between 60 and 30 days until expiration, rolling your position into a contract month with more time until expiration, even though it may cost more. A longer-term option gives you more time to be right.

A 0.30 delta option with 30 days until expiration will cost less than a 0.30 delta option with 90 days until expiration, but if your outlook is not soon realised, it will soon become a 0.10 delta option, and it will have cost you in time decay.

A near-term, 0.10 delta option is affordable, and if the market suddenly moves in its direction, it will profit handsomely, but it should be bought or held by those who feel comfortable making a short-term trade against 10 to 1 odds. A more prudent use of this option is to hedge another position.

Don't make the mistake of buying an option just because it is cheap. A low-priced, far out-of-the-money option also has a low probability of expiring in-the-money. It also has higher delta, theta and vega price ratios. If you want to reduce the cost of your call or put, you can do this by spreading.

Suppose you have bought a 0.30 delta option, and as a result of market movement, it now has a 0.60 delta, and you have a profit. This often happens sooner than you expect. Did your original outlook call for this option have a 0.80 delta? Don't kid yourself; if the market move has met your expectations, then the option has done its work. Rather than risk exposure to theta, you should close the position.

Selling an option

Options sellers should have declining volatility on their side, which means that the probability of smaller inter- and intraday price movement is increasing.

It is also advisable for options sellers to take advantage of time decay whenever possible by taking a short position close to expiration. How close depends on the delta of the option and the risk that is justifiable. As illustrated in Part 1, the further the strike is from the underlying, the more days until expiration its daily time decay accelerates.

If the underlying makes a sudden, unforeseen move that results in a loss, you must have sufficient capital to maintain your short strategy in order to take advantage of a return to stable market conditions. In any case, it is prudent to roll your short position to a further contract when your current contract has 30 DTE or less. A probability assessment least accounts for short-term price fluctuations, and an unexpected move when the underlying is close to expiration can severely damage your profit.

Should you wish to take advantage of decreasing probability, you may wish to sell a 0.20 delta option that is near-term, approximately 60 DTE. This option has less theta than a 0.30 or 0.50 delta option, but its delta indicates that it has a greater probability (80 per cent) of remaining out-of-the-money, and therefore has less potential risk.

If this option's delta eventually becomes 0.05, either through an underlying price movement or through time decay, then you have a profit. You may now be tempted to hold this position in order to continue to collect a small amount of theta, but instead you should ask yourself if your previous outlook for the underlying has been realised. If so, it is better to close your position than to risk exposure to an increased delta, i.e. an underlying move in the direction of your short call or put.

But suppose our short 0.20 delta option becomes a 0.50 delta option through an adverse market move. Clearly your outlook did not lead to success, and you have incurred a loss. You may hope for a market retracement, and you may fear a continued adverse market move, but instead you should use all available means to formulate a new outlook. You may even use your old outlook as a starting point; it may have been flawed in some respects, but it may have been accurate in others.

If your new outlook calls for a stable market in the near term, then your 0.50 delta option presents an opportunity to recoup some and possibly all of your loss through greater theta, and you should retain your position. Again, don't kid yourself; if you are uncertain, or too unsettled to formulate a new outlook, then you should close your position.

The major risk of a naked short call position is a sudden, unforeseen increase in the price of the underlying. Likewise the major risk of a naked short put position is a sudden, unforeseen decrease in the price of the underlying. Both of these risks can and should be limited by spreading.

Trading volatility trends

When trading vega, and therefore volatility, it is important to take advantage of, and not to fight, the volatility trend. Volatility can increase and decrease for long periods of time, just as stock, bond and commodity markets have their bull and bear trends.

It may seem obvious, but it is always preferable to buy options when volatility is increasing and to sell options when it is decreasing. Many options traders ignore the trend, perhaps because they are accustomed to, or simply better at, buying or selling premium. This makes for frustrating and difficult trading.

To be fair, it is often difficult to trade volatility because, like any other market trend, it can be erratic. When this is the case, you are fully justified to *stay out of the market.*

Remember that the vega of an out-of-the-money option increases or decreases as the implied volatility changes, whereas the vega of an at-the-money option remains unchanged. There needs to be a gamma of the vega calculation in the options business. Perhaps you might research this topic, and contact me with your findings (lenny@lennyjordan.com).

Durational outlook

A proper outlook tells you not only when to open a position, but also when to close a position, either by taking a profit or by cutting a loss with a stop order. There are many excellent books that describe how to trade the various types of markets; this guide teaches you how to be more flexible in your approach.

> A proper outlook tells you not only when to open a position, but also when to close a position, either by taking a profit or by cutting a loss with a stop order

When trading options you should always have a duration for your outlook because options work for a limited time. In all cases keep your duration in mind, and when it has ended, either close your position or formulate a revised outlook. A revised outlook can be formulated by asking yourself the following question: *If I wanted to enter the market now, is this the position I would take?* If the answer is no, then close your position. Otherwise, you are paying to hope.

Options vs basis points

An annualised return projection is not the way to think about options. Or trading, for that matter. You won't be making money day by day. It's not like receiving a coupon or getting a monthly paycheck.

Still, fund managers pressure their traders for weekly or monthly results. This leads to traders trying to meet short-term targets, and then to over-trading, and then to racking up commissions, and then to taking undue risk, and then sometimes to a blowout.

This is because a weekly or monthly return analysis favours collecting money from time decay. Income from time decay is the most numb-nut way of trading options. At the Chicago Board Options Exchange, we called it 'sellin' premo'. Sooner or later it blows up in your face.

An annualised return should be evaluated at the end of each quarter (barring an extraordinary event). But the best way to analyse a trader's performance is to review him after a year. The reason is that the best trades are few and far between.

The best traders I have known are those who are capable of *patience*. Patience requires experience and capital.

Some traders make only three or four trades per year. That means that they only execute six to eight times per year apart from adjustment trades. Most of the time they look for opportunities or they manage their position.

This is a difficult approach to sell under the fixed income model because the trading firm has monthly expenses. The firm needs monthly revenue.

I remember one prop trading firm based in Chicago that was doing very well, but who sold out to a group of well-capitalised investors who didn't understand trading. Within a year the prop firm was out of business. Of course, we hired a few of their traders.

One tip I can give you is to keep your costs low – and that includes personal expenses. Then you'll have more patience because you'll worry less about meeting your monthly expenses.

19

Options talk 3: troubleshooting and common problems

Investing with leverage

Options are leveraged investments: the risk/return potential is far greater per amount invested than with standard investment strategies. It is there-

options are leveraged investments

fore advisable to apportion less capital than with standard investments, unless you are very confident of your outlook.

One of the most prudent options strategies for trading a straight call or put position is to determine the amount of stock or shares that you are comfortably able to afford, then buy the number of call options that leverage the same number of shares and no more. The rest of your capital is then placed in a cash deposit.

For example, suppose you are bullish on a stock, and you are considering paying $95 for 500 shares. You could instead pay 10 for 5, April 95 calls with 180 DTE, and place the remainder in a six-month cash deposit. Your expenditure and cash deposit break down accordingly:

Amount to invest: $95 \times 500 = $47,500

Cost of options: $10 \times 100 \times 5 = $5,000

Amount deposited in CD: $85 \times 500 = $42,500

Of course, investors frequently leverage to a greater degree. The point to keep in mind is that a call can potentially expire worthless, and if it does, then you have still risked no more capital than you can afford.

The above guide to leverage is essential for those who sell calls naked. If you are the seller of the above 5, April 95 calls, you incur the potential obligation to buy 500 shares in order to transfer them to the long call holder. You should have at least the amount of the break-even level times the number of shares leveraged on deposit in order to meet the obligation of your short calls:

Short call break-even level: $10 + $95 = $105

Multiplied by number of shares: $105 × 500 = $52,500 on deposit

A short call spread faces the same potential capital requirement, although the risk is limited.

Covered call writing assumes that the short call holder has already purchased shares to deliver, and so the capital requirement is already on deposit.

The seller of a naked put incurs the potential obligation to buy stock at the break-even level. Therefore, this level of capital should be on deposit. For example, if you are bullish in a stock you might, if compelled by the devil to sell premium, sell 5, April 95 puts at 10. You may also wish to buy the stock on a price decline but, in either case, your prudent capital requirement would be as follows:

Short put break-even level: $95 – $10 = $85

Multiplied by number of shares: $85 × 500 = $42,500

The put buyer is in an advantageous position in terms of capital requirement. He has the potential right to sell the stock at a higher level than the market price at expiration.

Note that clearing firms often require less capital on deposit than we have mentioned. The above are merely prudent suggestions. They will also lead to more disciplined trading.

Contract liquidity and market making

Generally speaking, the more liquid an options contract, the tighter is the bid–ask spread for an option's price. The greater the bid–ask spread, the greater is the cost of opening and closing a position. This spread is often simply called 'the market' for the option. Eurodollar options, for example, have markets that are half to one tick wide, or $12.50 to $25.00. The markets for options on thinly traded stocks can be three or more ticks wide, or $300+.

The width of a bid–ask spread is a product of the opportunities for spreading risk, either with the underlying or with other options. If the underlying or the other options contracts are not liquid, then the options market-makers cannot hedge the positions that retail customers want them to assume. They may be forced to carry the positions in their inventory for periods of weeks or months, and during this time they are exposed to risk. In order to cover their risk, the market-makers need to widen their bid–ask spreads. Under these circumstances, to ask the market-makers to tighten their spreads is to ask them to put their jobs in jeopardy. No sensible trader, including yourself, will do this.

Bid–ask spreads also widen during highly volatile markets. If the underlying is leaping wildly, then the options market-makers cannot hedge. In order to cover their risk, they need to widen their markets to correspond to the wide range of the underlying's prices. You would do the same.

Common problems with straight call or put positions

This section offers observations on what may happen to a straight call or put position. The circumstances here presented are not those that necessarily will happen. These observations are given in case similar circumstances occur to you. The purpose is simply for you to have a basis for understanding the behaviour of your options position if one of these situations arises.

Stocks up, calls practically unchanged or underperforming

Occasionally when a stock or stock index rallies, purchased out-of-the-money calls underperform. This can occur when the implied volatility has been extremely high, after a sell-off, and long call positions have been seen either as defensive alternatives to buying the stock or as synthetic puts. This is discussed in Part 4. As the market rallies, the downside protection that the calls afford is needed less, and the market probably thinks that the potential upside is limited. As a result the implied volatility of the calls declines, and premium levels fall. The options still gain in value because they are trending towards the money, but profits are not optimum.

Under these circumstances, an alternative strategy would be the long call spread. With this strategy the long call position's exposure to declining volatility is offset by that of the short, further out-of-the-money call. Refer to Chapter 8 on this spread.

Stocks down, calls practically unchanged or down slightly (the opposite of the above)

Sometimes when an underlying breaks, short out-of-the-money calls in stocks or stock indexes stubbornly cling to their value. This can be due to a general rise in the implied volatility as traders seek downside protection from both calls and puts. The calls are losing value because the stock is moving away from them, but they are gaining value as the increasing implied volatility increases their premium. There is increased demand for them because they are alternatives to a stock purchase and because they can be converted into synthetic puts. This also discussed in Part 4.

When this occurs, it is advisable simply to hold the position until the market stabilises. This requires strong nerves, but keep in mind that the stock's price direction and time decay are on your side. If the stock rebounds, the implied volatility often decreases, and if so, the calls' premiums will also decrease. The potential problem is that the stock may suddenly rebound to a higher level than where you sold the calls. Be ready with a buy-stop order. The more prudent strategy is the short call spread.

Stocks down, puts practically unchanged or underperforming

Occasionally a stock or stock index sells off, and long, out-of-the-money puts underperform. This is often due to the fact that the stock has retraced to the lower end of its trading range, and the market thinks that it will remain supported at its present level. The implied remains stable, or decreases somewhat, because the stock decline has met expectations. This problem may also be due to a decrease in the implied volatility of the put because of a shift in the volatility skew, and for this, you should consult Chapter 9 on volatility skews.

An alternative strategy is the call sale, above, if properly managed. The long put spread is a better alternative because any decline in the implied, via the skew or otherwise, affects both the long and short put strikes. You are then taking advantage of downside price movement with little exposure to a change in the implied. Refer to Chapter 8 on the long put spread.

Personally, I have a different approach to buying a straight put. I use technical analysis to note the support level of the stock or index. If I think that the stock is more likely to break support than the market is indicating, I buy puts below the level of support. Not only are these puts cheaper but, more importantly, if the stock does break support, the implied often increases because the market is then uncertain of the extent of the down-side potential. If I am uncertain that the stock will break support, which I am most often, I use the long put spread.

Stocks up, puts down slightly or unchanged

Often when the stock market rallies, puts lose very little of their premium. This occurs when the market fears a retracement. A rally in the stocks may be seen as a put buying opportunity, and demand remains strong. This can be nerve-racking for put sellers, and they feel like sitting ducks. Often the market retraces and stabilises, and time decay begins to eat away at the puts, but by then the put sellers are only too glad to close their positions at a break-even level.

Another reason for this occurrence is that with a rally, the put skew often shifts horizontally with the underlying, causing the implieds of the puts to increase. Refer to Chapter 19 on volatility skews.

A sensible alternative to being short puts is the short put spread. This spread limits downside risk while still preserving the opportunity for income through time decay. The exposure to changes in the implied, via the skew or otherwise, is also limited. As we said before, you shouldn't sell naked puts unless you want to buy the stock or other underlying.

Straight calls and puts with commodities

Although it is difficult to generalise, with commodities you can often sub-stitute call strategies for the above anomalies with put strategies, and put strategies for the above anomalies with call strategies. In commodities, calls are often king because of potential supply shortages. They often have positive call skews instead of positive put skews. This is true for stocks with large commodity exposure as well. Generally speaking, with commodities the strategy with the most risk is the short call.

Misconceptions to clear up about straight call and put positions

Remember, there are two advantages to a call purchase. They must both be seen as alternatives to buying a stock or other underlying.

▪ The first is to take advantage of market gains.
▪ The second is to limit exposure to capital risk.

It is inaccurate and misleading to think of a call as simply 'a chance to win', when it is equally a chance not to lose. Furthermore, if you think of an option as a 'chance', you will most likely become prey to those traders who strive to minimise chance from their dealings.

Another advantage of a call purchase is that as the underlying advances, the call becomes a greater percentage of the underlying until eventually it trades at parity with the underlying. The alternative advantage is that as the underlying declines, the purchased call becomes less a percentage of the underlying until it eventually loses its correlation with the underlying.

Likewise, for stock-holders, long puts offer the dual benefit of downside protection while preserving potential upside gains. Puts are not simply a downside chance. As the stock or underlying declines, the long put position becomes a greater percentage of a sale at the strike price until it eventually trades at parity, or the full amount of the underlying's decline. But as the underlying increases in price, the long put gradually loses its correlation with the stock or underlying, and the upside profit is maintained.

It is no coincidence that at-the-money calls and puts are priced the same

It is no coincidence that at-the-money calls and puts are priced the same. They both offer the same amount of upside and downside volatility coverage. This amount, or price, is the expected range of the underlying through expiration.

In other words, if XYZ is trading at 100, both the 100 call and the 100 put have the same price, perhaps four, because the market expects XYZ to close between 96 and 104 at expiration. If you buy the call instead of buying XYZ, you have 96 points of potential savings, and unlimited profit potential above 104. If you buy the put instead of selling XYZ that you own, you have 96 points of potential savings, and unlimited profit potential above 104.

The above relationship between calls and puts is the basis of synthetic options positions, or put–call parity. This will be discussed in Part 4.

Volatility skews

We have previously discussed the relationship between implied volatility and historical volatility. We mentioned that the implied can have a life of its own based on expectations for future changes in the historical. This condition often creates variations in implied volatility from strike to strike. These variations often fall into patterns which can be plotted on a graph, and for which equations can be found to match. Such patterns in implied volatility are known as **volatility skews**.

In this chapter we will see how skews affect the profit/loss of straight options positions. We will also see that unless you are a skew wizard, your best way to reduce skew risk is to spread.

Observing skews: bonds

Figure 20.1 shows a graph of the volatility skew for options on March Treasury Bonds. Below that, Table 20.1 gives the data containing the implied volatilities used to plot the skew.

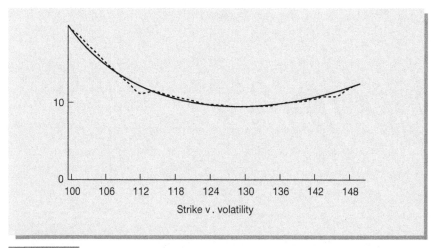

Figure 20.1 Options volatility skew: March Treasury Bond, underlying futures contract at 128.01

Source: Based on data from pmpublishing.com.

Table 20.1 March Treasury Bond options, 87 days until expiration, March futures at 128.01

Strike	Call value	Call implied volatility	Put value	Put implied volatility
112			0.01	11.21
114			0.03	11.47
116			0.06	11.21
118			0.11	10.84
120			0.19	10.38
122			0.33	10.01
124			0.57	9.76
126	3.31	9.57	1.30	9.55
*128	2.22	9.44	2.20	9.43

Strike	Call value	Call implied volatility	Put value	Put implied volatility
130	1.32	9.44	3.29	9.45
132	0.59	9.54		
134	0.34	9.58		
136	0.20	9.84		
138	0.11	9.98		
140	0.07	10.45		
142	0.04	10.70		
144	0.02	10.76		
146	0.01	10.86		

Source: Based on data from pmpublishing.com.

In Figure 20.1, the dotted line is the actual plot of the implieds from strike to strike, while the solid line has been generated with an algorithm. Some traders use the equation to determine if an option is undervalued or over-valued. The discrepancies as you can see are very small.

The ATM implied volatility is that of the 128 strike, at 9.44 per cent. Note that the implied volatility of the 136 call is 9.84 per cent, while the implied of the 120 put is 10.38 per cent, and that both these strikes are equidistant from the money.

Calls and puts of the strike prices ascending from the at-the-money strike are said to be on the **call skew**, while calls and puts of the strike prices descending from the at-the-money strike are said to be on the **put skew**. Here, both the call and put skews have increased implieds, and so they are said to be **positive**. This type of skew is often found in longer-term debt markets such as bonds, gilts and bunds.

(Personally, I refer to this type of skew as a 'parabolic' skew, because of its obvious resemblance to a parabola.)

Observing skews: stocks and stock indexes

Figure 20.2 shows a graph of the volatility skew for December options on the OEX. Table 20.2 gives the data containing the implied volatilities used to plot the skew.

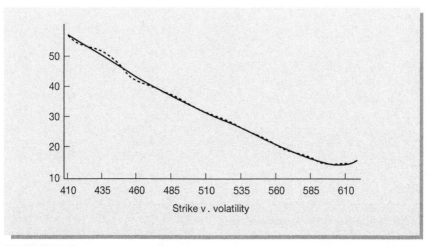

Figure 20.2   **Options volatility skew: December OEX, underlying index at 587.18, December synthetic future at 590.00**

Source: Based on data from pmpublishing.com.

Again, the dotted line is the actual plot of the implieds from strike to strike, while the solid line has been generated with an algorithm. The close match-up may seem arbitrary, but because skews continue to exhibit regular patterns over the years, they are calculable.

The ATM implied volatility is that of the 590 strike, at 17.82 per cent. Note that the implied volatility of the 610 call is 15.12 per cent, while the implied of the 570 put is 20.56 per cent, and that both these strikes are equidistant from the money. Note also that the implied of the 500 strike is 34.46 per cent, or almost double that of the ATM implied.

Here the put skew is positive while the call skew, with decreasing implieds, is negative. This type of skew is found in other stock index options, such as the FTSE.

(Personally, I refer to this type of skew as a 'linear' skew. It is simply more linear than a parabolic skew. Note that the tail of the call skew flattens out.)

Table 20.2 OEX December options

December OEX options
23 days until expiration
Underlying index at 587.18
December synthetic future at 590.00

Strike	Call value	Call implied volatility	Put value	Put implied volatility
420			0.13	53.67
430			0.19	52.77
440			0.25	51.16
450			0.25	47.66
460			0.19	42.59
480			0.31	38.71
490			0.44	37.19
500			0.50	34.46
515			0.81	31.92
545			2.00	25.98
550			2.38	25.06
555			2.75	23.90
570			4.50	20.56
575	21.00	20.75		
580	17.13	19.60	6.75	18.87
585	13.50	18.44	8.38	18.21
*590	10.50	17.82	10.50	17.82
595	7.75	16.98		
600	5.38	16.06		
605	3.63	15.49		
610	2.38	15.12		
615	1.56	15.05		
620	1.00	15.01		
630	0.50	15.84		

Source: Based on data from pmpublishing.com.

Volatility skews on individual stocks

Skews on individual stocks have basically the same characteristics as skews on the indexes. Figure 20.3 shows a recent skew of June options on Marks and Spencer.

On this day, M&S settled at 375.80.[1]

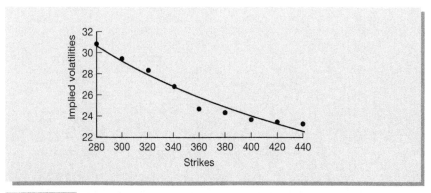

Figure 20.3   Recent skew of June options on Marks and Spencer

Observing skews: Commodities

volatility skews in commodities have their own special properties

Volatility skews in commodities have their own special properties. As an example, we can examine the skew for December 2010 Corn (see Figure 20.4).

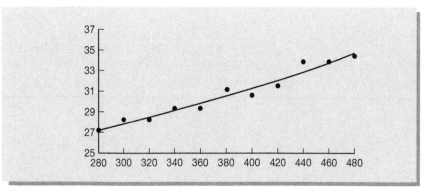

Figure 20.4   Skew for December 2010 Corn with Corn at $3.80 per bushell

---

[1] Data courtesy of the London International Financial Futures and Options Exchange, LIFFE.

Here, we have a typical commodities volatility skew. The call side is positive because producers and consumers wish to hedge shortage of supply. They buy calls.

The new skew

Recently we have seen a change in commodities' skews. Have a look at the crude oil chart in Figure 20.5.

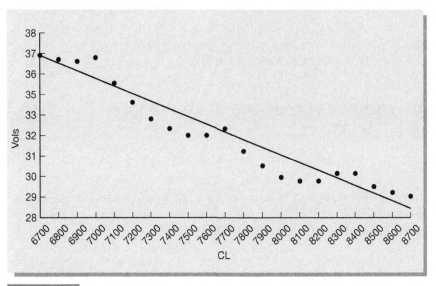

Figure 20.5 Crude oil skew

Here we have a positive put skew. It resembles the skew in stocks and bonds, not commodities. So what's going on? Here's my opinion.

Oil is now being traded by the banks and hedge funds. If you can think back a few years, then you'll remember that commodities were a niche market. They were traded by consumers and producers. This is no longer the case. Commodities are now an asset class, supposedly.

The result is that the current open interest in derivatives contracts overwhelms the available supply. The longs outnumber the shorts, and they have more money. Price is therefore supported. But in order to hedge their asset, the funds buy puts. That's why there's a positive put skew in oil. So, in the end, what's going to happen? A blow-out. No firm, no one, no body is bigger that the market. Think of the Hunt brothers who tried to corner silver in the 1970s.

Sooner or later, traders – and I mean big ones – will get wise to the weakness of the longs and they will short them. Then the longs will be routed. In the meantime, you might ask your bank manager if his firm has exposure to commodities.

Trading skews

So how to trade the skews? If there is a positive skew, one suggestion is to neutralise your exposure by buying the 1 × 1 call spread or put spread. You're then financing your long option with a short option that is more expensive in terms of implied volatility. You're financing option is value for money. There is more on this topic below.

Volatility skews versus the at-the-money implied volatility

Regardless of the nature of the skews, the implied volatility of any options contract, i.e. the implied that corresponds most closely to the current volatility of the underlying, is always the implied that is at-the-money. One can say that the at-the-money strike, however that may change, is always the focal point of both the call and put skews.

Why there are skews

There is no agreement as to why there are skews, apart from the obvious reason of supply and demand for the options. We know, however, by studying historical data that large price changes in many underlyings occur with greater frequency than are accounted for by normal distribution. At least once in a generation an asteroid hits the stock market. Skews might seem irrational, but then so do many market events.

Don't make the mistake of thinking that skews exist because brokers like to buy or sell out-of-the-money options, or because a particular house or group of houses always buys or sells certain options. One might as well say that short-term interest rates are at their current levels because the central banks hold them here.[2] Markets don't operate in this way; they are more powerful than the participants.

---

[2] True, central banks have in the past resisted monetary trends, but only by placing their nations' economies at risk.

For whatever reasons, skews continue to appear in most options contracts year after year, and they continue to display similar patterns in each contract. Most of us by now have learned to treat them with respect.

I have personal opinions on the reasons for volatility skews. A skew is a function of variations in implied volatility. Like the implied, it indicates market expectations for the near-term level of the historical volatility. It therefore indicates what the market expects the historical volatility will be if the underlying suddenly shifts to a new level in the direction of the skew. This is a form of discounting, which all markets do.

Further, a parabolic-shaped, positive skew indicates that the implied is likely to remain relatively stable when the underlying remains in the current trading range. The belly of the skew accounts for this. The increasing slopes of the parabolic skew indicate that the implied is likely to increase exponentially if the underlying suddenly moves towards the wings of the skew and breaks through the current trading range. Again, this is a form of discounting by the market.

Most stock index and long-term interest rate contracts have positive put skews because these markets, more often than not, become more volatile as they break. There is also perennial demand for puts in these markets to protect against loss of asset value.

Many commodities have positive call skews. Commodities become more volatile as prices increase, which they suddenly do when faced with supply shortages. Corn and soybeans have had positive call skews for years. If drought conditions occur, grain dealers find it difficult to honour forward commitments. Cash and futures prices, along with the implied volatilities of options, soar.

A flat or negative skew indicates that the volatility of an underlying is expected to be stable, or to decline slightly if the underlying moves in its direction. Bonds spend long periods of time with flat to slightly positive call skews during periods of interest rate stability. Commodities often have negative put skews because slackening demand results in their grinding lower. Negative call skews in stock indexes indicate that as their markets move steadily higher and the value of their indexes increases, an equivalent price change calculates to a lower historical volatility.

Skew behaviour towards expiration

Skews can change their degree of positiveness or negativeness. Positive skews most often become more positive as they approach expiration.

The underlying contract for this January set of T-Bond options is the same as for the previous March set of T-Bond options; it is the March futures contract. Here, the implied of the ATM call at the 128 strike is lower, at 8.14 (see Table 20.4). The implied of the January 122 put is greater, at 10.42, than the March 122 put at 10.01. The January 134 call has an implied of 9.19, while the March 134 call has an implied of 9.58. While both January skews are increased, the put skew exhibits the more radical change. You may compare the implied volatilities strike by strike (see Figure 20.6).

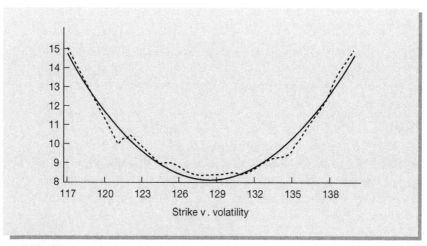

Figure 20.6 ■ January T-Bond options skew

Source: Based on data from pmpublishing.com.

Table 20.4 January Treasury Bond options

	January Treasury Bond options 24 days until expiration March future at 128.01					
Strike	Call value	Call implied	Call delta	Put value	Put implied	Put delta
121				0.01	10.02	0.01
122				0.03	10.42	0.03
123				0.05	9.92	0.06
124				0.07	9.00	0.08
125				0.14	8.91	0.14
126	2.26	8.59	0.77	0.25	8.68	0.23
127	1.44	8.44	0.65	0.42	8.42	0.35
*128	1.05	8.14	0.51	1.04	8.26	0.49
129	0.43	8.30	0.36	1.41	8.32	0.63
130	0.25	8.40	0.24	2.23	8.46	0.75
131	0.13	8.38	0.14			
132	0.07	8.62	0.09			
133	0.04	9.01	0.05			
134	0.02	9.19	0.03			
135	0.01	9.41	0.01			

Source: Based on data from pmpublishing.com.

Skews' shift with underlying

Skews most often shift horizontally with the price of their underlying contracts. If an underlying drifts back and forth in a range, the skew will most often range as well. The focal point clings to the at-the-money strike, with little change to the ATM implied. This effectively changes the implied of each strike.

For example, if the above March T-Bond contract rose to 129.01 then the implieds of all the strikes would be likely to shift to the next strike upward. The January 129 calls would have an implied of 8.14, and the January 123 puts would have an implied of 10.42, etc.

This occurrence presupposes no change in the historical or ATM implied volatility. Here the underlying is most often trading in a range. Sometimes the underlying moves but the focal point of the skew clings to a strike; this occurs when the market expects a retracement.

Skews' change of degree

A skew often becomes more positive if the underlying makes a sudden move, or threatens to make a sudden move, in its direction. A bond market put skew may become more positive if an inflation report is revealed to be worse than expected. Several days in advance, the put skew may behave in the same manner if the report is expected to be worse than expected.

Under these circumstances, the skew becomes more like a skew with fewer days until expiration. If and when the market's apprehension subsides, the skew may return to its former level.

A call skew in a stock index may become less negative to flat in anticipation of a Christmas or January rally, or an imminent cut in interest rates. Eventually, the skew will revert to its former position.

Skews' vertical shift

If the ATM implied increases or decreases, then the skew most often shifts vertically upward or downward. This effectively raises or lowers the implied of all strikes because the skew retains its shape. The focal point of the skew remains at the ATM strike (see Figure 20.7).

Caution

Do not assume that skews foretell directional moves or changes in volatility. Sometimes they do, but often they do not. A stock's put skew may be bid because earnings are expected to be bad. When the earnings are reported, they may be no worse than expected, the put skew may fall, the stock may rally and volatility may decline. Likewise, a flat call skew in a bond market is no indicator that events will continue to be dull and routine. If a shock

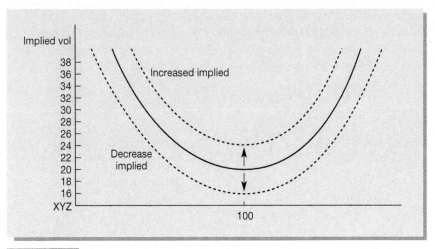

Figure 20.7 Skew vertical shift

hits the stock market, a flight to quality and so a flight to bonds may result, rapidly forcing their call implieds, and their call skews, higher.

Trading with skews

Volatility skews present additional opportunities for profit as well as additional risks. They are additional variables which should be considered when trading options, especially straight long or short calls and puts. Their risks are lessened through spreading. The following paragraphs offer guidelines on how to deal with some of the more common, but by no means all, market situations. Skew behaviour varies as much as market behaviour.

> Volatility skews present additional opportunities for profit as well as additional risks

As you might expect, there are two basic possibilities to skew trading:

■ buying or selling out-of-the money options on a positive skew

■ buying or selling out-of-the-money options on a negative skew.

Trading options on a positive skew

The purchase of an out-of-the-money option on a positive skew, like the purchase of any option, profits if the underlying moves in its direction and/or if the implied increases. If the underlying moves in the option's direction, but meets a support or resistance level, the option profits from direction but often underperforms. This is because the focal point of the skew shifts horizontally to the at-the-money strike, causing the implied of the option effectively to decrease (see Figure 20.8).

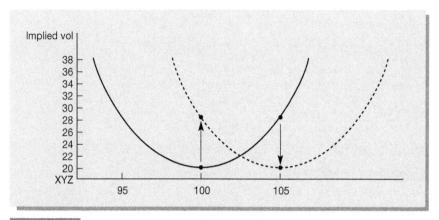

Figure 20.8   Positive skew, right horizontal shift

With XYZ at 100, the 105 call is purchased at an implied that is above the at-the-money level, and as the underlying moves to the 105 strike, the option's implied effectively decreases from 28 per cent to 20 per cent. The net result is still a profit if time decay has not been too costly. Note that the implied of the 100 call and put both increase from 20 per cent to 28 per cent.

For example, suppose you pay 25 ($^{25}/_{64}$) for the T-Bond January 130 call from the set in Table 20.4. You might estimate the profit potential for a two-point rally in bonds by multiplying two points (128 options ticks) by the average delta of the call over the course of the move. This average delta is determined by the delta of the 129 call, at 0.36: 128 × 0.36 = 46 ticks profit. Your estimated new value of the 130 call with bonds at 130 is 46 + 25 = $^{71}/_{64}$, or 1.07.

By looking at the 128 call with bonds at 128, you note that the current ATM call has a value of only 1.05. If the ATM implied remains stable, then the market is telling you that a 130 call with bonds at 130 will have a value of 1.05.

Effectively then, for a two-point rally, your 130 call may underperform by two ticks. In practice, this often happens. The reason for this is that you have purchased a call at an implied of 8.40 which will be reduced to 8.14 by a horizontal shift in the volatility skew.

In this case, the underperformance is not a great amount. But if the call were purchased further up the skew (at a higher strike), and if the skew were more positive, then the reduction due to a decrease in implied volatility would be greater.

In order to minimise this skew risk, you might instead purchase an out-of-the-money call spread. Here, you could buy the 130 call and sell the 132 call. As the skew shifts, both implieds decrease.

Another approach is simply to pay 1.05 ($^{69}/_{64}$) for the 128 call. Here, as the market rallies, the shift in the skew causes the implied of your call to increase. Using the delta of the 127 call at 0.65, your expected profit for a two-point rally would be 0.65 × 128 = 83. The new value of your call is estimated at 83 + 69 = $^{152}/_{64}$, or 2.24.

You note that the current 126 call has a value of 2.26. This is the expected value of your 128 call if bonds rally two points. Because the implied of your call increases from 8.14 to 8.59, your 128 call may, and often will, outperform by two ticks.

Still another approach is to buy the 128–130 call spread. Here, your spread's long strike profits from increased volatility, and your spread's short strike profits from decreased volatility.

You can use the preceding data to calculate the effect of a skew shift on the implieds and values of selected puts. If the underlying breaks, puts on a positive skew may underperform due to a decrease in their implieds.

Trading options on a linear skew

A long out-of-the-money option on a linear skew, or a skew that is call negative and put positive, presents a couple of possibilities. As the underlying rallies, you might expect the skew to shift horizontally, resulting in an increase in all the implieds. Often this happens.

In Figure 20.9, as XYZ rallies from 100 to 105, all the calls and puts increase their implied volatility. Note that the reverse situation often occurs: an underlying breaks, usually on a retracement, and the skew shifts to the left, resulting in a decrease in all the implieds.

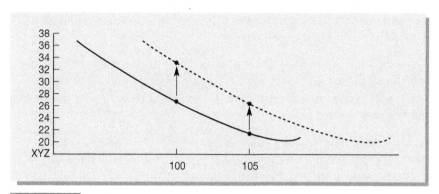

Figure 20.9   Horizontal skew shift, negative call skew, positive put skew

Frequently, however, on a rally the skew can remain in place, and the implieds of all strikes are unchanged. Effectively, the implied volatility decreases because the focal point of the skew moves to the new at-the-money strike. The solid line of Figure 20.9 illustrates this: XYZ rallies from 100 to 105, and the new ATM implied, now at the 105 strike, is less than that of the former 100 strike.

This situation often occurs with skews in stock indexes as they rally to former levels. The options market is unfazed by the upside retracement. This also occurs in commodities that have negative put skews as the commodities retrace from a rally; there the graph is the mirror image of Figure 20.9.

Another possibility is that on a break, the skew can remain in place. Effectively, the implied volatility increases because the focal point of the skew moves to the new at-the-money strike. The dotted line of Figure 20.9 illustrates this: XYZ breaks from 105 to 100, and the new ATM implied, now at the 100 strike, is greater than that of the former 105 strike.

This latter situation often occurs with skews in stock indexes as they break. The options market is fearful that this is the big one. When it really is the big one, then the entire skew will shift vertically upward, and the put wing will become more positive.

A note on market sentiment

In all cases where a straight long or short option is chosen for a directional strategy, skew risk can be minimised by trading the long or short call or put spread.

Volatility skews are indicators of market senti-ment. Positive skews indicate fear, while negative skews indicate complacence. Sentiment, as we know, can often be wrong, but it cannot be ignored.

Volatility skews are indicators of market sentiment

part

4

Basic non-essentials

Introduction

Most of us won't spend our options careers trading arbitrage, but when the opportunity arises, as it does from time to time, it's an almost risk-free way to make money. So if you learn about the arb, then you're prepared to take advantage of it when you see it.

Read Part 4 at least once. Think about it from time to time. When you're scanning the markets, ask yourself, 'Is there an arbitrage here? Can I lock in a profit with this trade until expiration?' If you keep this in mind, then some day you'll find yourself making a lot of money in a very short time.

If you're prepared.

21

Futures, synthetics and put–call parity

It is possible to combine options and underlying positions in ways that simulate straight call or put positions. An underlying itself may be simulated with a combination of options. As an example of the former, a long at-the-money call plus a short underlying position has the same risk/return profile as a long at-the-money put, and is therefore known as a synthetic put.

Synthetic positions are used primarily by professional market-makers to simplify the view of their options inventory in order to manage risk better. They are of little practical use to traders who take options positions based on market outlooks, but they can be studied in order to understand how options markets work.

In order to understand synthetics, it is best if you understand why they exist. Like all options positions, they are based on a relation to an underlying contract, which may be a cash investment or a futures contract. If we briefly take this subject step by step, then we will avoid future disorientation.

What a futures contract is

A **futures contract** is simply an agreement to trade a commodity, stock, bond or currency at a specified price at a specified future date. Because no cash is exchanged for the time being, the future buyer is said to have a **long position**, and the future seller is said to have a **short position**. As a result, the holder of the long position profits as the market moves up and takes a loss as the market moves down. The holder of the short position has the opposite profit/loss.

If short selling were not possible, investors would only be able to buy from those who wanted to sell physical holdings; liquidity would suffer and market volatility would increase. Most exchanges require a security deposit in order to open a futures contract, and this deposit is known as **initial margin**. The value of the contract as traded on the exchange invariably fluctuates, and so results in a profit to one party and a loss to the other. The party who has a loss is then required to deposit the amount of the loss, and this additional deposit is known as **variation margin**. Margin may be in the form of cash, or it may be in the form of liquid securities such as treasury bills or gilts, for which the depositor still collects interest. Meanwhile the party who has the profit is credited with variation margin, and he receives interest on the balance.

Futures contracts have traditionally been used in commodities markets in order to hedge supply shortages and surpluses. They are now used in stocks, stock indexes, bonds and currencies. Many excellent books describe how these forms of futures contracts operate.

An example of a futures contract

Consider the following example of a closing price of the S&P 500 index with the settlement price of the December futures contract and the settlement prices of the at-the-money call and put on the futures contract.

S&P index: 1133.68

December future: 1140.70

December 1140 call: 34.40

December 1140 put: 33.70

Here, the S&P futures contract multiplier is $250. An investor who trades one of the above December contracts is hedging 1140.70 × $250 = $285,175 worth of stocks that track the index. The options contract multiplier is $25.

We know that the December future, here with approximately six weeks until expiration, trades at a premium to the cash. This is because taking a long position in the futures contract instead of buying all the stocks in the index requires a margin deposit only. The holder of the futures position therefore has the use of his cash for the next six weeks. The value of the futures contract is increased by the cost of carrying on the stocks.

On the other hand, the holder of the long futures position forgoes the dividends payable for the next six weeks, and therefore the value of the December future is decreased by that amount. The formula for the value of the futures contract is approximated as follows:

Futures contract = cash value of index + interest or cost of carry on index until expiration – dividends payable until expiration

In practice, the formula is more complicated because annualised rates of carry and dividend yields are used. Here, we are simply concerned with why the above future trades above or below the cash.

Until recently short-term interest rates paid more than dividend yields, and so stock index futures traded at a premium to their underlying indexes. The situation is now reversed, and it is similar to the 1950s, where dividend yields paid more than short-term interest rates in order to compensate for the risk of owning stock. This was a holdover from the crash of 1929, when many stock-holders' investments were wiped out. The reason now, however, is that after the recent banking crisis, the central banks are trying to maintain liquidity by keeping interest rates low.

> The futures contract and the cash index converge at expiration because then there is no remaining differential between cost of carry and payable dividends

Occasionally, shortly before expiration, there may be a large amount of dividends payable in a stock or stock index. Then the dividend outweighs the interest amount and the future trades at a discount to the index. Once the dividend or dividends are paid, then the future trades above the cash.

In any event, the futures contract and the cash index converge at expiration because then there is no remaining differential between cost of carry and payable dividends. The futures contract simply expires to the current cash value of the index.

There, the holder of the long futures contract pays the cash value of all the stocks in the index. The holder of the short futures contract receives the cash value of all the stocks in the index. The ultimate amount exchanged is determined by the value of the index at expiration times the contract multiplier.

In the case of a physical commodity such as corn or crude oil, the futures contract is deliverable to the quantity of the commodity specified in the contract at the settlement price.

Synthetic futures contract

As we already know, a long XYZ 100 call, by virtue of its right to buy, equals a long XYZ position when XYZ is above 100 at expiration. We also know that a short XYZ 100 put, by virtue of its obligation to buy, equals a long XYZ position when XYZ is below 100 at expiration. The sum of these two options positions, therefore, equals a synthetic long XYZ position with a strike price of 100. This is a result of the combined right and obligation. Consider the example in Figure 21.1.

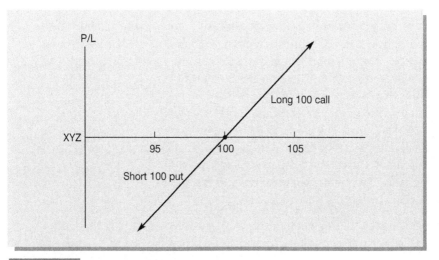

Figure 21.1   **Long XYZ synthetic**

We also know that a short XYZ 100 call, by virtue of its obligation to sell, equals a short XYZ position when XYZ is above 100 at expiration. A long XYZ 100 put, by virtue of its right to sell, equals a short XYZ position when XYZ is below 100 at expiration. The sum of these options positions, therefore, equals a synthetic short position with a strike price of 100. This again is a result of the combined right and obligation. Consider the example in Figure 21.2.

Assuming that interest rates will eventually rise, then the S&P 500 example above is typical of the modern era. A long December 1140 call plus a short December 1140 put equals a synthetic long futures contract valued at 1140. If you pay 34.40 for the call, and sell the put at 33.70, then you have paid a net 0.70 for the synthetic at 1140. In other words, you have paid 0.70 to go long the future at 1140. You have paid 1140.70 for the synthetic long future.

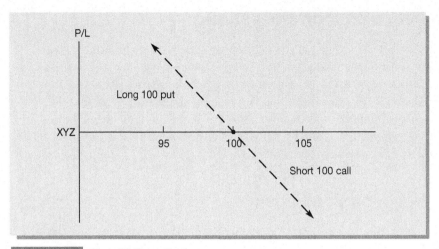

Figure 21.2   Short XYZ synthetic

Note that the actual December future is valued at 1140.70. Your synthetic options position is valued the same, and always will be, as a futures contract.

If, on the other hand, you sell the call at 34.40 and pay 33.70 for the put, then you have sold the synthetic future at 1140.70. Here, you have the obligation to sell the future above 1140, and the right to sell the future below 1140.

The profit/loss of the two synthetics is graphed in Figure 21.3.

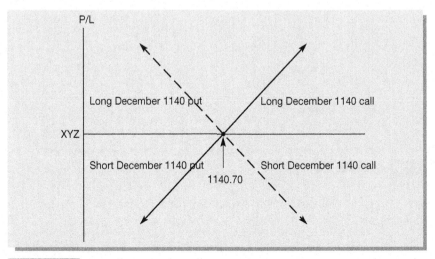

Figure 21.3   Synthetic long December SPZ futures contract + synthetic short December SPZ futures contract

Synthetics on individual stocks

In the case of individual stocks, there are also a synthetic futures position, because the holder of a long call plus short put position at any strike
controls a long stock position without having to pay for the stock. The
situation is the same as with the S&P example above, but often there is no
underlying future for comparison. Still,the synthetic future exists. In the
stock options the synthetic future is often spoken of simply as the synthetic, or occasionally, the combo.

Synthetic long call position

When a long XYZ 100 put is combined with a long underlying position,
the profit/loss's of the put and the underlying cancel each other below
100, leaving the upside, profit-making leg of the underlying. The sum
equals a synthetic long call. For the purpose of illustration, let's assume
that the call was purchased for free. At expiration, the synthetic position
would be as shown in Figure 21.4.

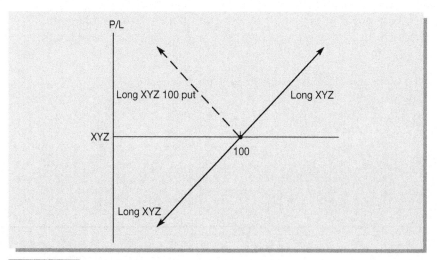

Figure 21.4   Synthetic long 100 call

Now let's return to the example based on the S&P 500 futures and options
on the futures:

S&P 500 December future: 1140.70

December 1140 call: 34.40

December 1140 put: 33.70

Suppose you take a long position in the futures contract at 1140.70 and at the same time you pay 33.70 for the December 1140 put. You know that below 1140 the profit/loss of the put and the futures contract offset each other because below 1140 you have the right to sell what you own at the price at which it was purchased less the cost of the put. Above 1140 you are simply long the futures contract. Being net long a futures contract above 1140 is the same as owning a December 1140 call. The cost of your synthetic call breaks down as follows.

The futures contract costs 1140.70, and the right to sell it at 1140 costs 33.70. With your futures contract you have paid 0.70 more for what you own than for your potential selling price. With your put your total cost is 0.70 + 33.70 = 34.40, or the price of the December 1140 call. Compare the profit/loss tables for the 1140 call (Table 21.1) and the 1140 synthetic call (Table 21.2).

Table 21.1 Profit/loss of SPZ December 1140 call at expiration

SPZ	1080.00	1140.00	1174.40	1200.00
Cost of December 1140 call	−34.40	----------	----------	----------
Value of call at expiration	0.00	0.00	34.40	60.00
Call profit/loss	−34.40	−34.40	0.00	25.60

Table 21.2 Profit/loss of SPZ December 1140 synthetic call at expiration

SPZ	1080.00	1140.00	174.40	1200.00
Profit/loss of long December futures at expiration	−60.70	−0.70	33.70	59.30
Cost of December 1140 put	−33.70	----------	----------	----------
Value of put at expiration	60.00	0.00	0.00	0.00
Profit/loss of synthetic long call	−34.40	−34.40	0.00	25.60

Synthetic short call position

If instead XYZ is sold at 100, and at the same time a 100 put is sold, a synthetic short 100 call results. Below 100 the profit on the short underlying position and the loss on the short put offset each other. Above 100, a loss is taken on the short underlying position. Let's assume that the put was sold for free. The graph at expiration would be as shown in Figure 21.5.

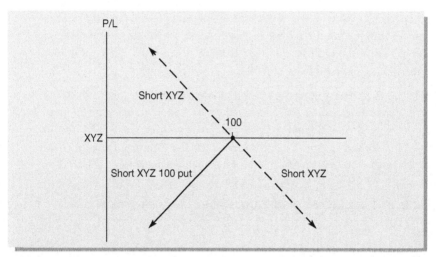

Figure 21.5 Synthetic short XYZ call

Returning to our SPZ example, suppose the above December 1140 put is sold for 33.70 and a short position is taken in the futures contract at 1140.70, the result is a synthetic short call. The profit/loss is the opposite to the above long synthetic long call (see Table 21.3).

Table 21.3 Profit/loss of synthetic short SPZ December 1140 call at expiration

SPZ	1080.00	1140.00	1174.40	1200.00
Profit/loss of short December futures at expiration	60.70	0.70	−33.70	−59.30
Income from December 1140 put	33.70	-------	-------	-------
Value of put at expiration	−60.00	0.00	0.00	0.00
Profit/loss of synthetic short call	34.40	34.40	0.00	−25.60

Synthetic long put position

When a long XYZ 100 call is combined with a short underlying position, the profit/loss of the call and the underlying cancel each other above 100, leaving the downside, profit-making leg of the underlying. The sum equals a synthetic long put. We'll assume that the put is traded for free. At expiration, the profit/loss graph is shown in Figure 21.6.

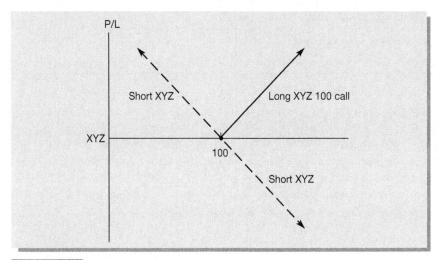

Figure 21.6 Synthetic long XYZ put

Returning to our SPZ example, suppose the December 1140 call is purchased for 34.40, and a short position in the futures contract is taken at 1140.70. The result is a synthetic long put purchased for 33.70. Tables 21.4 and 21.5 show a comparison of the profit/loss of the synthetic and the straight put.

Table 21.4 Profit/loss of long SPZ December 1140 put at expiration

SPZ	1080.00	1106.30	1140.00	1200.00
Cost of December 1140 put	–33.70			
Value of put at expiration	60.00	33.70	0.00	0.00
Put profit/loss	26.30	0.00	–33.70	–33.70

Table 21.5 Profit/loss of long SPZ December 1140 synthetic put at expiration

SPZ	1080.00	1106.30	1140.00	1200.00
Profit/loss of short December futures at expiration	60.70	34.40	0.70	−59.30
Cost of December 1140 call	−34.40	------	------	------
Value of call at expiration	0.00	0.00	0.00	60.00
Profit/loss of synthetic long put	26.30	0.00	−33.70	−33.70

Synthetic short put position

When a short XYZ 100 call is combined with a long underlying position, the profit/loss of the call and the underlying cancel each other above 100, leaving the downside, loss-taking leg of the underlying. The sum equals a synthetic short put. Again, we'll assume that the put is traded for free. At expiration, the profit/loss graph is shown in Figure 21.7.

Returning to our SPZ example, if the December 1140 call is sold at 34.40, and a long position is taken in the underlying at 1140.70, the result is a synthetic short put sold at 33.70. The profit/loss is the opposite of the above long synthetic put (see Table 21.6).

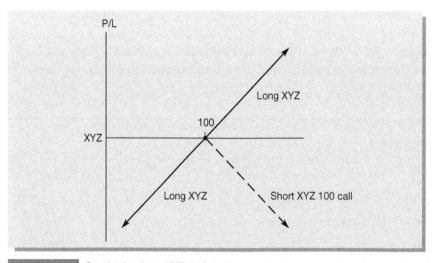

Figure 21.7 Synthetic short XYZ 100 put

Table 21.6 Profit/loss of short SPZ December 1140 synthetic put at expiration

SPZ	1080.00	1106.30	1140.00	1200.00
Profit/loss of long December futures at expiration	–60.70	–34.40	–0.70	59.30
Income from December 1140 call	34.40	---		
Value of call at expiration	0.00	0.00	0.00	–60.00
Profit/loss of synthetic short put	–26.30	0.00	33.70	33.70

The complex problem of put–call parity

The above are illustrations of **put–call parity**, which tells us that by know-ing the value of the underlying, the strike price, and either the call or put, the price of the unknown call or put can be determined. The formulas for determining the value of a corresponding call or put at a particular strike are as follows.

Call – put = futures – strike price (34.40 – 33.70 = 1140.70 – 1140),

therefore

Call = futures – strike price + put (34.40 = 1140.75 – 1140 + 33.70), or

Put = call – futures + strike price (33.70 = 34.40 – 1140.70 + 1140)

This equation can also be solved for the other two variables.

Futures = call – put + strike price (1140.70 = 34.40 – 33.70 + 1140), and

Strike price = futures + put – call (1140 = 1140.70 + 33.70 – 34.40)

All this really tells us is that a call and a put at the same strike have the same amount of time premium, or volatility coverage. If you've read this book with open eyes, you've already arrived at the same conclusion, at least intuitively. The mysterious and complex world of put–call parity is now exposed as a trifle. You, the intelligent reader, have more important things to think about, such as choosing your socks in the morning.

A call and a put at the same strike have the same amount of time premium, or volatility coverage

The real problem of put–call parity is that for many options contracts it doesn't apply. It assumes that in-the-money options have no early exercise premium, which is only true of European-style options. Put–call parity works with a straight Black–Scholes model only, and only when deep in-the-money options with their carrying costs are not involved.

If the above S&P 500 options were deep in the money, there would be small discrepencies in the put–call parity values. If the put–call parity formula were applied to options on the OEX or other American-style index options, large discrepencies would result due to early exercise premium. Significant discrepancies also result with American-style options on individual stocks, i.e. most stock options.

Put–call parity can be a helpful way of pricing options, but its limitations must be considered.

Conversions, reversals, boxes and options arbitrage

Conversions, reversals, and boxes are used almost exclusively by market-makers and risk managers to neutralise the risk of large options portfolios. At one time, they were traded in order to profit from small price discrepancies in synthetic positions, but now most mature options markets have eliminated this opportunity.

A short synthetic underlying position can be combined with an actual long underlying position to yield a **forward conversion**, or **conversion**. Likewise, a long synthetic position can be combined with an actual short underlying position to yield a **reverse conversion**, or **reversal**. The profit/loss of these positions does not change regardless of market movement, and their only practical risks are those of pin risk and early assignment.

> Conversions, reversals, and boxes are used almost exclusively to neutralise the risk of large options portfolios

A long box is the purchase of a synthetic underlying at a lower strike and the sale of a synthetic underlying at a higher strike. **A short box** is the opposite position. Because the box is both long and short the underlying, its profit/loss does not change regardless of market movement. Again, the only practical risks are pin risk and early assignment.

Conversion

A conversion is a long underlying plus a short call and a long put at the same strike.

If XYZ is at 100, you could sell one 100 call, buy one 100 put, and buy or go long XYZ to create a conversion. Because the sum of the position is short the synthetic and long the underlying there is no profit/loss change regardless of underlying price movement. At expiration, the synthetic pairs off against the underlying to leave no position.

Consider again the example from S&P 500 futures, and options on futures.

December S&P 500 future at 1140.70

December 1140 call at 34.40

December 1140 put at 33.70

Here, you could sell the call at 34.40, pay 33.70 for the put, and pay 1140.70 for the future. You have then sold the synthetic at 1140.70 and you have bought the future at the same price. There is no profit or loss to this position, nor will it change for the life of the options contract. At expiration the short synthetic pairs off against the long future, and the result is no position. There is minimal risk. Figure 22.1 shows is a graph of the conversion.

Occasionally, there is a small amount of profit to be made by trading the components of a conversion separately. For example, a trader might be able to sell the above call at 34.50, thereby making 0.10 profit on the whole position. This 0.10 is secure until expiration when all the components pair off. Some traders spend the best part of their youth trying to trade these small price discrepancies, and it is good for the rest of us that they do so. Their form of trading is called **arbitrage**.

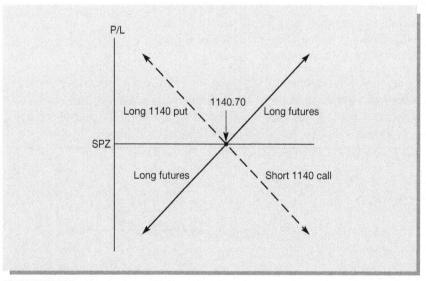

Figure 22.1   **SPZ 1140 conversion**

By keeping the conversions in line, the arbitrageurs, or arbs, help to maintain efficient pricing in the market. As a result, we benefit by getting a fair price for our options.

Reverse conversion, or reversal

A reversal is a short underlying plus a long call and a short put at the same strike.

If XYZ is at 100, you could buy one 100 call, sell one 100 put, and sell or go short one XYZ to create a reversal. Because the sum of the position is long the synthetic and short the underlying, there is no profit/loss change regardless of underlying price movement. At expiration, the synthetic pairs off against the underlying to leave no position.

With the S&P example, you could pay 34.40 for the call, sell the put at 33.70, and sell the future at 1140.70. Here you have paid 1140.70 for the synthetic and sold the future at the same price. Figure 22.2 shows a graph of the entire position.

Again, the arbs exploit the smallest price discrepancy with any of the components of the reversal. Here, they might pay 34.30 for the call, or sell the put at 33.80, or pay 1140.60 for the future. Rarely is more than one component out of line at one time.

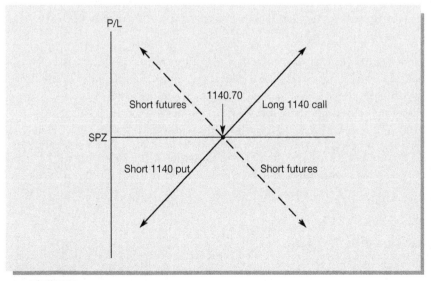

Figure 22.2   SPZ 1140 reversal

Conversion and reversals on individual stocks and on other stock indexes

The conversion and reversal markets on stocks operate in basically the same manner. Remember that with stocks there are no futures contracts, but that the options combine to form synthetic futures contracts. The situation is similar to the S&P 500 cash–futures–options relationship given in Chapter 20:

S&P 500 cash index at 1133.68

December future at 1140.70

December 1140 call at 34.40

December 1140 put at 33.70

If the futures contract were eliminated, and the options were exercisable instead to cash, then the relationship would be the same as between stocks and stock options.

The OEX options are traded in this manner, without an underlying futures contract; they are American style. Because there is no underlying cash instrument, apart from an unwieldy basket of stocks, there is no conversion or reversal tradable in the OEX.

The SPX options on the S&P 500 index, traded at the CBOE, are also based solely on the underlying index; they are European style. Traders here sometimes used the S&P 500 futures contract at the CME in order to create a conversion or reversal.

The FTSE-100 contract is a hybrid. The options are assigned to cash at monthly expirations like the OEX. There is a futures contract as well, like the S&P 500, which trades in the March–June–September–December cycle. During these four months, expiration for options and futures coincides at 10:30 on the third Friday, making conversions possible.

An example of a conversion in stocks is found in the following set of Marks and Spencer options:

M&S at 350.60

May options, 75 DTE

May 350 call: 15.75

May 350 put: 14.75

Here, you could sell the 350 synthetic at 1.00 and pay 350.60 for the shares to create the conversion. At May expiry the short synthetic converts to a short shares position which pairs off against the long shares position. You have effectively sold the synthetic at 351 for a net credit of 0.40 on the total position. This credit equals your cost of carry on the shares for the next 75 days as determined by the prevailing short-term interest rate (0.50 per cent). (Where applicable, dividends are a negative component in the long synthetic just as they are with a futures contract. In this example, there were no dividends through expiry.) During the next 75 days the difference between the synthetic and the stock will converge from 0.40 to zero.

Long box

The box is another spread that is occasionally employed by arbitrageurs in order to profit from small price discrepancies in the options markets. Again, it contains minimal risk.

If XYZ is at 100, you would go long the 100–105 box by going long the 100 synthetic and by going short the 105 synthetic. You would buy one 100 call, sell one 100 put, sell one 105 call, and buy one 105 put. The box itself always trades for a price that nearly equals the difference between the strike prices, in this case, a debit of five. Your purchase holds its value until expiration, at which time the synthetics pair off and you are credited with the difference between the strike prices.

As an example, consider the following set of May, Marks and Spencer options, with 75 DTE:

Marks and Spencer at 350.60

May options with 75 days until expiry

Table 22.1 Marks and Spencer May options

Strike	340	350	360
May calls	21.25	15.75	11.00
May puts	10.25	14.75	20.00

Here, the long 340–360 box is calculated as the 340 call minus the 340 put, minus the 360 call plus the 360 put, or $(21.25 - 10.25) - (11.00 - 20.00) = 20.00$. Until expiry this debit is your total profit/loss.

At expiration, the long 340 synthetic, through exercise or assignment, becomes a shares purchase at a price of 340. The short 360 synthetic, through exercise or assignment, becomes a shares sale at a price of 360. Your account is then credited with 20 ticks and your profit/loss is theoretically zero.

In practice, however, the value of the box is most often modified by time until expiration, early exercise, and interest rate factors; these are discussed below.

At expiration, your profit/loss summary is as shown in Table 22.2.

Table 22.2 Profit/loss of long M&S May 340–360 box at expiry

Marks and Spencer	330	340	350	360	370
Debit from long 340 synthetic	−11				
Value of long 340 synthetic at expiry	−10	0	10	20	30
Debit from short 360 synthetic	−9				
Value of short 360 synthetic at expiration	30	20	10	0	−10
Total profit/loss	0	0	0	0	0

The profit/loss graph shown in Figure 22.3 is simply an overlay of the two synthetics at expiration. The call synthetic goes from lower left to upper right. The put synthetic goes from lower right to upper left.

At any price level, the call plus the put combo equals 20. For example, at 350 the 340 call is worth 10, and the 360 put is worth 10. You're long them both. Meanwhile, the 340 put and the 360 call are worthless.

At 330 you're long the 360 put, which is worth 30, and you're short the 340 put which is worth 10. Your net is still +20.

If you connect the four dots at 340 and 360 then the picture looks like a box.

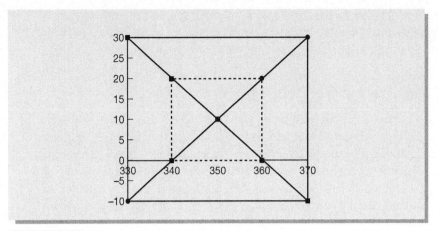

Figure 22.3 Marks and Spencer 340–360 box

Short box

If XYZ is at 100, you could sell one 100 call, buy one 100 put, buy one 105 call, and sell one 105 put to create a short box. Here, you are short the 100 synthetic and long the 105 synthetic for a credit of five. Your sale holds its value until expiry, at which time the synthetics pair off, and you pay the value of the box to the counterparty.

For an example, simply reverse the long box transaction in M&S, above. Sell the 340 synthetic and buy the 360 synthetic for a credit of 20. At expiry this credit returns to the counterparty.

Trading boxes

Boxes are seldom traded except as closing positions between market-makers; we trade them
close to expiration in order to clear options off
our books and to avoid pin risk. But then again,
the arbs try to pay 19.75 for the above box, and
they try to sell it at 20.25. They often do this by trading the components quickly and separately. They do this in large volume, so their costs are low. Their unit profit might be small, but once the position is on, it is almost risk free.

Boxes are seldom
traded except as
closing positions
between market-makers

With contracts that have early exercise, in-the-money boxes often trade for more than the difference between the strike prices. The options that are in-the-money have early exercise premium, and the option that is deeper in-the-money has more. Most often, the in-the money put will have extra value because it contains the right to exercise to cash.

Early exercise premium raises the value of the boxes in the OEX and other American-style options as well.

On contracts that are paid for up front, and where there is no early exercise, the purchase of a box results in cash tied up. The box therefore trades at a discount equal to the difference between strikes minus the cost of carry through expiration. At expiration the value of the box is transferred at exactly the difference between strikes. Examples of this are FTSE options contract, and the SPX European-style options on the S&P 500 which are traded at the CBOE.

Cost of carry on boxes

To be precise, a box that has no early exercise premium will always trade at a discount equal to its cost of carry. For example, an at-the-money 20-point box in Marks and Spencer above, with 75 DTE, at a short-term interest rate of 1 per cent, will trade at $20 - (20 \times 0.01 \times 75/365) = 19.96$.

The sale of a box through cash-traded European-style options is often used as a means of short-term finance. If a trading house wanted to borrow money then it could sell the above 20-point box at 19.96. Cash would be credited to their account until expiration, and then the house would pay 20 to close the position. Commissions and exchange fees would effectively raise the borrowing rate to more than 1 per cent. Only firms that trade in large size and that benefit from low costs can take advantage of this opportunity, and most often they prefer to borrow and lend in the cash markets.

23

Conclusions

Recent problems

Recent problems in a major US insurance firm, a major British oil company and a UK bank have highlighted the lack of understanding of risk at the highest levels. If you have read the book assiduously, then you probably have more risk awareness than their CEOs.

In the case of the insurance firm it appears – and I can't say for certain – that they increased the volume of their derivatives exposure in order to maintain their profit level. Fair enough. But they also increased their leverage. They tried to apply the manufacturing model to derivatives. A disaster waiting to happen.

In the case of the oil company, it appears that in order to cut costs, they outsourced to a well drilling firm that gave them the cheapest bid. The outsourcing firm could only give the cheapest bid because they would not expend on physical risk provisions, i.e. hardware to control a well blow-up. Another disaster waiting to happen.

In the case of the bank, the CEO had had a previous success in taking over another bank. This gave him the false confidence to attempt a takeover of second bank. But he was in competition with a third bank. They both tried to outbid each other. Here was a classic trader's mistake: hubris ... The CEO's ego became inflated by his previous success. He then assumed that he could do no wrong. But when confronted by his risk manager, who had concerns about due diligence, what did he do? He fired his risk manager. He then outbid his rival and, lo and behold, it turns out that he bought a toxic asset. It was soon revealed that the takeover bank had a corrupt balance sheet. Unable to finance the takeover bank's liabilities, the CEO's bank was brought to bankruptcy.

In the end, the central government, with its power of taxation, rescued him and his firm.

The lesson is that the market punishes hubris. So beware of reading this book: it may lead to you being fired.

One thing they all had in common: they cut costs while increasing risk. In other words, they didn't buy the put, or worse, they sold the put. These firms, like many others, seem to think that you can save money by squeezing out precautions. They made the same mistakes that we made when options were first listed at the Chicago Board of Trade many years ago.

These are classic risk problems and classic options problems, and unless future players understand the trade-off between long-term risk and short-term profit, they will happen again and again.

Congratulations

If you have read this book in its entirety, I offer you my congratulations. You are willing to make the effort needed to become a serious trader. You now know what options are and what they do. You also know how to create spreads, and you have a basic understanding of volatility. Most importantly, you have an understanding of risk. You understand how the variables interact and how to employ those variables that suit your outlook. Before you place your hard-earned capital at risk, here is some advice:

- Learn the fundamentals cold. Even those of us who have been in the business a while are sometimes surprised by options behaviour because no two markets, and their effects on options, are alike. Never stop increasing your knowledge.
- Paper trade before you place capital at risk. Take a position based on closing prices and follow it daily or weekly. Do this with straight calls and puts, and do it with spreads.
- Begin trading with 1×1s, butterflies and condors, in order to minimise skew and implied volatility risk.
- When you first start to trade, keep your size to a mimimum, even if this makes your commision rates high. If this annoys your broker, offer to increase your size when your trading becomes profitable, or find another broker.

■ When you first start to trade, *do not sell more options contracts than you are long*. Selling naked options can take you to the door of the poorhouse.

■ Trade options on underlyings that you know, and improve your knowledge by studying the history of the underlyings and the options on them. Many data vendors, including all exchanges, have price history.

■ After you have traded the basic spreads, study volatility. This is the elusive variable, and in the end this is what options are really about. Volatility data is also available from data vendors and exchanges.

■ Trade options with a durational outlook; when the duration has ended, take your profits or cut your losses. Likewise, trade with a price objective; when the objective is reached (it often happens sooner than you expect), close your position and don't hope for unrealistic profits. Before you open a position, establish a stop-loss level.

■ With straight calls and puts, discipline yourself by basing your options investment on the value of the underlying controlled, not on the amount of premium bought or sold.

■ Analyse your trades, both good and bad. What was your outlook at the time you opened the trade? How did the market change while the trade was outstanding? What were your reasons for closing the trade?

■ Analyse your reactions to trading. How did *you* respond when the trade was going your way or going against you? Did you make reasonable decisions, or did you make decisions based on hope or fear?

■ The major benefit of trading options is that you can limit your risk. Use this benefit by choosing a risk-limiting strategy. You will then trade with confidence.

There is obviously much more to be said about options in terms of theory and in terms of trading. *The Financial Times Guide to Options*, and its precursor, *Options Plain and Simple*, are intended to be a practical guide to the most common strategies tradable under the most common market circumstances. Markets, of course, defy commonality, but their many variations occur again and again.

This book should be considered basic; in other words, able to impart fundamental awareness, not simply transmit rules. You may wish to read much of this book again. One head of options at a London spread-betting firm has read *Options Plain and Simple, three times*. By rereading this book, discussing its ideas with your financial adviser and following markets, the behaviour of options will become second nature to you. This will be the basis of sound and profitable trading.

If you have any comments or questions, I would like to know. Feel free to contact me at lenny@lennyjordan.com. I'll try to include your feedback in the next edition of this book.

A final word on trading

And so what's trading like? A few years ago I was a trainer for a London firm that sponsored day-traders in futures contacts on Euribor, Bund, FTSE, etc. I also gave training lectures. One of our new traders was a female graduate who was very astute. After one of my lectures she walked up to me and asked, 'C'mon now Lenny, what's it take to be a good trader?' I answered, 'Suppose your dad gave you a hundred pounds. Could you walk in and out of Harrods without spending a penny?' She gave me a defiant stare and said, 'My daddy gives me two hundred pounds!' This charming young woman did not make it as a trader.

May probability be on your side.

Questions and answers

Chapter 1 questions

Here are a few questions on call contracts. Don't expect to know all the answers. The answers are given, so you should treat the questions as additional examples from which to learn.

1 *GE is currently trading at 18.03, and the April 19 calls are trading at 0.18.*

(a) If you buy one of these calls at the current market price, what is your break-even level?

(b) What is the maximum amount that you can gain?

(c) What is the maximum amount that you can lose?

(d) Answer questions a–c for a sale of this call.

(e) The multiplier for this options contract is $100, or 100 shares. What is the cash value of this call?

(f) Write a profit/loss table for a buy of this call at expiration.

(g) Graph the profit/loss for a buy of this call at expiration.

(h) Answer questions f–g for a sale of this call

(i) If at April expiration, GE closes at 19.00 what is the profit/loss for the call buyer and for the call seller?

(j) If at April expiration, GE closes at 19.10 what is the profit/loss for the call buyer and for the call seller?

2 *This is a question to get you thinking about risk and return.*

Unilever is currently trading at 553p (£5.53)[1], and the March 550 calls are trading at 74p (£0.74). This year, Unilever shares have ranged from 346.75 to 741. You foresee a continued volatile market and you think that food producers will attract buying interest as defensive investments. Because of market volatility you hesitate to risk an outright purchase of shares, and you would like to compare the risk of a call purchase.

(a) If you buy one of these calls at the current market price, what is your break-even level?

(b) What is the maximum amount that you can gain?

(c) What is the maximum amount that you can lose?

(d) Answer questions a–c for a sale of this call.

(e) The multiplier for this options contract is £1,000, or 1,000 shares. What is the cash value of one of these calls?

(f) If at March expiry Unilever closes at 650, what is the profit/loss for the call buyer, and for the call seller?

(g) What is the amount of capital at risk for the call buyer versus the buyer of 1,000 shares? Calculate the difference.

(h) If by March Unilever has retraced to its former low, what would be the amount lost on buying the shares versus buying the call? Calculate the difference.
Calculate the risk/risk ratio.

(i) If by March of next year Unilever has rallied to its former high, what would be the amount gained on buying the shares versus buying the call?
Calculate the difference.
Calculate the return/return ratio.

(j) Looking at the above risk scenario h), and the above return scenario i), compare the risk/return ratios of the shares position versus the call position.
This is just one method of accessing risk/return. The point is that you do need to have a method.

---

[1] A recent price of Unilever is 1961p. If you wish, you can substitute another share at this price level. Examples like this are why this book is used in university courses.

3 *In the UK, the FTSE-100 share index is currently trading at 5133, and the December 5300 call is trading at 253. Assume that you are a large unit trust, and if you miss a year-end rally, your investors will be disappointed. You could buy a basket of all the stocks in the index for a cost of £51,330, or you could take a long futures position with an exposure of £51,330. Lately the market has been volatile, however, and you don't want the downside risk.*

(a) If you buy one of these calls at the current market price, what is your break-even level?

(b) What is the maximum amount that you can gain?

(c) What is the maximum amount that you can lose?

(d) Answer questions a–c for a sale of this call.

(e) The multiplier for this options contract is £10. What is the cash value of one of these calls?

(f) This year, the trading range of the FTSE-100 index has been 4648.7 to 6179. If the market retraces part of its recent gains, at what level would the retracement equal the cost of the call?

(g) Write a profit/loss table at expiry for a *sale* of this call with the FTSE in a range of 5000 to 6000 at intervals of 100.

(h) Write a graph at expiry for a sale of this call with the FTSE in a range of 5000 to 6000 at intervals of 100.

4 *March soybeans are currently trading at 573.75 and the March 575 calls are trading at 22.75.*

(a) If you buy one of these calls at the current market price, what is your break-even level?

(b) What is the maximum amount that you can gain?

(c) What is the maximum amount that you can lose?

(d) Answer questions a–c for a sale of this call.

(e) The multiplier for this options contract is $50. What is the cash value of one of these calls?

(f) Write a profit/loss table for a buy of this call at expiration, which will be in February.

(g) Graph the expiration profit/loss for a buy of this call.

(h) If at March expiration, which is in February, the March futures contract settles at 590, what is the profit/loss for the call buyer and the call seller?

Chapter 1 answers

1 (a) 19.18

(b) unlimited

(c) 0.18

(d) 19.18, 0.18, unlimited

(e) $18

(f)

GE	18.00	18.50	19.00	19.18	19.50	20.00	20.50	21.00
Cost of call	−0.18 ---							
Value of call at expiration	0	0	0	0.18	0.50	1.00	1.50	2.00
Profit/loss	−0.18	−0.18	−0.18	0	0.32	0.82	1.32	1.82

(g)

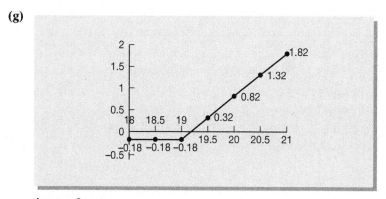

Answer 2g

(h)

GE	18.00	18.50	19.00	19.18	19.50	20.00	20.50	21.00
Income from call	0.18 ---							
Value of call at expiration	0	0	0	0.18	0.50	1.00	1.50	2.00
Profit/loss	0.18	0.18	0.18	0	−0.32	−0.82	−1.32	−1.82

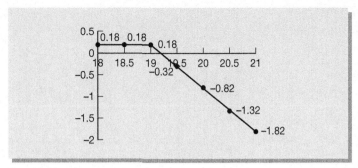

Answer 2h

(i) The call expires worthless: 0.18 loss for the buyer; 0.18 profit for the seller.

(j) Value of call is price of stock minus strike price minus cost of call, or 19.10 – 19.00 – 0.18 = –0.08: Loss for buyer; profit for seller.

2 (a) 624

   (b) unlimited

   (c) 74

   (d) 624, 74, unlimited

   (e) 740

   (f) Price of stock at expiration minus strike price, 650 – 550 = 100, or expiration value of call
   100 minus traded value of call at 74 = 26
   0.26 × contract multiplier of £1,000 = £260 profit for buyer, loss for seller

   (g) £740 versus £5,530, or a difference of £4,790

   (h) 553 – 346.75 = 206.25 loss for the shares, versus 74 loss for the call
   206.25 – 74 = 132.25 greater loss for the shares
   206.25 ÷ 74 = 2.79, or risk of 2.79 with shares purchase per 1.00 risk with call purchase

   (i) 741 – 553 = 188 gain for the shares, versus 741 – 624 = 117 gain for the call
   188 – 117 = 71 greater gain for the shares
   188 ÷ 117 = 1.61 or return of 1.61 shares per 1.00 return with call

   (j) Shares risk/return = 206.25 ÷ 188 = 1.10 = risk of 1.10 to return of 1.00. Call risk/return = 74 ÷ 117 = 0.63 to return of 1.00

3 **(a)** 5553

  (b) unlimited

  (c) 253

  (d) 5553, 253, unlimited

  (e) £2,530

  (f) 5133 – 253 = 4880

  (g) Answer 3g

FTSE at expiry	5000	100	5200	5300	5400	5500	5600	5700	5800	5900	6000
Income from call	253	--------									
Value of call at expiry	0	0	0	0	–100	–200	–300	–400	–500	–600	–700
Profit/ loss	253	253	253	253	153	53	–47	–147	–247	–347	–447

  (h) See answer 3h on next page

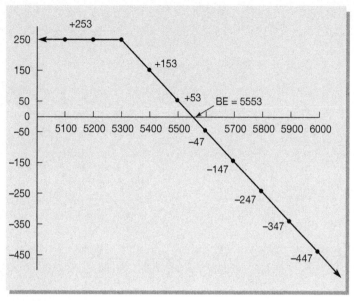

Answer 3h

4 (a) 597.75

(b) unlimited

(c) 22.75

(d) 597.75, 22.75, unlimited

(e) $1,137,50

(f)

March soybeans	550	575	600	625	650	675	700
Cost of call	−22.75						
Value of call at expiration	0	0	25	50	75	100	125
Profit/loss	−22.75	−22.75	+2.25	+27.25	+52.25	+77.25	+102.25

(g)

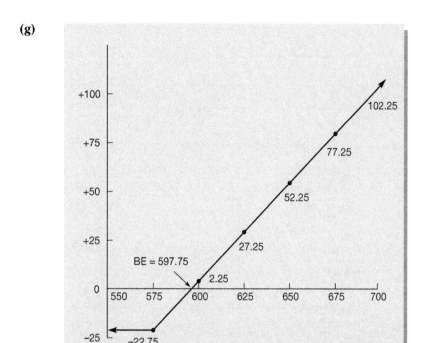

Answer 4g

(h) Futures price at expiration minus strike price of call equals
590 – 575 = 15, or expiration value of call
Traded price of call minus expiration value of call, 22.75 – 15 = 7.75
7.75 × contract multiplier of $50 = $387.50 profit for seller, loss for buyer

Chapter 2 questions

Here are some questions on puts, and on the difference between calls and puts. Again, don't expect to know all the answers.

1 *What is the similarity and difference between:*

    (a) a long call and a short put?

    (b) a long put and a short call?

2 *A long call provides downside protection, while a long put provides upside protection. True or false? Why or why not?*

3 *Suppose your outlook calls for a more extensive decline in GE. With the stock at 18.03, the April 17.00 puts are offered at 0.21.*

    (a) If you buy one of these puts at the current market price, what is your break-even level?

    (b) What is the maximum amount that you can gain?

    (c) What is the maximum amount that you can lose?

    (d) Answer questions a–c for a sale of this put.

    (e) If you sell one of these puts at the current market price, what is the potential effective purchase price of the stock at expiration?

    (f) The multiplier for this options contract is $100. What is the cash value of one of these puts?

    (g) If at April expiration GE closes at 16.50, what is the profit for the put buyer, and what is the loss for the put seller?

    (h) Write a profit/loss table for a sale of this put at expiration.

    (i) Draw a graph of the expiration profit/loss for a sale this put.

4 *Boeing is currently trading at 74.16, and the June 70.00 puts are trading at 1.51.*

    (a) If you buy one of these puts at the current market price, what is your break-even level?

    (b) What is the maximum amount that you can gain?

    (c) What is the maximum amount that you can lose?

    (d) Answer questions a–c for a sale of this put.

    (e) If you sell one of these puts at the current market price, what is the potential effective purchase price of the stock at expiration?

    (f) The multiplier for this options contract is $100. What is the cash value of one of these puts?

(g) If at May expiration Boeing closes at 30, what is the profit for the put buyer, and what is the loss for the put seller?

(h) Write a profit/loss table for a sale of this put at expiration.

(i) Draw a graph of the expiration profit/loss for a sale this put.

5 *This question involves put options on the Chicago Board of Trade (CBOT) Treasury Bond futures contract. The futures contract trades in ticks of 32 per full futures point, i.e. $1.00 = {}^{32}/_{32}$. The options contract, however, trades in ticks of 64 per full futures point, i.e. $1.00 = {}^{64}/_{64}$. An options tick is simply half the value of a futures tick. Both contracts have a multiplier of $1,000, therefore ${}^1/_{32} = \$31.25$, and of course, ${}^1/_{64} = \$15.625$.*

December Bonds are currently trading at 129.26 $(129^{26}/_{32})$, and the December 129 puts are currently trading at 0.58 $({}^{58}/_{64})$. (A 129 price for bonds is possible during a flight to quality.)

(a) What is the value of the December 129 put?

(b) If you buy one of these puts at the current market price, what is your break-even level? [The formula is the same for all put options, i.e. break-even = strike price minus price of put. Here, you must first convert the futures strike price from a decimal listing into the equivalent number of options ticks. Next you subtract the put price from the converted strike price. Then you reconvert the break-even level into a decimal listing. The process is tedious but not difficult.]

(c) What is the maximum amount that you can gain?

(d) What is the maximum amount that you can lose?

(e) Answer questions a–c for a sale of this put.

(f) If you sell one of these puts at the current market price, what is the potential effective purchase price of the December futures contract at expiration?

6 *At Euronext LIFFE, British Airways is currently trading at 233.5p (£2.335), and the June 220 puts are trading at 9.75 (0.0975). The contracts are for 1,000 shares, so the cash outlay for them would be £2335 and £97.5. This year's range for British Airways is 174 to 255.5. The airlines sector is currently under pressure because the global ecomomy is sluggish and the price of oil is rising. The economic indicators are looking positive, however, and you think that BA would be a profitable medium-term investment. However, the shares are in a zone of technical resistance and an outright purchase risks a short-term decline. You want to compare a purchase of shares to a sale of the June 220 put.*

(a) If you sell the put, what is your potential purchase price?

(b) If you bought the shares at 233.50, at what level would an increase in their price by April equal the income from the put?

(c) Suppose you sell the put instead of buying the shares. Consider that if BA reaches 280 that would signal a technical break out. What is the potential savings from a purchase of shares if assigned on the put compared to the potential opportunity cost of not buying the shares, should BA reach 280, by June expiry?

(d) Suppose you sell the put and place a stop order to buy the shares at 280. BA rallies to 280 and you are filled on your stop order at that price. Your put eventually expires worthless. What is the effective purchase price of the shares?

(e) If you buy 1,000 shares at the current market price of 233.5 and you sell one June 220 put at 9.75, what is your average cost if the shares decline and you are assigned on the put?

Chapter 2 answers

1 (a) Both are a potential purchase or a potential long position. The long call has the right, while the short put has the obligation.

(b) Both are a potential sale or a potential short position. The long put has the right, while the short call has the obligation.

2 *True, because a long call is a limited risk alternative to the purchase of an underlying, while a long put is a limited risk alternative to the sale of an underlying.*

3 (a) $17.00 - 0.21 = 16.79$

(b) 16.79 minus the value of the stock at expiration (in theory, 16.79)

(c) 0.21

(d) 16.79, 0.21, 16.79

(e) $17.00 - 0.21 = 16.79$

(f) $0.21 \times \$100 = \$21$

(g) $17.00 - 16.50 - 0.21 = 0.29$

(h)

	15.50	16.00	16.50	16.79	17.00	17.50	18.00
Cost of put	0.21	----	----	----	----	----	----
Value of put at expiration	1.50	1.00	0.50	0.21	0	0	0
P/L	1.29	0.79	0.29	0	–0.21	–0.21	–0.21

(i)

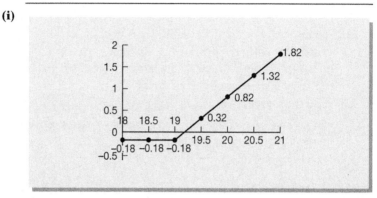

Answer 3i

4 **(a)** 68.49

(b) 68.49

(c) 1.51

(d) 68.49, 1.51, 68.49

(e) Obligation to buy stock at the strike price minus income from put: 70.00 – 1.51 = 68.49

(f) $151

(g) Strike price minus price of stock at expiration minus value of put: 70.00 – 65.00 – 1.51 = 3.49

(h)

	55.00	60.00	65.00	68.49	70.00	75.00	80.00
Income from put	1.51	----	----	----	----	----	----
Value of put at expiration	15.00	10.00	5.00	1.51	0.00	0.00	0.00
P/L	–13.49	–8.49	–3.49	0	1.51	1.51	1.51

(i)

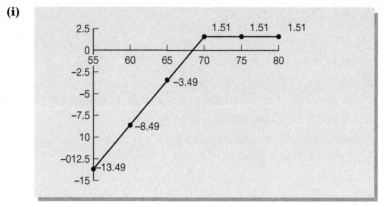

Answer 4i

5 **(a)** $^{58}/_{64} \times \$1,000 = \$906.25$

(b) $129.00 = 128^{32}/_{32} = 128^{64}/_{64}$, or strike price in options ticks $128^{64}/_{64} - {}^{58}/_{64} = 128^{6}/_{64} = 128^{3}/_{32} = 128.03$, or break-even level

(c) 128.03

(d) 0.58

(e) 128.03, 0.58, 128.03

(f) Obligation to buy futures contract at strike price minus income from put, or $129.00 - 0.58 = 128^{6}/_{64} = 128.03$ futures price

6 **(a)** Strike price minus income from put: $220 - 9.75 = 210.25$

(b) Shares purchase price plus income from put: $233.5 + 9.75 = 243.25$

(c) $233.5 - 210.25 = 23.25$ potential savings: $280 - 233.5 = 46.5$ potential opportunity cost

(d) Cost of shares minus income from put: $280 - 9.75 = 270.25$. But remember that before expiry your put contract is still outstanding, and if BA retraces to below 220, you will be obligated to buy 1,000 shares. If you don't want to make an additional purchase, then buy back your put as soon as you buy your shares. This will raise the effective purchase price of your shares.

(e) Cost of purchase via put is strike price minus income from put, or $220 - 9.75 = 210.25$. Average cost of shares is $(233.5 + 210.25) \div 2 = £221.875$.

Chapters 3 questions

1 *If GE is trading at 18.03, the 17.00 puts and the 19.00 calls are both out-of-the-money. True or false?*

2 *At the NYSE-LIFFE, British Airways is trading at 233.5. The June 235 calls are quoted at 12.75, and the June 235 puts are quoted at 16.75. What are the intrinsic and time values of the options?*

3 *Parity options contain approximately equal amounts of intrinsic and time premiums. True or false?*

4 *Why do at-the-money options contain the most time premium?*

5 *Which option or options have the most accelerated time decay as they approach expiration?*

   (a) In-the-money option

   (b) At-the-money option

   (c) Out-of-the-money option

6 *Which options always require margin?*

   (a) Long puts

   (b) Short calls

   (c) Short puts

   (d) Long calls

7 *Concerning options on stocks or shares, which of these statements are true?*

   (a) The short-term interest rate is added to the price of a call.

   (b) The dividends until expiration are added to the price of a call.

   (c) The dividends until expiration are subtracted from the price of a put.

   (d) The short-term interest rate is subtracted from the price of a put.

8 *Which positions are potentially long the underlying, and which positions are potentially short the underlying?*

   (a) Long calls

   (b) Short puts

   (c) Long puts

   (d) Short calls

9 *You are short one GE 19.00 put at expiration, and GE has closed at 17.50. Do you exercise, or will you be assigned? What is your resulting position and at what price?*

10 *It is the third week in November, and the December Corn options contracts have expired. You are short one December 280 Corn call, and the December futures contract has settled at 284.25. Do you exercise, or will you be assigned? What is your resulting position, if any, and at what price?*

11 *You are long one OEX 520 call at expiration and the closing index price is 529.45. Do you exercise, or will you be assigned? What is your resulting position, if any, and at what price?*

12 *At NYSE-LIFFE, you are short one FTSE 5525 put at expiration and the closing index price is 5479.6. Do you exercise, or will you be assigned? What is your resulting position, if any, and at what price?*

13 *You have previously sold naked (beware!) one XYZ May 80 call at 3.35. It is now three weeks until expiration and the call is worth 0.28. The stock is at 74.16, and it has been ranging from 72.50 to 77.00 during the past two weeks, and you expect it to continue to do so for the foreseeable future. You would like to continue to collect time decay. What do you do?*

14 *A European styled call can only be exercised when it is in-the-money. True or false?*

15 *Early exercise premium is a minor component of all in-the-money American styled put options. True or false?*

Chapter 3 answers

1 *True.*

2 *Call, no intrinsic; time value is 12.75. Put intrinsic is 235 − 233.5 = 1.5; time value is 16.75 − 1.5 = 15.25.*

3 *False; parity options contain only intrinsic value or premium.*

4 *Because they are the only options that hedge the underlying for equal amounts of upside and downside movement.*

5 *All have accelerated time decay, but the at-the-money options accelerate more quickly because they contain the most amount of time premium.*

6 *b and c, all short options require margin.*

7 **(a)** True

   (b) False

   (c) False

   (d) True

8 **(a)** Long

   (b) Long

   (c) Short

   (d) Short

9 *You will be assigned a purchase of 100 shares at 19.00*

10 *You will be assigned one short December futures contract at 280.*

11 *Your clearing firm will exercise for you, and you will receive the cash differential between the index price and the strike price of the option: 529.45 – 520 = 9.45. You have no remaining position. Remember the contract multiplier is $100, therefore you receive $945.*

12 *You will be assigned, and you will pay the cash differential between the strike price and the index price: 5525 – 5479.6 = 45.4. You have no remaining position. Remember that the multiplier is £10, therefore you pay £454.*

13 *You have a profit. You don't want the risk of a large, unforeseen move by the stock to the upside, which could result in a loss and an unwanted assignment to a short stock position. You also want to avoid pin risk. You should soon buy this call back. If you want to continue with a short call position, you could sell the November–December or November–January time spread, thereby rolling your short call position to a more distant month.*

14 *False; there is no early exercise possible for European options.*

15 *False; stock and stock index puts have significantly greater early exercise premium than puts on futures contracts because they can be exercised to gain cash and, therefore, interest.*

Chapter 4 questions

1 *What is the difference between the historical and the implied volatility?*

2 *Suppose that the S&P 500 index has just made a 5 per cent downside correction. If the implied volatility of the near-term at-the-money put has increased, then the implied volatility of the near-term at-the-money call has decreased. True or false?*

3 *The implied volatility always adjusts to the 20-day historical volatility within several days. True or false?*

4 **(a)** A five-day historical volatility gives a more accurate indication of an underlying contract's volatility than a 30-day historical volatility. True or false?

　　(b) What do these different readings tell you?

5 *The December US 30-Year Treasury Bond Futures contract is currently trading at 129.01. The December 129.00 calls, with 60 days till expiration, are trading at 1.43 with an implied volatility of 8 per cent. Bonds suddenly break to 128.00 on the monthly employment report, but gradually retrace throughout the day to settle at 129.01. The settlement price of the December 129 calls is 1.49.*

　　What has happened to the implied volatility, and what does this tell you about the historical volatility? What market explanation could you give for this?

6 *Referring to question 5, above, if an options trader expects the implied volatility trend to continue, he will most likely do which of the following? Why?*

　　(a) Buy calls and sell puts.

　　(b) Buy puts.

　　(c) Sell calls and buy puts.

　　(d) Buy calls and buy puts.

7 *The S&P 500 index has closed at 1085.93, up 17.84. What is a layman's estimate for the day's annualised volatility of the index?*

8 *You note that the daily volatility in question 4, above, is about average for the past five days. You also note that the current, at-the-money implied volatility is 35 per cent. What are these figures telling you?*

9 *During the course of several weeks, the average day-to-day price range of Shell Transport has been increasing. Is the ten-day historical volatility of Shell Transport increasing or decreasing?*

10 *Last night the FTSE-100 index settled at 4800, and this morning, after an overnight fall in the US market, it has opened at 4400. The front-month* *at-the-money options are bid with an implied volatility of 70 per cent (October 1997). Are you a seller?* (Hint: First, estimate the volatility of the index at the opening, then compare it to the implied volatility of the options.)

Chapter 4 answers

1   *The historical volatility is an average of a set of daily annualised volatilities of the underlying, while the implied volatility is an indication, by the price of an option, of the historical volatility expected through expiration.*

2   *False. Both implieds have increased the same amount because they are at the same strike price. Both options hedge the same expected range of underlying price movement.*

3   *False. The two volatilities can differ for months at time.*

4   **(a)**   False. The five-day volatility only gives a more recent indication. A 30-day volatility gives a better indication of the volatility trend.

     (b)   The five-day can lead the 30-day if the short-term trend continues. But if the five-day is a short-term aberration based on a special event that has no long-term consequences, then the volatility will revert to the 30-day.

5   *The implied has increased (to 8.25 per cent), which indicates that the near-term historical volatility is expected to increase. The options market may indicate that there are components in the employment report that will continue to unsettle the futures market.*

6   *The trader is likely to do b or d, i.e. any combination of buying calls and puts. He is buying the volatility trend, which is increasing. This is comparable to a trader in the stock market who buys stocks because his outlook is for increased prices.*

7   *1085.93 – 17.84 = 1068.09 was yesterday's closing price*
17.84/1068.09 = 0.0167, or 1.67%
1.67 × 16 = 26.72% estimate of day's annualised volatility

8   *One possibility is that the options have yet to account for a decrease in the historical volatility, and that they may be overvalued. Another possibility is that the options are anticipating a near-term increase in the historical volatility, and if so, they are correctly valued.*

9 *Ten-day historical volatility is increasing*
4800 – 4400 = 400 points change at opening
400/4800 = 0.0833, or 8.33% price change
8.33% × 16 = 133% volatility of index

The options, at 70 per cent, are extremely undervalued. On the other hand, the implied volatility is at an exceptionally high level and it may average down during the next few days. You may not want to buy these options because of their high cost, but you certainly wouldn't go short them unless you are well capitalised.

10 *It's your choice.*

Chapter 5 questions

1 *State whether the following positions are equivalent to a long or short underlying position.*

(a) short call

(b) long put

(c) short put

(d) long call

2 *A 0.20 delta put decreases at 80 per cent of the underlying if the underlying moves up. True or false?*

3 *For a small upward move in the underlying a 0.50 delta call changes more than a 0.50 delta put, but for a small downward move in the underlying a 0.50 delta put changes more than a 0.50 delta call. True or false? Why or why not?*

4 *Given the following set of options with their deltas, what is the new price of each option if the underlying moves* up *by one point?*

Underlying	Option	Price	Delta	New price
Sainsbury	April 340 call	8.75	0.48	
Sainsbury	April 300 call	38.25	0.96	
December Corn	December 400 call	$5^3/_8$	0.28	
December Corn	December 380 put	$12^1/_2$	0.48	

5 *Given the following set of options with their deltas, what is the new price of each option if the underlying moves* down *by one point?*

Underlying	Option	Price	Delta	New price
FTSE-100	March 5700 put	199.5	0.48	
FTSE-100	March 4700 call	935.0	0.98	
IBM	January 120 call	2.5	0.25	
IBM	January 90 put	1	0.12	

6 *A 0.50 delta option has the same correlation with the underlying from 50 to 10 days until expiration. True or false? Why or why not?*

7 *Five long 0.20 delta calls have the same delta equivalence as five (long or short?) 0.20 delta puts.*

8 *A delta neutral hedge can be created with 20 short, 0.30 delta calls and how many long or short underlying contracts?*

9 *As time passes, the deltas of out-of-the-money calls and in-the-money puts both decrease. True or false?*

10 *Given the following position in March US Treasury Bond options, calculate the total delta for the position.* (Figures courtesy of pmpublishing.com.)

Long	Short	Option	Delta per option	Deltas per strike
5		March 128 call	0.51	
	2	March 124 call	0.75	
	10	March 132 call	0.27	
10		March 120 put	0.14	
	Total delta position			

(a) What is the equivalent futures position?

(b) How would you create a delta neutral hedge for the above options position?

11 *For the above example in US T-Bond options, the March futures contract is currently at 128.01 with 87 days until expiration. Suppose you are short two, March 124 calls. What is the probability of your being assigned two short futures contracts at expiration?*

Chapter 5 answers

1 **(a)** short underlying

(b) short underlying

(c) long underlying

(d) long underlying

2 *False, a 0.20 delta put decreases in price by 20 per cent for a small upwards move in the underlying.*

3 *False, they both change the same amount in either case. If the underlying moves up, the 0.50 delta call increases in value at half the rate of the underlying, while the 0.50 delta put decreases in value at half the rate of the underlying. If the underlying moves down, the call decreases while the put increases.*

4 *New price*

9.25 (rounded)

39.25

$5^5/_8$

12.00

5 *New price*

200

934.00

2.25

1.10

6 *True, a 0.50 delta, at-the-money option correlates the same with the underlying because its delta is not affected by time.*

7 *Short.*

8 *A delta neutral hedge is here created with six long underlying contracts assuming, as in most cases, that the options contract and the underlying contract have the same multiplier.*

9 *False. As time passes, the deltas of out-of-the-money calls decrease because they have less probability of becoming in-the-money, while the deltas of in-the-money puts increase because they have more probability of staying in-the-money.*

10 *Deltas per strike*

+2.55
−1.50
−2.70
−1.40
———
−3.05 Total delta position.

(a) Short three futures contracts.

(b) Buy, or go long, three futures contracts.

11 *75 per cent.*

Chapter 6 questions

1 *50 delta options in the same contract month have more gamma and theta than 0.80 delta options. True or false? Why?*

2 *Given the following options with their deltas and gammas, what is the approximate new delta if the underlying moves up by one point?*

Underlying	Option	Delta	Gamma	New delta
CBOT US T-Bonds	January 128 call	0.51	0.15	
CBOT US T-Bonds	January 125 put	0.14	0.08	
NYMEX Crude oil	Sep 83.00 call	0.36	0.05	
NYMEX Crude oil	Sep 83.00 put	0.64	0.05	

3 *Given the following options with their deltas and gammas, what is the approximate new delta if the underlying moves* down *by one point?*

Underlying	Option	Delta	Gamma	New delta
CBOT Corn	December 360 call	0.76	0.010	
CBOT Corn	December 380 put	0.48	0.013	
NYMEX Crude oil	Sep 74.00 call	0.64	0.040	
NYMEX Crude oil	Sep 74.00 put	0.36	0.040	

4 *Given the following options, which are expressed in ticks and whose multiplier is $50, and given their thetas expressed in dollars and cents, calculate the approximate new value of the options after seven days' time decay. Both options have 30 DTE.*

Underlying	Option	Value	Theta	New value
CBOT Corn	December 380 call	$12^{1}/_{2} \times \$50$	$11.5	
CBOT Corn	December 400 call	$5^{3}/_{8} \times \$50$	$5.5	

5 *High theta options have a greater probability of making a profit than low theta options. True or false? Why?*

6 **(a)** Referring to Tables 6.3 and 6.4, what is the percentage increase in gamma of the December 380 call from 90 to 30 DTE?

(b) What is the percentage increase in theta for this option over the same time period?

7 *What is the correlation between gamma and theta?*

8 *Is it possible to have positive gamma and positive theta? Why is this?*

Chapter 6 answers

1 *True, because at-the-money options always have the largest gamma and theta in any contract month.*

2 *New delta*

   0.66

   0.06

   0.41

   0.59

3 *New delta*

   0.75

   0.49

   0.60

   0.40

4 *New value*

   For the 380 call: $(12^1/_2 \times \$50) - (7 \times \$11.5) = \$544.50$

   For the 400 call: $(5^3/_8 \times \$50) - (7 \times 10) = \$198.75$

5 *False, because there is no correlation between theta and profit/loss. High theta options, those with 0.50 deltas are more likely to expire in-the-money than low theta options with 0.20 deltas, but their greater time premium, and therefore their greater theta, is a fair exchange for this.*

6 **(a)** $(0.013 - 0.008)/0.013 = 38\%$

   (b) $(11.5 - 6.65)/6.65 = 73\%$

7 *Increased gamma correlates to increased theta.*

8 *Not possible, because positive gamma indicates that the options position profits from market movement, while positive theta indicates that the options position profits from market stasis.*

Chapter 7 questions

1   *A short call position has negative vega, and therefore it takes a loss from an increase in the implied volatility. True or false?*

2   **(a)** Given the following OEX options, which have a contract multiplier of $100, what is their new value both in dollars and rounded into ticks if the implied increases by 3 percentage points? The December OEX is currently at 590.00, and the January OEX is currently at 592.75.

Option	Option value	DTE	Implied	Vega	New value
December 590 call	10.5	23	17.82	0.60	
December 610 call	2.4	23	15.12	0.40	
January 590 call	19.1	51	20.21	0.90	
January 610 call	8.8	51	17.80	0.80	

   (b) If the implied increases by 3 percentage points, which of the above options gains the most in percentage terms?

3   *Increased implied volatility leads to increased vegas. True or false? Why?*

4   *In the example in question 2, the January at-the-money implied volatility is 20 per cent, and the range of the OEX implied volatility during the past year is 18 per cent to 25 per cent. In dollar terms, what is the vega risk/return ratio for a position that is short ten of the January 590 calls if the implied remains within its range during the next week?*

Chapter 7 answers

1   *True for both short calls and puts, because negative vega profits from decreased implied volatilities, while positive vega profits from increased implieds.*

2   **(a)** *New value*
       12.3, $1230
       3.6, $360
       21.8, $2180
       11.2, $1120

   (b) December 610 call increases 0.40 × 3/2.4 = 50 per cent.

3   *False, because only vegas of out-of- and in-the-money options increase with an increase in the implied. At-the-money options vegas remain practically unchanged.*

4   *The simple answer is a vega risk of = $^5/_2$ 2.5. An answer that better communicates the amount at risk is as follows: vega equals 0.90, or $90; 2 × $90 = $180 reduction in one option's value if the implied decreases from 20 per cent to 18 per cent; 10 × $180 = $1,800 total potential vega return. 5 × $90 = $450 increase in one option's value if the implied increases from 20 per cent to 25 per cent; 10 × $450 = $4,500 total potential vega risk. R/R = $4,500/$1,800 = $2.50 potential risk for each potential return of $1.*

Chapter 8 questions

1 *Refer again to the Spider options prices in Table 8.1. Suppose you are bearish on the stock for the short term, and you wish to buy the June 111–109 put spread.*

  (a) What is the net debit in ticks and in dollars for this spread?

  (b) What is the maximum profit?

  (c) What is the maximum loss?

  (d) What is the break-even level?

  (e) What is the risk/return ratio?

  (f) The SPDR is currently at 115.22. In percentage terms, how much would the index need to retrace in order for the spread to break even?

  (g) Construct a table and draw a graph of the expiration profit/loss.

2 *At the LIFFE, Sainsbury is currently priced at 323p. The June 330 calls are priced at 7.75p, and the June 340 calls are priced at 4.75p. There are 30 days until expiry. Remember that the contract multiplier here is £1,000, so the value of the 330 calls is 0.0775 × £1,000 = £77.50, and that of the 340 calls is 0.0475 × £1,000, or £47.50.*

  (a) What is the cost of a going long one June 330–340 call spread?

  (b) What is the break-even level of the spread?

  (c) What is the maximum profit?

  (d) What is the maximum loss?

  (e) What is the risk/return ratio?

  (f) Construct a table and draw a graph of the profit/loss at expiry.

  (g) Now suppose you're a bear. Construct a table and draw a graph of the P/L at expiry for a *sell* of this call spread.

3 *In London, the FTSE-100 index is currently trading at 5422. Suppose you're bearish for the next several weeks, with a target of 5300 by December expiry. You would like to buy one December 5400 put, but the cost of 193p (£1,930) is too great, especially with accelerated time decay. You note that the 5300 puts are priced at 154p, and you decide to buy this put spread. The contract multiplier is £1,000.*

  (a) What is the cost of buying this spread, in ticks and in actual pounds sterling?

  (b) What is the break-even level?

  (c) What is the maximum profit?

(d) What is the maximum loss?

(e) What is the risk/return ratio?

4 *The following options on the Dow Jones Industrial Average trade at CBOE. Here, the value of the Dow Jones Index is divided by 100 in order to give the value of the index, known as DJX, on which the options are based. For example, if the Dow closes at 9056, the DJX settles at 90.56. You may think of the index as a stock with a price of 90.56, etc. The options contract multiplier is $100, so the December 91 call at 1.90 is worth 1.90 × $100, or $190.*

DJX at 90.56

30 days until December expiration

Strike	87	88	89	90	91	92	93	94
December calls			3.2	2.6	1.9	1.3	1.1	0.6
December puts	1	1.1	1.5	1.8	2.2			

(a) What is the break-even level for a purchase of one straight December 91 call?
What value of the Dow would this break-even level correspond to?
What is the break-even level for a purchase of one straight December 90 put?
What value of the Dow would this break-even level correspond to?

(b) Suppose you think that the Dow has topped out for the time being, and you anticipate a Christmas break, i.e. a correction of 3 per cent by December expiration. What index level would this correspond to?

(c) Which out-of-the-money put spread would completely cover this range?

(d) If you buy, or go long, this spread, what is your net debit in options ticks?

(e) What is your maximum profit?
What is your maximum loss?
What is your break-even level
What is your risk/return ratio?

(f) Suppose you believe in the Christmas rally. Your chart analysis, however, tells you that there is resistance at 9300 in the Dow. What out-of-the-money call spread could you buy?

(g) What is your debit for this spread?
What is the maximum profit?
What is the break-even level?
What is the maximum loss?
What is the risk/return ratio?

Chapter 8 answers

1 **(a)** 2.60 – 2.15 = 0.45 ticks; 0.45 × $100 = $45

(b) 111 – 109 – 0.45 = 1.55

(c) 0.45

(d) 111 – 0.45 = 110.55

(e) 0.45/1.55 = $29 at risk for each potential return of $1.00, or 1/3

(f) 115.22 – 110.55 = 4.67; 4.67/115.22 = 4%

(g)

SPDR	107.00	108.00	109.00	110.00	110.55	111.00	112.00	113.00
Spread debit	–0.45	----	----	----	----	----	----	----
Value of spread at expiration	2.00	2.00	2.00	1.00	0.45	0.00	0.00	0.00
Profit/loss	1.55	1.55	1.55	0.55	0	–0.45	–0.45	–0.45

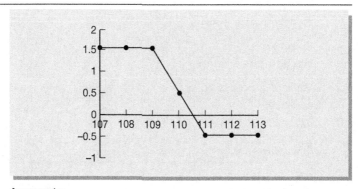

Answer 1g

2 (a) 7.75p – 4.75p = 3p; 0.03 × £1,000 = £30

(b) 330 + 3 = 333

(c) [340 – 330] – 3 = 7

(d) 3

(e) $^3/_7$ = 43p at risk for each £1 of potential return (risking 1 to make 2.33)

(f)

Sainsburys	below	320	330	333	340	350	above
Cost of spread	–3	–3	–3	–3	–3	–3	–3
Value of spread at expiration	0	0	0	3	10	10	10
P/L	–3	–3	–3	0	7	7	7

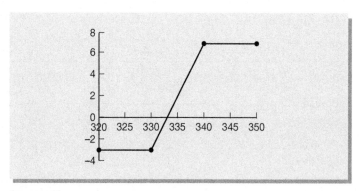

Answer 2f

(g)

Sainsburys	below	320	330	333	340	350	above
Credit from spread	3	3	3	3	3	3	3
Value of spread at expiration	0	0	0	–3	–10	–10	–10
P/L	3	3	3	0	–7	–7	–7

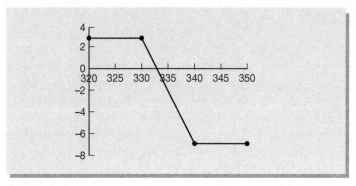

Answer 2g

3 (a) 193 − 154 = 39p; 0.39 × £1,000 = £390

(b) 5400 − 39 = 5361

(c) [5400 − 5300] − 39 = 61

(d) 39

(e) 39 ÷ 61 = 64p at risk for each potential return of £1 (£1 at risk for each return of £1.56)

4 (a) 91 + 1.9 = 92.90; 9290; 90 − 1.80 = 88.20; 8820

(b) 90.56 × 0.03 = 2.72; 90.56 − 2.72 = 87.84

(c) Long December 90–87 put spread

(d) 1.8 − 1 = 0.8

(e) 3 − 0.8 = 2.2 = $220; $80; 90 − 0.8 = 89.20; 0.8/2.2 = 0.36 for 1 (2.8/1)

(f) December 91–93 call spread

(g) 1.9 − 1.1 = 0.8 = $80; 2 − 0.8 = 1.2 = $120; 91 + 0.8 = 91.8; $80; 80/120 = 0.67 for 1, or 1.5 for 1

Chapter 9 questions

1 *It's now the third week in November, and the global stock markets have overcome their annual October nervousness and have begun to rally. You want to take a bullish position because you expect the rally to continue until Christmas. The S&P 500 index is currently at 1152.61, but your technical analysis tells you that there is resistance between 1180 and 1200. You think that the index will eventually meet resistance and settle at approximately 1200 for December expiration. You want to give your assessment a try, but you don't want to risk too much.*

   At the CBOE the following SPX options on the S&P 500 are trading at the following prices. The contract multiplier is $100. This is a European-style option, so there is no early exercise.

S&P index at 1152.61

December options with 30 days until expiration

Strike	1175	1200	1225
Call prices	17	7.5	2.5

(a) i)   What is the cost of the December 1175–1200, one by two call spread in ticks and in dollars?

ii)   What is the lower break-even level?

iii) At December expiration, what index level will give the maximum profit?

iv)   What is the maximum profit?

v)   What is the upper break-even level?

vi)   What is the maximum loss?

vii) What is your profit/loss if the index settles at 1212?

viii) If, one week after you open this position, i.e. with approximately three weeks till expiration, the index reaches 1200, how can you manage the risk?

(b) Suppose instead you want to pay more for your spread in exchange for less upside risk.

i)   What is the cost of the December 1175–1200–1225 call ladder in ticks and in dollars?

ii)   What is the lower break-even level?

iii) At December expiration, what index level will give the maximum profit?

iv)   What is the maximum profit?

v)   What is the upper break-even level?

vi)   What is the maximum loss?

vii) What is your profit/loss if the index settles at 1212?

(c) Perhaps you think the upside risk of the above two spreads is still too great, and you think the index might reach 1225 before settling into a range. You are willing to pay more to reduce your exposure, and to profit more from the upside potential.

    i)   What is the cost of the December 1175–1225, one by two call spread?

    ii)   What is the lower break-even level?

    iii) At December expiration, what index level will give the maximum profit?

    iv) What is the maximum profit?

    v)   What is the upper break-even level?

    vi) What is the maximum loss?

    vii) What is your profit/loss if the index settles at 1212?

2 *Because of perennial lawsuits in the US, you are bearish on British American Tobacco. The current price of the shares is 479.5p (£4.795).[1] You think that the shares are well supported below 400p, and you note the prices of the following January puts. (Remember, the contract multiplier is £1,000.)*

British American Tobacco at 479.5p

January puts with 70 days until expiry

Strike	390	420	460
January puts	4.5	10	22.5

(a) i)   What is the cost of the January 460–390, one by two put spread in ticks and in sterling?

    ii)   What is the upper break-even level?

    iii) At January expiry, what price level of the shares will give the maximum profit?

    iv) What is the maximum profit?

    v)   What is the lower break-even level?

    vi) What is the maximum loss?

    vii) At expiry, what is your profit/loss if the shares close at 370?

(b) Suppose you decide to be more economical, and you don't mind raising your lower break-even level.

    i)   What is the cost of the January 460–420–390 broken put ladder in ticks and in sterling?

    ii)   What is the upper break-even level?

---

[1] Another great example. Overlook the former prices, or substitute other shares, and you'll learn a great deal.

iii) At January expiry, what price level of the shares will give the maximum profit?

iv) What is the maximum profit?

v) What is the lower break-even level?

vi) What is the maximum loss?

vii) At expiry, what is your profit/loss if the shares close at 370?

(c) If instead you think that the maximum downside potential for the shares is approximately 420, you might buy the January 460–420, one by two put spread.

i) What is the cost of this spread in ticks and in sterling?

ii) What is the upper break-even level?

iii) At January expiry, what price level of the shares will give the maximum profit?

iv) What is the maximum profit?

v) What is the lower break-even level?

vi) What is the maximum loss?

vii) If, two weeks after you open this position, the shares are trading at 420, how can you manage the risk?

viii) At expiry, what is your profit/loss if the shares close at 370?

(d) For a favourable price you are willing to buy shares in British American Tobacco. This year's range for the shares is 584.5–329.5. You realise that by trading the above three spreads, you may be obligated to buy shares via your extra short put. What would be the effective purchase price of your shares with spreads a, b and c above?

Chapter 9 answers

1 (a) i) $17 - [2 \times 7.5] = 2$, or \$200

ii) $1175 + 2 = 1177$

iii) 1200

iv) $[1200 - 1175] - 2 = 23$

v) $1200 + 23 = 1223$

vi)   potentially unlimited

vii) $23 - 12 = 11$ profit

viii) Buy either one 1200 call, or one 1225 call.

(b) i) $17 - 7.5 - 2.5 = 7$, or \$700

ii) $1175 + 7 = 1182$

iii) 1200 to 1225

iv) $[1200 - 1175] - 7 = 18$

v) $1225 + 18 = 1243$

vi) potentially unlimited

vii) 18 profit

(c) i) 17 – [2 × 2.5] = 12, or $1200

ii) 1175 + 12 = 1187

iii) 1225

iv) [1225 – 1175] – 12 = 38

v) 1225 + 38 = 1263

vi) potentially unlimited

vii) [1212 – 1175] – 12 = 25 profit

2 (a) i) 22.5 – [2 × 4.5] = 13.5, or £135

ii) 460 – 13.5 = 446.5

iii) 390

iv) [460 – 390] – 13.5 = 56.5

v) 390 – 56.5 = 333.5

vi) 333.5, if the shares go to zero

vii) 56.5 – [390 – 370] = 36.5p profit

(b) i) 22.5 – 10 – 4.5 = 8, or £80

ii) 460 – 8 = 452

iii) 420 to 390

iv) [460 – 420] – 8 = 32

v) 390 – 32 = 358

vi) 358, if the shares go to zero

vii) 32 – [390 – 370] = 12p profit

(c) i) 22.5 – [2 × 10] = 2.5, or £25

ii) 460 – 2.5 = 457.5

iii) 420

iv) [460 – 420] – 2.5 = 37.5

v) 420 – 37.5 = 382.55

vi) 382.5, if the shares go to zero

vii) Buy one 420 put, or buy one 390 put.

viii) 37.5 – [420 – 370] = 12.5 p loss

(d) 390 – 56.5 = 333.5; 390 – 32 = 358; 420 – 37.5 = 382.5

Chapter 10 questions

1   *Can you see a freight train coming? Then you can trade the grain markets during the growing season. It's only May, and December Corn seems like a long way away, but you know that if it gets a full head of steam, it can roll over price levels. Besides, Corn, like other commodities, is now a mainstream investment supported by hedge funds, and even banks.*[1]

   On this day, December Corn settles at 380, or $3.80 per bushel, and you note the following set of December options. These options expire on the third Friday of November, and they are exercisable to the December futures contract. (If you want a grain silo, then take delivery.) Their contract multiplier is $50, which means that the $4 call, priced at 25, costs 25 × $50 = $1,250. Corn options trade in 1/8ths, so 1 = $^1/_8$, 2 = $^1/_4$, 3 = $^3/_8$, etc.

December Corn at 380

December options, with 176 days until expiration.

Strike	300	320	340	360	380	400	420	440	460	480	500
Calls				41'6	32'2	25	19'4	15'3	12'1	9'6	7'7
Puts	3'4	7'4	13'5	21'7	32'2	44'7					

(a) i)   What is the cost of the long $5 call, short $3 put combo in ticks and in dollars?

   ii)   At expiration, what is the upside break-even level?

   iii)   What is the maximum upside profit?

   iv)   What is the downside price of a potential long position in the December futures contract?

   v)   What is the potential downside loss?

   vi)   What is the profit/loss if the December futures contract settles between 420 and 440 at the expiration of the December options?

(b) Suppose, instead, your outlook for December Corn calls for a maximum price appreciation of $5.

   i)   What is the cost of the long $4.40–$5.00 call spread, short $3.20 put, three-way spread?

   ii)   At expiration, what is the upside break-even level?

   iii)   What is the maximum profit?

---

[1] As if your mortgage lender has any business speculating in commodities.

iv) What is the downside price of a potential long position in the December futures contract?

v)   What is the potential downside loss?

2 *The CBOT December Treasury Bond futures contract is currently trading at 129.26 (129²⁶/₃₂), which corresponds to a yield of 5.08 per cent. Lately, Treasuries have attracted buying interest through a flight to quality based on problems in emerging markets. You think that the bullishness has run its course, however, and you note the following December options. These options expire in the third week of November and they are exercisable to the December futures contract. As specified earlier, they trade in 64ths, and the contract multiplier is $1,000, which means that the cost of the 132 call is ³²/₆₄ × $1,000, or $500.*

December T-Bond futures at 129.26

December options with 22 days until expiration

Strike	128	129	130	131	132
Calls		1.46	1.12	0.50	0.32
Puts	0.37	0.58	1.24		

(a) You decide to buy the 129 put and sell the 132 call as a combo. What is the cost of your spread in ticks and in dollars?

(b) At expiration, what is the downside break-even level?

(c) What is the maximum downside profit?

(d) If the December futures contract rallies, what is the price of your potential short position?

(e) What is your potential upside loss?

(f) What is your profit/loss if the December futures contract is between 129 and 132 when the December options expire?

Chapter 10 answers

1 (a) i) $7^7/_8 - 3^1/_2 = 4^3/_8 × \$50 = \$218.75$

ii) $500 + 4^3/_8 = 504^3/_8$

iii) The full amount that the December futures contract rallies above $504^3/_8$.

iv) $300 + 4^3/_8 = 304^3/_8$

v)   The full amount that the December futures contract declines below 300, plus $4^3/_8$.

vi) $4^3/_8$ loss

(b) i) $[15^3/_8 - 7^7/_8] - 7^1/_2 = $ zero

ii) $4.40

iii) $[500 - 440] = 60 \times \$50 = \$3,000$

iv) $3.20 per bushel

v)   The full amount that the December futures contract declines below 320.

2 **(a)** $0.58 - 0.32 = 0.26;$ $^{26}/_{64} \times \$1,000 = \$406.25$

(b) 26 options ticks = 13 futures ticks. Futures trade in 32nds. 129.00 – 0.13 = 128.32 – 0.13 = 128.19

(c) The full amount that the December futures contract declines below 128.19.

(d) Futures price of 132.00 – 0.26 options ticks = 131.32 – 0.13 = 131.19

(e) The full amount that the December futures contract rallies above 132, plus the spread debit of 26 options ticks.

(f) Loss of spread debit, 26 options ticks

Chapter 11 questions

1   *Coca-Cola's earnings prospects are good, but the stock market as a whole has been bearish and volatile lately. The market could rally, or it could retrace to recent lows, dragging Coca-Cola along with it. The stock price is 52.67, and the following August options are listed with 90 days until expiration:*

Coca-Cola at 52.67

August options with 90 days until expiration:

Coca-Cola strike	45.00	47.50	50.00	52.50	55.00	57.50	60.00
Calls			4.04	2.52	1.45	0.79	0.34
Puts	0.82	1.30	2.05	2.90	4.25		

(a) i)   What is the cost of the August 52.50 straddle?
   ii)   At expiration, what is the upside break-even level?
   iii) What is the downside break-even level?
   iv)   What is the maximum profit?
   v)   What is the maximum loss?
   vi)   What is the profit/loss if the stock closes at 57.50 at expiration?

(b) i)   What is the cost of the long August 50–55 strangle?
   ii)   At expiration, what is the upside break-even level?
   iii) What is the downside break-even level?
   iv)   What is the maximum profit?
   v)   What is the maximum loss?
   vi)   What is the profit/loss if the stock closes at 47.50 at expiration?

(c) Why is the 50 put priced higher than the 55 call?

2   *In the UK, the outlook for Sainsbury during the next several months is for continued good, but not spectacular, trading, and you expect the shares to be stable. The implied volatility for the options is 38 per cent, down from over 50 per cent. It is November, and the January options are entering their accelerated time decay period. Sainsbury is trading at 537.5, and the following options prices are listed:*

Sainsbury at 537.5

January options with 70 days until expiry:

Strike	420	460	500	550	600	650	700
Calls				34	17.5	8	3
Puts	3	8	17.5	39.5			

i)   What is the income from selling the January 500–600 strangle?
ii) At expiry, what is the upside break-even level?
iii) What is the downside break-even level?
iv) What is the maximum profit?
v)   What is the maximum loss?

Chapter 11 answers

1 (a) i)   2.52 + 2.90 = 5.42
ii) 52.50 + 5.42 = 57.92
iii) 52.50 – 5.42 = 47.08
iv) upside unlimited; downside, value of the stock
v)   5.42
vi) [57.50 – 55] – 5.42 = –2.92 loss

(b) i)   2.05 + 1.45 = 3.50
ii) 55 + 3.50 = 58.35
iii) 50 – 3.5 = 46.5
iv) upside unlimited; downside 50 – 3.5 = 46.5
v)   3.50
vi) 5 – 3.5 = 1.5

(c) Because of the put volatility skew. This explained in Part 4.

2   i)   17.5 + 17.5 = 35
ii) 600 + 35 = 635
iii) 500 – 35 = 465
iv) 35
v)   unlimited upside, 465 on the downside.

Chapter 12 questions

1 *Refer to the previous set of Sainsbury January options:*

Sainsbury at 537.5

January options with 70 days until expiry

Strike	420.0	460.0	500.0	550.0	600.0	650.0	700.0
Calls				34.0	17.5	8.0	3.0
Puts	3.0	8.0	17.5	39.5			

(a) i)   What is the income from the short January 460–500–600–650 iron condor? This is an asymmetric spread.

ii)   At expiry, what is the upside break-even level?

iii) What is the downside break-even level?

iv)   What is the maximum upside loss?

v)   What is the maximum downside loss?

vi)   What is the maximum profit from this spread?

vii) What is the profit range?

(b) i)   What is the income from the short January 460–550–650 iron butterfly? This is also an asymmetric spread.

ii)   At expiry, what is the upside break-even level?

iii) What is the downside break-even level?

iv)   What is the maximum upside loss?

v)   What is the maximum downside loss?

vi)   What is the maximum profit?

vii) What is the profit range?

2 *Given the previous set of Coca-Cola options.*

Coca-Cola at 90

August options with 90 days until expiration

Strike	45.00	47.50	50.00	52.50	55.00	57.50	60.00
Calls			4.04	2.52	1.45	0.79	0.34
Puts	0.82	1.30	2.05	2.90	4.25		

(a) i)   What is the cost of the long August 45–50–55–60 iron condor?

ii)   At expiration, what is the upside break-even level?

iii)   What is the downside break-even level?

iv)   What is the maximum upside profit?

v)   What is the maximum downside profit?

vi)   What is the maximum loss?

(b) i)   What is the cost of the long August 45–52.50–60 iron butterfly?

ii)   At expiration, what is the upside break-even level?

iii)   At expiration, what is the downside break-even level?

iv)   What is the maximum upside profit?

v)   What is the maximum downside profit?

vi)   What is the maximum loss?

Chapter 12 answers

(a) i)   17.5 + 17.5 – 8 – 8 = 19 credit

ii)   600 + 19 = 619

iii)   500 – 19 = 481

iv)   [650 – 600] – 19 = 31

v)   [500 – 460] – 19 = 21

vi)   19

vii) 619 – 481 = 138

(b) i)   34 + 39.5 – 8 – 8.5 = 57.5 credit

ii)   550 + 57.5 = 607.5

iii)   550 – 57.5 = 492.5

iv)   [650 – 550] – 57.5 = 42.5

v)   [550 – 460] – 57.5 = 32.5

vi)   57.5

vii) 607.5 – 492.5 = 115

2 (a) i)   2.05 + 1.45 – 0.82 – 0.34 = 2.34 debit

ii)   55 + 2.34 = 57.34

iii)   50 – 2.34 = 47.66

iv)   [60 – 55] – 2.34 = 2.66

v)   [50 – 45] – 2.34 = 2.66

vi)   2.34

(b) i) 2.52 + 2.90 – 0.82 – 0.34 = 4.26 debit

ii) 52.50 + 4.26 = 56.76

iii) 52.50 – 4.26 = 48.24

iv) [60 – 52.50] – 4.26 = 3.24

v) [52.50 – 45] – 4.26 = 3.24

vi) 4.26

Chaper 13 Questions

1 *In the UK, the FTSE-100 index has been bullish since the end of October, and you expect this trend to continue through the end of the year. The December futures contract is currently at 5470. Using technical analysis, you determine that there is resistance at a former support area between 5700 and 5800. You note the following European-style December call options:*

December FTSE contract at 5470

December options with 40 days until expiry

Strike	5625.0	5675.0	5725.0	5775.0	5825.0	5875.0	5925.0	5975.0	6025.0
Calls	159.5	137.5	117.0	97.5	81.0	68.0	57.0	46.5	35.5

(a) i) What is the cost of the long 5675–5775–5875 call butterfly?
ii) At expiry, what is the maximum profit of the spread?
iii) What is the lower break-even level?
iv) What is the upper break-even level?
v) What is the profit range?
vi) What is the maximum loss?

(b) i) What is the cost of the long 5625–5725–5825–5925 call condor?
ii) At expiry, what is the maximum profit of the spread?
iii) What is the lower break-even level?
iv) What is the upper break-even level?
v) What is the profit range?
vi) What is the maximum loss?

(c) How do you account for the greater profit range of the condor?

2 *Because of budget deficit problems in Western economies the stock markets have been extremely volatile. However, bail-out packages with the IMF and the more solvent nations have finally been agreed upon. The global stock markets have sold off, and you expect them to range for the next two months.*

DJ Eurostoxx 50 at 2831

June puts with 57 days until expiration

Strike	2700	2750	2800	2850
Puts	54.50	68.40	85.80	107.00

(a) i)   What is the price of the long June 2850–2800–2750 put butterfly?

ii)   At expiration, what is the maximum profit?

iii)   What is the upper break-even level for this butterfly?

iv)   What is the lower break-even level?

v)   What is the profit range?

vi)   What is the maximum loss?

(b) i)   Suppose you prefer to leave yourself a margin of error in your outlook. You are range bearish. What is the cost of the 2850–2800–2700–2650 put condor?

ii)   At expiration, what is the maximum profit?

iii)   What is the upper break-even level?

iv)   What is the lower break-even level?

v)   What is the profit range?

vi)   What is the maximum loss?

(c)   Compare the advantages and disadvantages of the put butterfly to the put condor.

Chapter 13 answers

1 (a) i) $137.5 + 68 - [2 \times 97.5] = 10.5$

ii) $[5775 - 5675] - 105 = 89.5$

iii) $5675 + 10.5 = 5685.5$

iv) $5875 - 10.5 = 5864.5$

v) $5864.5 - 5685.5 = 179$ points

vi) $10.5 = £105$

(b) i) $159.5 + 57 - 117 - 81 = 18.5$

ii) $[5725 - 5625] - 18.5 = 81.5$

iii) $5625 + 18.5 = 5643.5$

iv) $5925 - 18.5 = 5906.5$

v) $5906.5 - 5643.5 = 263$ points

vi) $18.5 = £185$

(c)   The condor has a gross profit range that is 100 points greater. The 8p extra cost reduces eight points of profit from both the lower and upper break-even levels. The net profit range of the condor is therefore 84p greater.

2 (a) i) $107 + 68.40 - (2 \times 85.80) = 3.8$

ii) $(2850 - 2800) - 3.8 = 46.2$

    iii) 2850 – 3.8 = 2846.2

    iv) 2750 + 3.8 = 2753.8

    v)   2846.2 – 2753.8 = 92.4 points

    vi) 3.8

(b) i)   107 + 54.5 – 85.8 – 68.4 = 7.3

    ii)   (2850 – 2800) = 42.7

    iii) 2850 – 7.3 = 2842.7

    iv) 2650 + 7.3 = 2657.3

    v)   2842.7 – 2657.3 = 185.4 points

    vi) 7.3

(c) The condor has a gross profit range that is 185.4 – 92.4 = 93 points greater at an additional cost of 3.5.

Chapter 14 questions

1 *Your shares in Intel have performed well in the past, but now, with the possibility of a global recession, Intel's orders are down, and the stock is in a trading range. You are looking to supplement your dividend by writing one call on each 100 shares that you own. You realise that if the stock rallies above the call strike price, it will be called away from you. Intel is currently trading at 21.42, and the July 24 calls, with 46 days until expiration, are trading at 0.21. They are 12 per cent out-of-the-money.*

(a) What is the maximum profit from writing one July 24 call?

(b) What happens if at expiration the stock closes above 24?

(c) What is the break-even level?

(d) What is your percentage return over the next 46 days with your stock valued at 21.42?

2 *Sainsbury's range this past year is no less than 370 to 588.5. You have held onto your shares, riding the market turbulence. Because supermarkets are currently cutting prices, you forsee reduced profit margins for the near term.*

Sainsbury is currently trading at 537.5. With 70 days until expiration, the January 550 calls are trading at 34, and the January 600 calls are trading at 17.5. You would like to sell one of these as a covered write on 1,000 shares that you own.

(a) i) What is the maximum profit from writing one January 550 call?

ii) What happens if at expiry the shares closes above 550?

iii) What is the break-even level?

iv) What is your percentage return over the next 70 days with your shares valued at 537.5?

(b) i) What is the maximum profit from writing one January 600 call?

ii) What happens if at expiry the shares closes above 600?

iii) What is the break-even level?

iv) What is your percentage return over the next 70 days with your shares valued at 537.5?

3 *It is late November, and IBM is currently trading at 159.75. You expect IBM to remain at approximately 160 for the next month. You note the following prices for 160 calls.*

November 160 calls, with one day until expiration: 0.69

December 160 calls, with 29 days until expiration: 5.13

January 160 calls, with 64 days until expiration: 7.5

(a) What is the cost of the December–January 160 call calendar?

(b) Barring a special dividend or takeover within the next 29 days, what is the maximum loss of your calendar spread?

(c) i)   Although there are 28 days between November and December expirations, and 35 days between December and January expirations, you would like to estimate the profit potential of the December–January spread. What is your estimate for the value of this spread with IBM at 160 and one day until December expiration?

ii)   Would you expect the December–January spread to be worth more or less than the November–December spread?

Chapter 14 answers

1 (a) $[24 - 21.42] + 0.21 = 2.79$

(b) Your stock will be called away, or sold, but you will still have your maximum profit.

(c) $21.42 - 0.21 = 21.21$

(d) $0.21/21.42 = 1\%$

2 (a) i) $[550 - 537.5] + 34 = 46.5$

ii)   Your shares will be called away, or sold, but you will still have your maximum profit.

iii) $537.5 - 34 = 503.5$

iv) $34/537.5 = 6.33\%$

(b) i) $[600 - 537.5] + 17.5 = 80$

ii)   Your shares will be called away, or sold, but you will still have your maximum profit.

iii) $537.5 - 17.5 = 520$

iv) $17.5/537.5 = 3.26\%$

3 (a) $7.5 - 5.13 = 2.37$

(b) 2.37

(c) i)   Estimate would equal the November–December spread's value, 5.13 – 0.69 = 4.44.

ii)   More, because the long January call will have more days until expiration than the long December call. This doesn't imply greater profit potential, however, because the November–December spread would have cost less to begin with. This analysis assumes that the three implied volatilities are equal and will remain constant.

Chapter 15 questions

1 *Coca-Cola is trading at 52.67 For the September 60 calls with 90 days until expiration, note whether time passing causes the following Greeks to increase, decrease or remain unchanged.*

(a) delta

(b) gamma

(c) vega

(d) theta

2 *Answer the above questions for the September 52.50 calls.*

(a) delta

(b) gamma

(c) vega

(d) theta

3 (a) If the manager of your pension fund wants to hedge a portfolio of stocks and Treasury Bills against a possible interest rate increase during the next two weeks, which options position or positions might he employ?

(b) In terms of the Greeks, compare the advantages and disadvantages that he might consider by employing out-of-, or at-the-money options.
   i)   delta
   ii) gamma
   iii) vega
   iv) theta

(c) Suppose he considers an at-the-money option. In terms of the Greeks, compare the advantages of employing a 30-day option to a 60-day option.
   i)   delta
   ii) gamma
   iii) vega
   iv) theta

(d) Now suppose he considers an out-of-the-money option. In terms of the Greeks, compare the advantages of employing a 30-day option to a 60-day option, each at the same strike.
   i)   delta
   ii) gamma
   iii) vega
   iv) theta

(e) Getting settlements from exchange websites, choose an option or two from the major stock indexes: DJ Eurostoxx 50, SPDRS or SPX, FTSE-100, CAC or DAX, etc. Follow the options for the next two weeks.

4 *The December FTSE futures contract is currently at 5530 and you are long one the December 5575 call which is currently trading at 190. A rumour circulates that a certain tabloid baron has dropped his opposition to European monetary union because he has formed a partnership with an Italian media mogul, and the December futures contract rallies to 5620. You know that your call position has made a profit, and while awaiting a price quote (and a possible change in the tabloid's editorial policy), you decide to evaluate the effect of the market move on your call's Greeks. How will they be affected by the change in the December futures contract?*

(a) delta

(b) gamma

(c) vega

(d) theta

5 *Coca-Cola is currently trading at 52.67. The January options have 60 days until expiration and the December options have 30 days until expiration. Is each of the following statements true or false?*

(a) If the implied volatility increases, then the delta and theta of the January 47.50 put will also increase.

(b) If the implied increases, then the gamma of the January 57.50 call will increase, and the vega will decrease.

(c) If the implied decreases, then the vega of the December 52.50 call will decrease.

(d) If the implied decreases, then the gamma and delta of the January 47.50 call will increase.

6 *Under what circumstances can an increase in the implied cause an increase in an out-of-the-money option's gamma?*

7 *Suppose the S&P 500 index is at 1030, and you are long a number of 975 puts. The chairman of the US Federal Reserve bank, who is liked by the financial markets, announces that he is to retire when his term expires. What may happen to the implied volatility of your put options?*

Chapter 15 answers

1 **(a)** decrease

   (b) increase

   (c) decrease

   (d) increase

2 **(a)** practically unchanged

   (b) increase

   (c) decrease

   (d) increase

3 **(a)** Purchase puts on a stock index and/or eurodollars.

   (b) i)   ATM puts provide more coverage per option.
         ii) ATM puts respond more to market movement.
         iii) ATM puts are more sensitive to an increase or decrease in the implied.
         iv) OTM puts cost less in time decay.

   (c) i)   No difference.
         ii) Near-term has greater gamma, it responds more to market movement.
         iii) Not-so-near is more sensitive to change in the implied.
         iv) Near-term costs more in daily time decay.

   (d) i)   60-day has larger delta, therefore more coverage per option.
         ii) 30-day has greater gamma.
         iii) 60-day is more sensitive to change in the implied.
         iv) 30-day costs more in daily time decay.

4 **(a)** Increased.

   (b) Practically unchanged because the call is now as equally far in-the-money as it was formerly out-of-the money.

   (c) Unchanged, for the above reason.

   (d) Unchanged, for the above reason.

5 **(a)** True.

   (b) False, the gamma will decrease but the vega will increase.

   (c) False, it will remain practically unchanged.

   (d) True.

6 *If the implied is increasing from a very low level then the gammas of the far out-of-the-money options will increase.*

7 *If his retirement is unexpected, then the implied may increase due to uncertainty; if his retirement is expected, then the implied will most likely remain unchanged.*

Chapter 21 questions

1 *Given the following set of FTSE December European-style options, calculate the price of the missing call or put using the put–call parity formulas.*

FTSE December futures contract at 5470

Strike	5325.0	5475.0	5525.0	5725.0
December calls	306.5	?	?	97.5
December puts	?	217.0	238.5	?

(a) December 5325 put

(b) December 5475 call

(c) December 5525 call

(d) December 5725 put

2 *Given the following May options on Marks and Spencer, determine the price of the synthetic futures contract and the prices of the missing options. Bear in mind that these are settlements and that there can be small discrepancies between their values and the synthetic that they equal.*

M&S at 350.60

May options with 75 days until expiry

Strike	330.00	340.00	350.00	360.00	370.00
December calls	28.50	?	15.75	11.00	?
December puts	?	10.25	14.75	?	

(a) May synthetic futures contract

(b) May put

(c) May 340 call

(d) May 360 put

(e) May 370 call

Chapter 21 answers

1 **(a)** $306.5 - 5470 + 5325 = 161.5$

   (b) $5470 - 5475 + 217 = 212$

   (c) $5470 - 5525 + 238.5 = 183.5$

   (d) $97.5 - 5470 + 5725 = 352.5$

2 **(a)** $15.75 - 14.75 + 350 = 351$

   (b) $28.50 - 351 + 330 = 7.50$

   (c) $351 - 340 + 10.00 = 21.00$

   (d) $11.00 - 351 + 360 = 20.00$

   (e) $351 - 370 + 26 = 7.00$

Chapter 22 questions

1 *Suppose the current Bank of England interest rate is 3 per cent.*

   (a) With 37 days until expiry what is the price of a December 1,000 point box in the FTSE-100 European-style options? (Hint: the box trades at a discount.)

   (b) Suppose you want to borrow or lend money for the next 37 days at the above rate in the FTSE options market. What strategy, bought or sold, would enable you to trade money at approximately 3 per cent?

   (c) The December FTSE futures contract is trading at 5470, and three legs of the 4975–5975 box are trading as indicated below. What is the price of the fourth leg?

   FTSE December futures at 5470

Strike	4975.0	5975
December calls	572.5	35.5
December puts	81.0	?

2 *The purpose of the following questions is to help you understand how conversions and reversals form the basis of bid–ask spreads, or markets, for options.*

   M&S at 350.60

   May options, 75 days until expiry

   Bank of England rate at 0.50 per cent

Strike	350.00
January calls theoretical value	15.75
January puts theoretical value	14.75

   (a) What is the value of the May synthetic future, and why is it so valued?

   (b) To be realistic, there is probably a bid–ask market for Marks and Spencer of 350–351 and the spread is certain to increase during volatile markets. In order to price the May 350 conversion, the market assumes that the shares are bought at 351. At what price must the call and put be traded in order to break even, or make a small profit on the cost of carry on the shares?

(c) Now determine the market price of May 350 reversal. Here the shares must be sold at 350. At what prices must the call and put be traded in order to break even, or make a small profit on the cash income from the shares?

(d) If the prices in the options markets correspond to the current Bank of England rate, what would be the minumum bid–ask markets for the May 350 calls and puts?

Chapter 22 answers

1 (a) $1000 \times 0.03 \times 37/360 = 3$ points discount from 1,000. The box is priced at $1,000 - 3 = 997$. The market for the box is probably 995 – 999.

(b) Purchase boxes in the FTSE to lend, sell boxes to borrow.

(c) $997 = (572.5 - 81) - (35.5 + ?)$
$? = 997 - 572.5 + 81 + 35.5$

(d) $? = 541$

2 (a) $350 + 15.75 - 14.75 = 351$. The £0.40 price above the shock is due to the cost of carry on the shock for 75 days: $350.60 + (350.60 \times 0.005 \times {}^{75}/_{365}) = 0.36$, traded at 0.40.

(b) The synthetic must be sold at £0.40 over the ask price of the stock in order to recoup the cost of carry. Bearing in mind that the options contract trades in multiples of 0.25, the synthetic must be sold at 351.50. This is possible if the call is sold at 16.00, and 14.50 is paid for the put.

(c) If the return on a sale of the stock is 0.50 per cent, then no more than £0.40 must be paid for the synthetic over the bid price of the stock. Bearing in mind that the options contract trades in multiples of 0.25, the synthetic must be traded at 350.25. Therefore 15.25 will be paid for the call, while the put will be sold at 15.00.

(d) Call market is 15.25 – 16.00
Put market is 14.50 – 15.00

Glossary

The following glossary is best used as a quick reminder of basic options definitions. Alternatively, it may be used as a source of jargon for small talk at wine bars. (Make sure you're overheard.) It is no substitute for proper learning.

American style An American-style option can be exercised at any date during the life of the option's contract.

Asymmetric spread A spread whose strikes are not equidistant.

At-the-money (ATM) Calls and puts closest to the underlying.

Bear call spread Short call spread.

Bear put spread Long put spread.

Box A long box is a long synthetic plus a short synthetic at a higher strike. A short box has the opposite long/short position.

Broken spread An asymmetric spread.

Bull call spread Long call spread.

Bull put spread Short put spread.

Butterfly A long call butterfly is a long one by two call spread plus a long call at a third, higher strike. All strikes are equidistant. A long put butterfly is a long one by two put spread plus a long put at a third, lower strike. Again, all strikes are equidistant. For shorts of these spreads, reverse the long/short positions.

Calendar spread A long calendar spread is a long option plus a short option that is closer to expiration. Both options have the same strike.

Call A call option is the right to buy the underlying asset at a specified price for a specified time period. The call buyer has the right, but not the obligation, to buy the underlying. The call seller has the obligation to sell the underlying at the call buyer's discretion.

Call spread A long call spread is a long call plus a short call at a higher strike. A short call spread is the opposite.

Christmas tree See *Ladder*.

Combo A long out-of-the-money call plus a short out-of-the-money put, or vice versa. This is also known as the *cylinder*. The short call, long put version is also known as the *fence*. Occasionally this term applies to the synthetic underlying.

Condor A long call condor is a long call spread plus a short call spread at higher strikes. All strikes are equidistant. A long put condor is a long put spread plus a short put spread at lower strikes. Again, all strikes are equidistant.

Conversion A long underlying plus a short synthetic.

Covered write A long underlying plus a short out-of-the-money call. This is also know as the *buy-write*.

Cylinder See *Combo*.

Delta The rate of change of an option with respect to a change in the underlying.

Delta neutral Any combination of options and an underlying position whose delta sum is practically zero.

Delta/price ratio The percent that an option's value changes with respect to a change in the underlying.

Diagonal spread A long diagonal is a long option plus a short option that is closer to expiration and further out-of-the-money.

European style A European-style option can only be exercised at expiration.

Extrinsic value See *Time premium*.

Fence See *Combo*.

Future A contract to buy or sell a physical asset at a specified price at a specified future date. This asset can be a commodity, bond or stock. In the case of a stock index, the contract is for a cash value of all the stocks that comprise the index.

Gamma The rate of change of the delta with respect to a change in the underlying.

Hybrid spread A spread combination that is not one of the standard spreads.

In-the-money (ITM) Apart from at-the-money options, calls below the underlying and puts above the underlying.

Intrinsic value The amount that an option is in the money, or the parity component of an in-the-money option.

Iron butterfly A long iron butterfly is a long straddle plus a short strangle with all strikes equidistant. A short iron butterfly has the opposite long/ short position.

Iron condor A long iron condor is a long strangle plus a short strangle that is further out of the money. A short iron condor has the opposite long/ short position.

Ladder A long call ladder is a long call spread plus a short call at a third, higher strike. Usually all strikes are equidistant. A long put ladder is a long put spread plus a short put at a third, lower strike. Again, all strikes are usually equidistant. Also known as the *Christmas tree*.

Leverage The right or obligation to trade the full value of the underlying by trading only the value of the option.

Long To be long is to own. A long futures contract owns a cash or physical asset when the contract expires. A long options contract owns the right to buy, for a call, or the right to sell, for a put.

Long deltas Any combination of long calls, short puts and long underlying.

Margin Cash or liquid security deposited by holders of futures or options contracts.

Multiplier Part of a contract specification: the cash amount by which a futures or options value is multiplied.

Naked A short option not spread with a long option or underlying.

One by two A long one by two call spread is a long call plus two short calls at a higher strike. A long one by two put spread is a long put plus two short puts at a lower strike.

Out-of-the-money (OTM) Apart from at-the-money options, calls above the underlying and puts below the underlying.

Parity An in-the-money option with no time premium that consequently has a 100 per cent correlation with the underlying.

Pin risk The risk of an underlying closing exactly at the options strike price at expiration. The risk lies primarily with the short option holder because he is uncertain of assignment.

Put A put option is the right to sell the underlying asset at a specified price for a specified time period. The put buyer has the right, but not the obligation, to sell the underlying. The put seller has the obligation to buy the underlying at the put buyer's discretion.

Put spread A long put spread is a long put plus a short put at a lower strike. A short put spread is the opposite.

Reversal Short underlying plus long synthetic.

Rho The change of an option's value through a change in the interest rate.

Short To short is to sell. A short futures contract sells a cash or physical asset when the contract expires. A short options contract sells the right to buy, for a call, or the right to sell, for a put.

Short deltas Any combination of short calls, long puts and short underlying.

Stop order An order to buy or sell at the market price when a market reaches a pre-specified price level.

Straddle A call plus a put at the same strike, both either long or short.

Strangle An out-of-the-money call plus an out-of-the-money put, both either long or short.

Strike price The price of the underlying that forms the basis of an options contract.

Synthetic call A long synthetic call is a long put plus a long underlying. A short synthetic call is a short put plus a short underlying.

Synthetic put A long synthetic put is a long call plus a short underlying. A short synthetic put is a short call plus a long underlying.

Synthetic underlying A long synthetic is a long call plus a short put at the same strike. A short synthetic is a short call plus a long put at the same strike. Sometimes referred to as the *combo*.

Theta The amount that an option decays in one day.

Theta/price ratio The percent of an option's value diminished by one day's time decay.

Time decay The decline in an option's value through all or a portion of the option's life. Usually expressed as *theta*.

Time premium The premium apart from intrinsic value of an option. The amount of an option's value that corresponds to volatility coverage.

Time spread See *Calendar spread.*

Underlying An asset upon which an option's value is based. This can be a stock or stock index, bond, commodity or futures contract.

Vega The amount that an option changes through a 1 per cent change in the implied volatility.

Vega/price ratio The percent that an option's value changes through a 1 per cent change in the implied volatility.

Vertical spread A call or put spread.

Volatility A one-day, one standard deviation move, annualised.

Volatility, historical Volatility averaged over a time period such as 10, 20 or 30 days.

Volatility, implied The volatility that is implied by an option's price. In the case of an ATM option, this is the expected historical volatility of the underlying through expiration.

Volatility skew A pattern of implied volatility variations exhibited by in-the-money and out-of-the-money options.

Further reading

There are now many helpful books on options, and below are a few that can be recommended. Also included are books of a more general interest in order to help you make trading decisions. They all are, or will be, classics. The list is limited because your time is limited, and your priority is to take the shortest route to a more advanced level.

Technical books

Option Volatility and Pricing (1994) by Sheldon Natenberg, McGraw-Hill.
An excellent next step

Options, Futures and Other Derivatives (2009) by John Hull, Prentice Hall.
Another classic. For those with an advanced mathematical background

Paul Wilmott Introduces Quantitative Finance (2007) by Paul Wilmott, John Wiley & Sons.
Heavy on the maths, but readable. Wilmott is a super-quant.

Technical Analysis of the Financial Markets by John J. Murphy, New York Institute of Finance.
Thorough and readable

An Introduction to the Global Financial Markets (2010) by Stephen Valdez, and Philip Molyneux, Palgrave Macmillan.
A first-rate intro to this business.

Options Plain and Simple (2000) by Lenny Jordan, Prentice Hall.
A classic, generally agreed. Some traders have read it three times. Just get over the fractions.

Books about trading

The Gambler by F.M. Dostoyevsky (various editions).
To know the difference between trading and gambling.

Reminiscences of a Stock Operator (2004) by William J.O'Neil and Edwin Lefevre, John Wiley & Sons.
A classic, for market awareness about stock manipulators.

The Big Con (2000) by David W. Maurer, Arrow/Random House.
Written in the 1930s. Anyone involved in the Bernie Madoff scandal could read this and weep. The rest of you should read it before you contract a financial adviser.

Traders' website

www.nakedtrader.com

Mostly about cash futures trading, but very helpful with technical analysis. It will also bring you into the mind of the trader.

And finally…

The Meditations of Marcus Aurelius (various editions).
Advice from a battle-hardened emperor. Stoicism will help you manage your *self*.

Index

Page numbers in **bold** indicate a glossary entry.